# GROWING UP IN SLAVERY

# GROWING UP IN SLAVERY

## Stories of Young Slaves As Told By Themselves

EDITED BY YUVAL TAYLOR

ILLUSTRATIONS BY KATHLEEN JUDGE

Lawrence Hill Books

Library of Congress Cataloging-in-Publication Data
Is available from the Library of Congress.

Cover and interior design: Joan Sommers Design

First edition
Published by Lawrence Hill Books
An imprint of Chicago Review Press, Incorporated
814 North Franklin Street
Chicago, Illinois 60610
ISBN 1-55652-548-6
Printed in the United States of America
5 4 3 2 1

# CONTENTS

# FOREWORD

*"Pity me!... You never knew what it is to be a slave; to be entirely unprotected by law or custom.... You never exhausted your ingenuity in eluding the power of a hated tyrant; you never shuddered at the sound of his footsteps, and trembled within hearing of his voice."*

*H*arriet Jacobs wrote those words shortly after she escaped to freedom, addressing the readers of her masterly and moving account of her slave experiences, *Incidents in the Life of a Slave Girl*. Like many other former slaves, Jacobs was burning with a desire to tell her story to as many people as possible: people who, while living in the same era as she did, were even more unfamiliar with the life of the slave than we are today.

In this book, ten slaves introduce to us, in their own words, their lives: what it was like to grow up enchained, robbed of their liberty and their very identity, forbidden even to read and write. They range from Olaudah Equiano, William Wells Brown, Frederick Douglass, and Elizabeth Keckley, who all became famous, to William H. Robinson, whose book has long been out of print and forgotten.

Each of these accounts, excerpted from their books, remains a singular story told in a singular voice. Each one shows a black youth— all under the age of nineteen—trying to come to terms with almost inconceivable circumstances: being torn from mother and family, not getting enough to eat, being constantly watched, being whipped and even tortured, being prey to their masters' sadistic fancies. But these are not all tales of deprivation and violence. These slaves overcame tremendous obstacles to learn to read and write, and they tell how; they challenged authority in numerous ways, from trickery to outright rebellion; and they did the things that young people all do, from playing games to telling jokes to falling in love. And in telling their tales, they illuminate the unique conditions of slavery, from the passage in slave ships across the Atlantic, to daily life both on large plantations and in small city dwellings, to escaping slavery and even fighting in the Civil War.

Slavery in the United States affected millions of black Americans, often crushing them underfoot. But in the spirited accounts of these ten slaves, we see not only the horror and misery, but the vital human spirit that enabled them to survive.

# INTRODUCTION

## TRANSFORMING SLAVERY INTO LIBERATION

o matter how many years may pass, the shame of slavery will color our country's heritage. It was an established fact long before our birth as a nation; it caused our greatest war; it has shadowed every struggle, defeat, and victory of our land. Whites still apologize for it, blacks still resent it, and we are all oppressed by its legacy.

The slaves whose stories are collected here tried to lift the burden of that oppression. They transformed themselves from victims into agents of resistance just by telling their stories and protesting the vast injustice that was done to them. Along with other writers who had been slaves, they established a popular literary genre, sold hundreds of thousands of books, and advanced the antislavery cause. While they wrote mainly for their contemporaries, they produced works of lasting literary and historical value. In doing so, they performed an act of liberation.

This book presents the stories of ten slaves who wrote eloquently of their experiences as young men and women trapped in an intolerable situation. But these are only a small portion of a whole body of inventive, lucid, thoughtful, and passionate works of art: the literature of the slaves.

## SLAVE NARRATIVES

Between the arrival of the first documented shipload of Africans in Virginia in 1619 and the death of the last former slave in the 1970s, some six thousand North American slaves told their own stories in writing or in written interviews. Most of these accounts are brief (many were included in periodicals, collections, or other books), but approximately 150 of them were separately published as books or pamphlets ranging from eight pages to two volumes. These accounts are commonly referred to as "slave narratives."

At first, the slaves who wrote their stories seemed to think of their lives as adventures or spiritual journeys, instead of as tales of horror and abuse; in the titles of their books they called themselves Africans, not slaves. But beginning in 1824, with the publication of the *Life of William Grimes, the Runaway Slave,* the situation was reversed. Now the books were explicitly slaves' stories, and almost always featured graphic scenes of cruelty. Over the years the books also became more like novels—those published after 1852, the date of Harriet Beecher Stowe's bestseller *Uncle Tom's Cabin,* were far more likely to use re-created dialogue and other conventions of fiction.

Between 1836 and the end of the Civil War, slave narratives enjoyed great popularity, and over eighty were published. These narratives, which we may all call the *classic* or most typical narratives, share a number of similarities: most include a preface, written by someone else, describing the book as a "plain, unvarnished tale"; the first sentence of the book is usually "I was born . . ."; the plot often includes a slave auction, the separation of the narrator from his family, an exceptionally strong and proud slave who refuses to be whipped, and at least two escapes, one of them successful.

The slave narratives published after the Civil War were not nearly as angry; they often ended with the narrator adjusting to newfound freedoms, rather than calling for them from exile; and certain aspects of slave life began to seem quaint or colorful rather than horrifying. Now, instead of trying to convince their readers that slavery was evil, these writers were trying to present a balanced picture of their lives. The emphasis on *freedom* in the classic narratives was replaced by an emphasis on *progress*.

The slave narratives, with very few exceptions, were all written or dictated by *former* slaves. In the history of slavery in the United States, probably between 1 and 2 percent of the slave population managed to escape. The young men and women who wrote or told their stories were therefore more courageous, hardy, resourceful, or imaginative than those who were left behind. Most of them hailed from near the Mason-Dixon line (which separated the slave states from the free). They often knew how to read and write, even though that was forbidden by law; a large number had served as "house slaves" and had thereby learned something of the outside world by watching their masters; most had excellent memories and were extraordinarily intelligent. Also, quite a few of the narrators were of mixed race, or mulatto. While mulattoes constituted only between 7 and 12 percent of the slave population, they were not only more likely to be house slaves, but it was easier for them to pass as white when escaping. The age at which they wrote their tales varied from their early twenties to their mid-seventies, and between 10 and 12 percent of them were women.

More than half of these books were written by the slaves themselves, and many were also self-published. A large number, however, were dictated by the slave to an editor, usually a white man, called an *amanuensis*. In many cases, it seems that the amanuensis followed the words of the slave quite carefully; but sometimes editors added passages based on their own research, and once in a while the slave's story was more or less rewritten.

The central purpose of the classic slave narratives is clear: *to speak truth to power*. But this is not the only goal. One can find many others:

1. **To document the conditions of slavery.** The slave narratives are the richest firsthand source for information about plantation life. Some of the narratives are very clear about this goal. Charles Ball's was called *Slavery in the United States* and John Brown's was called *Slave Life in Georgia*. In his preface, one ex-slave, Louis Hughes, asked, "To what purpose is the story which follows?" and responded, "the narrator presents his story…in the hope that it may add something of accurate information regarding the character and influence of an institution which for two hundred years dominated the country." Many passages of the narratives spell out in detail the daily duties of the slave, the method of growing crops, what and when the slaves ate, the different kinds of whips, and so on.

2. **To persuade the reader of the evils of slavery.** Many narratives are also political appeals. Publishing a narrative could be a more effective political act than giving an abolitionist speech. Although many a narrative called itself a "plain, unvarnished tale," most of them spiced up their accounts with more general talk of the evils of slavery and its conflict with Christian principles or those upon which this country was founded.

3. **To impart religious inspiration.** The narratives were often fundamentally religious in character. For example, the *Life of John Thompson* concludes with a sermon that makes the narrator's experiences aboard a whaling ship into an allegory of faith. And in his preface to *The Fugitive Blacksmith*, James W. C. Pennington declares, "Especially have I felt anxious to save professing Christians, and my brethren in the ministry, from falling into a great mistake."

4. **To affirm the narrator's identity.** The slave not only identified writing with his newfound freedom, but his book with his new-

found self. Austin Steward goes so far as to say, "The author... sends out this history—presenting as it were his *own body*, with the marks and scars of the tender mercies of slave drivers upon it." Slaves were, of course, property, and therefore did not own themselves; they were also forbidden to read and write. Self-expression, then, was one of the greatest gifts of freedom—witness the joy of Harriet Jacobs's exclamation, "What a comfort it is, to be free to *say* so!" Even if they did not put it into words, many fugitive slaves may have considered writing to be the ultimate act of self-affirmation, the ultimate denial of enslavement.

5. **To redefine what it means to be black.** Books of the slavery era are full of stereotypes of meek, idiotic, or savage Negroes, and slave narratives tried to correct such racist views. Even the fact that there existed a book written by a black person could easily make white readers reconsider their beliefs, since many of them thought such a thing impossible. Beyond that, slaves needed to set straight readers who believed, as most did, what Southern slaveholders told them—that slaves were "happy darkies" who adored being protected and watched over by their father-like masters. In the slave narratives there are no "lush green fields with singing slaves working hard but happily [near] the big plantation house staffed by authoritarian house slaves and beautiful women in billowing gowns," as Kenny J. Williams has described the literature of the South.

6. **To make money.** Naturally, one usually publishes a book with the expectation of profit. Several narrators made this explicit. Moses Grandy wrote, "Whatever profit may be obtained by the sale of this book... will be faithfully employed in redeeming my remaining children and relatives from the dreadful condition of slavery." William Grimes said at the end of his narrative, "I hope some will buy my books from charity; but I am no beggar. I am now entirely destitute of property; where and how I shall live I don't know." The "Advertisement to the Second Edition" of Moses Roper's narrative states that its

sale will help the author "create a fund which may enable him to qualify himself to instruct the heathen"; six years later Roper wrote, "by the sale of my book . . . [I] have paid for my education and supported myself."

7. Last but not least, **to delight or fascinate the reader.** The slave narratives owe their success to this more than to any other factor, but the writers consistently denied that this was their aim. For example, Olaudah Equiano denies the fact that his narrative "abound[s] in great or striking events," and asks the reader's pardon for "a work wholly devoid of literary merit." The *Narrative of the Life of J. D. Green* clearly aims to amuse the reader with the many farcical incidents it describes, but one would never guess that from the prefatory material, which simply invokes the "horrors" of slavery. But the method of storytelling in the narratives—which reminds one of adventure stories or sentimental novels—makes clear that delighting the audience was indeed one of the goals of the writers. This goal may have been seen at the time as inconsistent with their *central* goal (speaking truth to power). In the eighteenth and nineteenth centuries, when the conventions used to distinguish fiction from nonfiction were not as clear as those of today, it was important that the narratives deny being even remotely fictional—especially since a number of fictional slave narratives were published in the period as well.

THE LEGACY OF THE SLAVE NARRATIVES

Their power to fascinate, delight, and thrill may be the primary reason the slave narratives were so widely read. A number of them went through more than a dozen editions, and sold tens of thousands of copies. (Compare that to *Walden, Moby Dick,* and *Leaves of Grass,* which sold fewer than two thousand copies each and then went out of print.) They were popular among both men and women, young and old, black and white, Northerners, Southerners (as evidenced by the large number of proslavery Confederate romances published to rebut slave narratives), British, and, considering the number of translations into a host of languages, practically all literate people. In short, their appeal was universal. An 1855 issue of *Putnam's Monthly* explained:

Our English literature has recorded many an example of genius struggling against adversity, ... yet none of these are so impressive as the case of the solitary slave, in a remote district, surrounded by none but enemies, conceiving the project of his escape, teaching himself to read and write to facilitate it, accomplishing it at last, and subsequently raising himself to a leadership in a great movement in behalf of his brethren.

Other readers remarked on the narratives' romantic nature. Senator Charles Sumner called the fugitive slaves "among the heroes of our age. Romance has no storms of more thrilling interest than theirs. Classical antiquity has preserved no examples of adventurous trial more worthy of renown." Part trickster, part pilgrim, the fugitive slave—wandering the wilderness and defying death on a quasi-religious quest for freedom—proved to be the ideal American hero. And his narrative was just what readers were thirsting for.

In the first half of the twentieth century, slave narratives fell out of print and, because they were products of African American consciousness, were largely ignored by American historians. But black writers have always appreciated them for their originality, complexity, and power. Nineteenth-century works influenced by slave narratives include Stowe's *Uncle Tom's Cabin* (1852), William Wells Brown's *Clotel* (1853), Harriet Wilson's *Our Nig* (1859), Martin R. Delaney's *Blake* (1861), and Mark Twain's *The Adventures of Huckleberry Finn* (1884). The number of twentieth-century works is too large to count, but some of the more prominent titles include James Weldon Johnson's *Autobiography of an Ex-Colored Man* (1912), Claude McKay's *Home to Harlem* (1928), Arna Bontemps's *Black Thunder* (1936), Zora Neale Hurston's *Their Eyes Were Watching God* (1937), W. E. B. Du Bois's *Dusk of Dawn* (1940), Richard Wright's *Black Boy* (1945), Ralph Ellison's

*Invisible Man* (1952), James Baldwin's *Go Tell It on the Mountain* (1953), *The Autobiography of Malcolm X* (1965), Margaret Walker's *Jubilee* (1966), Maya Angelou's *I Know Why the Caged Bird Sings* (1970), Ernest Gaines's *The Autobiography of Miss Jane Pittman* (1971), Alex Haley's *Roots* (1976), Ishmael Reed's *Flight to Canada* (1976), Charles Johnson's *Oxherding Tale* (1982), Sherley Anne Williams's *Dessa Rose* (1986), Toni Morrison's *Beloved* (1987), and Caryl Phillips's *Cambridge* (1991). Indeed, most if not all post–Civil War African American prose works are descended from the slave narrative, not only because it was the first distinctive African American literary genre, but because of its powerful mix of storytelling, racial awareness, social critique, and self-reflection—elements of the greatest black literary achievements.

## A CONCISE HISTORY OF SLAVERY IN THE UNITED STATES

Lincoln's Gettysburg Address maintained that the United States was "conceived in Liberty." But it was no less conceived in slavery, which had stained the New World from the moment of its discovery. Christopher Columbus wrote of the Caribbean natives that "there are no better people.... They love their neighbors as themselves, and they have the sweetest speech in the world; and are gentle and always laughing"; but he did not hesitate to enslave them upon his ships. John Smith, the leader of the early British colonists, had been a slave himself, in Turkey, where he killed his master and fled northward; in Jamestown, Virginia, he was frustrated by the colonists' refusal to endure hard labor. So he was dismissed from the governorship, and his replacement, Sir Thomas Dale (as Frederick Law Olmsted later wrote), "ordered them all, gentle and simple, to work in gangs under overseers, and threatened to shoot the first man who refused to labor, or was disobedient."

A few years later Africans were introduced to the British settlements—the first documented shipload arrived in Virginia in 1619, but some may have been landed even earlier. Many black slaves were in Spanish Florida by that time, and tens of thousands in the West

Indies, but only small numbers of Africans were shipped to the British colonies prior to the 1680s. Not until 1661 were these legally called slaves, and indeed many of them were only indentured servants (who worked without pay for a specified number of years).

At first, children who were born to white fathers and slave mothers were free, just as in the French, Dutch, Danish, German, Spanish, and Portuguese colonies. In 1662, however, Virginia enacted a law that the children of female slaves should be slaves themselves, which made it advantageous for a slave owner to rape his female slaves. Soon it was lawful in Virginia to do almost anything to one's slaves—even kill them.

It didn't take long for people to notice the horrifying results of slavery, especially with the arrival of huge numbers of Africans between 1680 and 1750. For example, when the colony of Georgia was founded in 1733, slavery was prohibited within its borders. William Byrd II, a prominent Virginia farmer and slaveholder, wrote in 1736:

I am sensible of many bad consequences of multiplying these Ethiopians [Africans] amongst us. They blow up the pride, & ruin the industry of our white people, who seing a rank of poor creatures below them, detest work for fear it shoud make them look like slaves....

Another unhappy effect of many Negros, is, the necessity of being severe. Numbers make them insolent, & then foul means must do, what fair will not.... Yet even this is terrible to a good naturd man, who must submit to be either a fool or a fury. And this will be more our unhappy case, the more Negros are increast amongst us.

But the institution of slavery was not widely questioned until the late eighteenth century. After all, it predates recorded history. Slave labor was used in building the Egyptian pyramids, and the Bible includes laws concerning the treatment—and freeing—of slaves. Modern slavery had its origins in the fifteenth century, when the Portuguese— followed by the British, Dutch, French, and Spanish—began to exploit Africans as slaves. And while it was in the Americas that their use was most widespread, it was in Europe that the idea of abolition—of getting rid of slavery—arose. In America, criticism of slavery remained mild at best.

Despite the tens of thousands of slaves who ran away during the American Revolution, slaves numbered 20 percent of the U.S. population by 1790, and the next two decades would witness the largest importation of Africans yet.

In 1787 the U.S. constitution declared a slave to count as three-fifths of a person in calculating representation for the states, which meant that a slaveowner with fifty slaves would get 31 votes, while a Northerner with no slaves got only one (slaves were not allowed to vote, and were property, not people, in the eyes of the law). Ninety percent of the slaves lived in the South, where slavery had become an important part of the plantation system of agriculture; and by 1804, mostly due to the influence of Quakers, all except one of the Northern states (Delaware) had at least begun to abolish slavery. It had become clear by this time that slavery was the great factor dividing the northern from the southern states. By 1807 the African slave trade had been outlawed by both the British Empire and the United States (though the illegal slave trade flourished for a long time thereafter), and in 1833, slavery itself, which had been abolished in England in 1772, was abolished throughout the British Empire. But in the United States, slavery seemed to be not only impossible to get rid of, but had come to be the most important political, economic, and social issue of the age.

In the North, the 1830s witnessed the rise of the abolitionist movement, which grew out of the evangelical religious revivals of the 1820s. In 1829 David Walker, a free black man, had published his *Appeal,* one of the most vigorous denunciations of slavery ever written. The first issue of William Lloyd Garrison's *The Liberator,* a radical abolitionist journal, followed in 1831. The American Anti-Slavery Society, which grew out of Garrison's New England Anti-Slavery Society, was organized two years later in Philadelphia. The society integrated its black and white members, advocated nonviolence, and included in its goals equal rights for free blacks. In 1835 it launched a massive propaganda campaign, flooding the slave states with abolitionist literature, sending agents throughout the North to organize antislavery societies, and petitioning Congress to abolish slavery in the District of Columbia.

The mood quickly turned violent. Mobs attacked the abolitionists in the North, in the South their pamphlets were suppressed, the House of Representatives enacted a gag rule that prevented the discussion of antislavery proposals, and in 1837 the abolitionist editor Elijah P. Lovejoy was murdered while a mob destroyed his press for the fourth time. Despite these setbacks, by 1838 almost a quarter-million Americans belonged to antislavery societies.

In the South the suppression of freedoms was fed by fear. In 1831 Nat Turner had led the Southampton Insurrection in Virginia, killing between fifty-seven and sixty-five whites in the most deadly slave revolt in U.S. history. This uprising, like earlier ones led by Gabriel Prosser and Denmark Vesey, sparked violent reprisals and the passage of more oppressive laws throughout the South. In Virginia, for example, black ministers were forbidden to preach, education for free blacks was denied, and free blacks who had left the state could not return. Similarly, after the Denmark Vesey insurrection, black sailors landing in South Carolina were locked up in jail until their vessels put out to sea.

The North-South divide was further encouraged by the passage of a series of federal laws designed to delimit slavery. The Missouri Compromise, passed by Congress in 1820 and 1821, included a provision prohibiting slavery in the remainder of the Louisiana Purchase north of 36° 30′ (the southern boundary of Missouri). The Compromise of 1850 included the admission of California as a free state, the prohibition of the slave trade in the District of Columbia, and a more stringent fugitive slave law. And the Kansas-Nebraska Act of 1854, which overruled the Missouri Compromise, allowed Kansas and Nebraska, both of which were north of the line, to decide themselves the question of slavery in their territories. While all of these laws were compromises between Northern and Southern congressmen, they did little to calm the conflict between the regions, instead entrenching each side more adamantly in its position.

Legislative compromises were not the only ways that Americans tried to resolve the slavery issue. The American Colonization Society was set up to deal with the problem of free blacks, who did not enjoy the same freedoms as whites anywhere in the United States, by resettling them in Africa. In 1819 Congress appropriated one hundred thousand dollars for returning blacks to Africa. The result was the founding of Liberia in 1821. Abraham Lincoln would later profess to be in favor of colonization. But the movement was savagely attacked by abolitionists, who argued that it strengthened slavery in the South by removing free blacks; and blacks themselves were unenthusiastic about the project, maintaining that they were Americans, not Africans.

In contrast to the compromisers and colonizers, the abolitionists were mostly unconcerned about making peace or preserving the Union. The 1850s witnessed a huge rise in the popularity of abolitionism. The 1793 fugitive slave law, providing for the return between states of escaped slaves, had been loosely enforced, with some Northern states allowing fugitives trials before their return and others forbidding state officials to capture them. So, as part of the Compromise of 1850, a new fugitive slave law was passed, commanding "all good citizens" to "aid and assist" Federal marshals in recapturing fugitive slaves, and imposing extraordinarily heavy penalties upon anyone who helped a slave escape. When captured, any black could be taken before a special commissioner, where he would be denied a jury trial, his testimony would not be admitted, and the affidavit of anyone claiming ownership would be enough to establish it in the eyes of the law. Thus all free blacks, whether fugitives or not, were put in danger of being enslaved. The result was an increase in kidnappings, in active resistance to the law, and in antislavery feeling in the

North. Abolitionists, who had been widely considered extremists, finally started to gain widespread popularity.

Meanwhile the cotton the slaves produced had become not only the United States' leading export, but exceeded in value all other exports combined. After the slave trade was outlawed in 1807, approximately one million slaves were moved from the states that produced less cotton (Maryland, Virginia, the Carolinas) to those that produced more (Georgia, Alabama, Mississippi, Louisiana, Texas)—a migration almost twice as large as that from Africa to the British colonies and the United States. With the increase in cotton production, the price of slaves went up—to $1,800 per slave, or the equivalent of $40,000 today, in 1860—to such an extent that by then the worth of the Southern slaves—who now numbered close to four million, or one-third of the population—was greater than the worth of anything else, including land.

Due to the increased economic importance of slavery, and in reaction to the North's ever more fiery condemnations of it, between 1830 and 1860 freeing one's slaves was increasingly prohibited in Southern states, freed blacks were expelled, black churches were eliminated, and penalties for hurting or killing blacks were largely ignored. Proslavery literature was published at an alarming rate, owning abolitionist literature was made a serious crime, freedom of speech regarding slavery was effectively ended, and prices were even put on the heads of the leading abolitionists. The large majority of slaves were still owned by a small minority of landowners—only one-quarter of Southern whites owned slaves, and only 12 percent of those (or 3 percent of the total number of whites) owned more than twenty slaves. But whether slaveholders or not, whites now wielded absolute power over blacks.

The rising popularity of slave narratives in the fifteen years before the Civil War is only one example of the power of abolitionist literature. Harriet Beecher Stowe's novel *Uncle Tom's Cabin*, based in part on slave narratives, was a major factor in turning Northerners against slavery. It sold over three hundred thousand copies in 1852 and helped bring respect to the antislavery movement worldwide. Its influence was so strong that upon meeting the author, Lincoln is said to have commented, "So this is the little lady who made this great war."

The Underground Railroad is another powerful example of the success of abolitionists in changing public views of slavery. As you can tell by reading the slave narratives, escaping slaves relied mostly on their own resourcefulness, although free blacks, Quakers, and sympathetic Northern sailors certainly helped them. The stories of the Underground Railroad, on the contrary, created the impression that a highly systematic and secret organization, run mostly by white abolitionists, conducted most of the fugitive slaves along secret routes from the South to the North. No such national coordinated organization existed; and regional Underground Railroads were responsible for a relatively small number of successful escapes. The Underground Railroad was partly a way to dramatize abolitionist heroism, thereby attracting followers in the North and increasing alarm in the South.

The most important change in the legal status of blacks during this period was the decision by the Supreme Court in the 1857 Dred Scott case that Congress had no power to prohibit slavery in the territories, that the Missouri Compromise was unconstitutional, and that a black "whose ancestors were ... sold as slaves" was not entitled to the rights of a Federal citizen and therefore had no standing in court. According to Chief Justice Roger B. Taney, who gave the majority decision, blacks had not been citizens at the time of the adoption of the Constitution and had not become citizens of the nation since. By coming down strongly on the side of the South in the question of slavery in the territories, the decision caused a decisive split in the Democratic Party.

The Kansas-Nebraska Act of 1854 had already caused considerable violence in "bleeding Kansas." Both proslavery and antislavery groups pushed settlers into Kansas, hoping to influence elections. Each camp founded its own towns, Lawrence and Topeka being antislavery and Leavenworth and Atchison proslavery. The first elections were won by the proslavery group, but armed Missourians had intimidated voters and stuffed ballot boxes. Then the legislature ousted all free-state members, removed the governor, and adopted proslavery statutes. In retaliation, the abolitionists set up a rival government, and a bloody local war ensued—all despite the fact that slaves in Kansas in 1856 probably numbered only four hundred at most.

One of the most active abolitionists in Kansas was John Brown (not to be confused with the slave of the same name), a white man who killed five proslavery men in the Pottawatomie massacre in 1856. Three years later, with twenty-one followers, he captured the U.S. arsenal at Harper's Ferry, Virginia (now West Virginia), imprisoned the inhabitants, and took possession of the town, intending to liberate the slaves by setting up an armed stronghold to which they could flee and from which revolts could be initiated. The U.S. Marines assaulted the arsenal, however, killing ten of Brown's men and wounding Brown himself. Brown, who was hanged after a spectacular trial, became a martyr of the abolitionist cause, galvanizing the North with his boldness; his raid so alarmed slaveholders that the whole South began to get ready for war.

We won't discuss Lincoln's election, the Civil War, and the emancipation of the slaves here. But we should note that slavery in the United States by no means ended at the close of the Civil War in 1865. Following a period called Reconstruction, during which the civil rights of Southern blacks were to some degree protected by the federal government, in 1876 the government effectively pulled out of the South and allowed local control, in all its racist fury, to reassert itself. Although they were not called *slavery*, the post-Reconstruction Southern practices of peonage, forced convict labor, and to a lesser degree sharecropping essentially continued the institution of slavery well into the twentieth century, and were in some ways even worse. Peonage, for example, was a complex system in which a black man would be arrested for "vagrancy," another word for unemployment, ordered to pay a fine he could not afford, and jailed. A plantation owner would pay his fine and "hire" him until he could afford to pay off the fine himself. The peon was then forced to work, locked up at night, and, if he ran away, chased by bloodhounds until recaptured. One important difference between peonage and slavery was that while slaves had considerable monetary value for the plantation owner, peons had almost none, and could therefore be mistreated—and even murdered—without monetary loss. However, these practices were ignored by post-emancipation slave narratives, which aimed to emphasize the progress blacks had made since emancipation and to minimize their status as victims.

## ABOUT THIS BOOK

This book collects excerpts from ten slave narratives. Each excerpt focuses on one or more stories from the writer's life prior to his or her nineteenth birthday. *The words of the slaves remain unchanged.* But I have emended spellings and punctuation to some degree, I have corrected minor factual errors, I have removed sentences and paragraphs in the interest of brevity, and I have added paragraph breaks and section breaks for ease of reading. The titles of the sections rely on words from the narratives themselves—sometimes from section or chapter titles, sometimes from summaries printed at heads of chapters, and sometimes from the body of the slave's account.

The selections are organized according to the date of first publication of the slave's story. Later writers had usually read earlier writers, and their books contain evidence of this. In some instances the writers based their own accounts on earlier ones; more frequently they attempted to distinguish theirs from those preceding them.

Each selection is introduced with a few words of biographical detail, publication history, and interpretation. At the end of the selection,

I summarize the remainder of the narrative and tell the story of what happened to the narrator after its publication. I have added in square brackets explanations of the more difficult or uncommon words, biographical information about people mentioned in the text, and geographical information, all where appropriate. At the end of the volume is a list of further reading.

With two exceptions, I have based the text on the first American edition of the slave's narrative. The exceptions are the stories of Olaudah Equiano, which is based on the first British edition, and Frederick Douglass, which combines the first edition of his first narrative, the 1845 *Narrative of the Life of Frederick Douglass, an American Slave*, with that of his second, the 1855 *My Bondage and My Freedom*.

Much of this book is adapted from an earlier book I compiled, *I Was Born a Slave: An Anthology of Classic Slave Narratives*, which includes the complete narratives of seven of these ten slaves. In closing, I would like to acknowledge and thank those who assisted me in preparing that earlier book—Samuel Baker, Vincent Carretta, Charles Johnson, Curt Matthews, Linda Matthews, the University of Chicago Library, and my wife, Kathryn Anne Duys. Cynthia Sherry and Linda Matthews came up with the idea for the present book, and together with Jerome Pohlen and Mary Rowles have been tremendously supportive and given me much insight into how the book should be shaped. Linda Matthews was especially helpful in cutting the narratives down to size and selecting which ones should be included. Many thanks to Kathleen Judge for her fresh and revelatory illustrations. Lastly, I would like to thank my own children, Thalia and Jacky, whose cheerfulness has helped me see that these pages contain not only the woes of oppression but the joys of being alive.

# OLAUDAH EQUIANO
## (GUSTAVUS VASSA)

y the end of his life, **Olaudah Equiano** (a.k.a. Gustavus Vassa; c. 1745–97) seems to have accomplished practically everything that it was possible for a black man to accomplish in his time. If we can believe everything he tells us in his brilliant autobiography, *The Interesting Narrative of the Life of Olaudah Equiano, or Gustavus Vassa, the African* (1789), Equiano grew up in remotest Africa; was sold as a slave; was transported across the Atlantic in a slave ship; was cheated out of his freedom by an unscrupulous master; witnessed the worst aspects of slavery in the West Indies; made close friends with whites of both sexes; became a successful businessman; managed a slave estate; saved the crew of a shipwreck; captained a ship; officiated as a pastor at a funeral; made war in Canada and in the Mediterranean; went on a voyage to the North Pole; worked as a hairdresser; became an accomplished French horn player; stayed with Turks in Smyrna and Miskito Indians in Central America; was employed by the British government to help resettle free blacks in Africa; wrote letters, poetry, and memoirs; cut a handsome figure in "superfine clothes"; gave evidence before a British parliamentary committee on the slave trade; petitioned the queen for its abolition; knew many of the most famous people of his day; and was visited by the Lord himself.

His book was the most famous and influential black auto-biography of its time. Equiano, who was known by his slave name, Gustavus Vassa, throughout his life, has rightly been called "the father of Afro-American autobiography," and while his book ranges, in more than one sense, all over the map, it is masterfully written. In writing it, Equiano did more than any other black man before Frederick Douglass to stir up antislavery sentiment. It became the most popular book ever written by a black author up to that point, selling about twenty thousand copies in twenty-two editions over fifty years.

Below are Equiano's accounts of his kidnapping from the home of his parents (probably in present-day Nigeria), his horrific voyage on a slave ship (the most detailed first-hand account we have from a slave's point of view), and his arrival in the New World. It may prove to be somewhat more difficult to read than the narratives that follow it, for not only does it substantially predate them, but it was written for a more educated audience, and by a more educated man.

## HIS BEING KIDNAPPED WITH HIS SISTER

My father, besides many slaves, had a numerous family, of which seven lived to grow up, including myself and a sister, who was the only daughter. As I was the youngest of the sons, I became, of course, the greatest favourite with my mother, and was always with her; and she used to take particular pains to form my mind. I was trained up from my earliest years in the art of war; my daily exercise was shooting and throwing javelins; and my mother adorned me with emblems, after the manner of our greatest warriors. In this way I grew up till I was turned the age of eleven, when an end was put to my happiness in the following manner:

Generally when the grown people in the neighbourhood were gone far in the fields of labour, the children assembled together in some of the neighbours' premises to play; and commonly some of us used to get up a tree to look out for any assailant, or kidnapper, that might come upon us; for they sometimes took those opportunities of our parents' absence to attack and carry off as many as they could seize. One day, as I was watching at the top of a tree in our yard, I saw one of those people come into the yard of our next neighbour but one, to kidnap, there being many stout young people in it. Immediately on this I gave the alarm of the rogue, and he was surrounded by the stoutest of them, who entangled him with cords, so that he could not escape till some of the grown people came and secured him. But alas! ere long it was my fate to be thus attacked, and to be carried off, when none of the grown people were nigh.

One day, when all our people were gone out to their works as usual, and only I and my dear sister were left to mind the house, two men and a woman got over our walls, and in a moment seized us both, and, without giving us time to cry out, or make resistance, they stopped our mouths, and ran off with us into the nearest wood. Here they tied our hands, and continued to carry us as far as they could, till night came on, when we reached a small house, where the robbers halted for refreshment, and spent the night. We were then unbound, but were unable to take any food; and, being quite overpowered by fatigue and grief, our only relief was some sleep, which allayed our misfortune for a short time.

The next morning we left the house, and continued travelling all the day. For a long time we had kept the woods, but at last we came into a road which I believed I knew. I had now some hopes of being delivered; for we had advanced but a little way before I discovered some people at a distance, on which I began to cry out for their assistance: but my cries had no other effect than to make them tie me faster [more firmly] and stop my mouth, and then they put me into a large sack. They also stopped my sister's mouth, and tied her hands; and in this manner we proceeded till we were out of the sight of these people.

When we went to rest the following night they offered us some victuals; but we refused it; and the only comfort we had was in being in one another's arms all that night, and bathing each other with our tears. But alas! we were soon deprived of even the small comfort of weeping together.

The next day proved a day of greater sorrow than I had yet experienced; for my sister and I were then separated, while we lay clasped in each other's arms. It was in vain that we besought them not to part us; she was torn from me, and immediately carried away, while I was left in a state of distraction not to be described. I cried and grieved continually; and for several days I did not eat any thing but what they forced into my mouth.

## THE EFFECT THE SIGHT OF A SLAVE SHIP HAD ON HIM

The first object which saluted my eyes when I arrived on the coast was the sea, and a slave ship, which was then riding at anchor, and waiting for its cargo. These filled me with astonishment, which was soon converted into terror when I was carried on board. I was immediately handled and tossed up to see if I were sound by some of the crew; and I was now persuaded that I had gotten into a world of bad spirits, and that that they were going to kill me. Their complexions too differing so much from ours, their long hair, and the language they spoke, (which was very different from any I had ever heard) united to confirm me in this belief. Indeed such were the horrors of my views and fears at the moment, that, if ten thousand worlds had been my own, I would have freely parted with them all to have exchanged my condition with that of the meanest slave in my own country. When I looked around the ship too and saw a large furnace or copper [cooking pot] boiling, and a multitude of black people of every description chained together, every one of their countenances expressing dejection and sorrow, I no longer doubted of my fate; and, quite overpowered with horror and anguish, I fell motionless on the deck and fainted.

When I recovered a little I found some black people about me, who I believed were some of those who brought me on board, and had been receiving their pay; they talked to me in order to cheer me, but all in vain. I asked them if we were not to be eaten by those white men with horrible looks, red faces, and loose hair. They told me I was not; and one of the crew brought me a small portion of spirituous [alcoholic] liquor in a wine glass; but, being afraid of him, I would not take it out of his hand. One of the blacks therefore took it from him and gave it to me, and I took a little down my palate, which, instead of reviving me, as they thought it would, threw me into the greatest consternation at the strange feeling it produced, having never tasted any such liquor before.

Soon after this the blacks who brought me on board went off, and left me abandoned to despair. I now saw myself deprived of all chance of returning to my native country, or even the least glimpse of hope of gaining the shore, which I now considered as friendly; and I even wished for my former slavery in preference to my present situation, which was filled with horrors of every kind, still heightened by my ignorance of what I was to undergo.

I was not long suffered [allowed] to indulge my grief; I was soon put down under the decks, and there I received such a salutation [welcome] in my nostrils as I had never experienced in my life: so that, with the loathsomeness of the stench, and crying together, I became so sick and low that I was not able to eat, nor had I the least desire to taste anything. I now wished for the last friend, death, to relieve me; but soon, to my grief, two of the white men offered me eatables; and, on my refusing to eat, one of them held me fast by the hands, and laid me across I think the windlass [a barrel around which a rope was tied; used to hoist the anchor], and tied my feet, while the other flogged me severely. I had never experienced any thing of this kind before; and although, not being used to the water, I naturally feared that element the first time I saw it, yet nevertheless, could I have got over the nettings [placed along the sides of slave ships to prevent slaves from jumping overboard], I would have jumped over the side, but I could not; and, besides the crew used to watch us very closely who were not chained down to the decks, lest we should leap into the water: and I have seen some of these poor African prisoners most severely cut for attempting to do so, and hourly whipped for not eating. This indeed was often the case with myself.

In a little time after, amongst the poor chained men, I found some of my own nation, which in a small degree gave ease to my mind. I inquired of these what was to be done with us; they gave me to understand we were to be carried to these white people's country to work for them. I then was a little revived, and thought, if it were no worse than working, my situation was not so desperate: but still I feared I should be put to death, the white people looked and acted, as I thought, in so savage a manner; for I had never seen among any people such instances of brutal cruelty; and this not only shewn towards us blacks, but also to some of the whites themselves. One white man in particular I saw, when we were permitted to be on deck, flogged so unmercifully with a large rope near the foremast, that he died in the consequence of it; and they tossed him over the side as they would have done a brute. This made me fear these people the more; and I expected nothing less than to be treated in the same manner.

I could not help expressing my fears and apprehensions to some of my countrymen: I asked them if these people had no country, but lived in this hollow place (the ship): they told at me they did not, but came from a distant one. 'Then,' said I, 'how comes it in all our country we never heard of them?' They told me because they lived so very far off. I then asked where were their women? had they any like themselves? I was told they had: 'and why,' said I, 'do we not see them?' they answered, because they were left behind. I asked how the vessel could go? they told me they could not tell; but that there were cloths put upon the masts by the help of the ropes I saw, and then the vessel went on; and the white men had some spell or magic they put in the water when they liked in order to stop the vessel.

I was exceedingly amazed at this account, and really thought they were spirits. I therefore wished much to be from amongst them, for I expected they would sacrifice me: but my wishes were vain; for we were so quartered that it was impossible for any of us to make our escape.

While we stayed on the coast I was mostly on deck; and one day, to my great astonishment, I saw one of these vessels coming in with the sails up. As soon as the whites saw it, they gave a great shout, at which we were amazed; and the more so as the vessel appeared larger by approaching nearer. At last she came to an anchor in my sight, and when the anchor was let go I and my countrymen who saw it were lost in astonishment to observe the vessel stop; and were now convinced it was done by magic.

Soon after this the other ship got her boats out, and they came on board of us, and the people of both ships seemed very glad to see each other. Several of the strangers also shook hands with us black people, and made motions with their hands, signifying I suppose we were to go to their country; but we did not understand them.

## HORRORS OF A SLAVE SHIP

At last, when the ship we were in had got in all her cargo, they made ready with many fearful noises, and we were all put under deck, so that we could not see how they managed the vessel. But this disappointment was the least of my sorrow. The stench of the hold while we were on the coast was so intolerably loathsome, that it was dangerous to remain there for any time, and some of us had been permitted to stay on the deck for the fresh air; but now that the whole ship's cargo were confined together, it became absolutely pestilential [deadly]. The closeness of the place, and the heat of the climate, added to the number on the ship, which was so crowded that each had scarcely room to turn himself, almost suffocated us. This produced copious perspirations, so that the air soon became unfit for respiration [breathing], from a variety of loathsome smells, and brought on a sickness among the slaves, of which many died, thus falling victims to the improvident [shortsighted] avarice, as I may call it, of their purchasers. This wretched situation was again aggravated [worsened] by the galling [irritation] of the chains, now become insupportable [unbearable]; and the filth of the necessary tubs [makeshift toilets], into which the children often fell, and were almost suffocated. The shrieks of the women, and the groans of the dying, rendered the whole a scene of horror almost inconceivable.

Happily perhaps for myself I was soon reduced so low here that it was thought necessary to keep me almost always on deck; and from my extreme youth I was not put in fetters. In this situation I expected every hour to share the fate of my companions, some of whom were almost daily brought upon deck at the point of death, which I began to hope would soon put an end to my miseries. Often did I think many of the inhabitants of the deep much more happy than myself. I envied them the freedom they enjoyed, and often wished I could change my condition for theirs. Every circumstance I met with served only to render my state more painful, and heighten my apprehensions, and my opinion of the cruelty of the whites.

One day they had taken a number of fishes; and when they had killed and satisfied themselves with as many as they thought fit, to our astonishment who were on the deck, rather than give any of them to us to eat as we expected, they tossed the remaining fish into the sea again, although we begged and prayed for some as well as we could, but in vain; and some of my countrymen, being pressed by hunger, took an opportunity, when they thought no one saw them, of trying to get a little privately; but they were discovered, and the attempt procured them some very severe floggings.

One day, when we had a smooth sea and moderate wind, two of my wearied countrymen who were chained together (I was near them at the time), preferring death to such a life of misery, somehow made through the nettings and jumped into the sea: immediately another

quite dejected fellow, who, on account of his illness, was suffered to be out of irons, also followed their example; and I believe many more would very soon have done the same if they had not been prevented by the ship's crew, who were instantly alarmed. Those of us that were the most active were in a moment put down under the deck, and there was such a noise and confusion amongst the people of the ship as I never heard before, to stop her, and get the boat out to go after the slaves. However two of the wretches were drowned, but they got the other, and afterwards flogged him unmercifully for thus attempting to prefer death to slavery.

In this manner we continued to undergo more hardships than I can now relate, hardships which are inseparable from this accused trade. Many a time we were near suffocation from the want of fresh air, which we were often without for whole days together. This, and the stench of the necessary tubs, carried off many.

During our passage I first saw flying fishes, which surprised me very much: they used frequently to fly across the ship, and many of them fell on the deck. I also now first saw the use of the quadrant [a navigational measuring device]; I had often with astonishment seen the mariners make observations with it, and I could not think what it meant. They at last took notice of my surprise; and one of them, willing to increase it, as well as to gratify my curiosity, made me one day look through it. The clouds appeared to me to be land, which disappeared as they passed along. This heightened my wonder; and I was now more persuaded than ever that I was in another world, and that every thing about me was magic.

## ARRIVES AT BARBADOES, WHERE THE CARGO IS SOLD AND DISPERSED

At last we came in sight of the island of Barbadoes, at which the whites on board gave a great shout, and made many signs of joy to us. We did not know what to think of this; but as the vessel drew nearer we plainly saw the harbour, and other ships of different kinds and sizes; and we soon anchored amongst them off Bridge Town.

Many merchants and planters now came on board, though it was in the evening. They put us in separate parcels [groups], and examined us attentively. They also made us jump, and pointed to the land, signifying we were to go there. We thought by this we should be eaten by these ugly men, as they appeared to us; and, when soon after we were all put down under the deck again, there was much dread and trembling among us, and nothing but bitter cries to be heard all the night from these apprehensions, insomuch that at last the white people got some old slaves from the land to pacify us. They told us we were not to be eaten, but to work, and were soon to go on land, where we should see many of our country people. This report eased us much; and sure enough, soon after we were landed, there came to us Africans of all languages.

We were conducted immediately to the merchant's yard, where we were all pent up together like so many sheep in a fold, without regard to sex or age. As every object was new to me every thing I saw filled me with surprise. What struck me first was that the houses were built with stories, and in every other respect different from those in Africa: but I was still more astonished on seeing people on horseback. I did not know what this could mean; and indeed I thought these people were full of nothing but magical arts. While I was in this astonishment one of my fellow prisoners spoke to a countryman of his about the horses, who said they were the same kind they had in their country. I understood them, though they were from a distant part of Africa, and I thought it odd I had not seen any horses there; but afterwards, when I came to converse with different Africans, I found they had many horses amongst them, and much larger than those I then saw.

We were not many days in the merchant's custody before we were sold after their usual manner, which is this:—On a signal given, (as the beat of a drum) the buyers rush at once into the yard where the slaves are confined, and make choice of that parcel they like best. The noise and clamour with which this is attended, and the eagerness visible in the countenances of the buyers, serve not a little to increase the apprehensions of the terrified Africans, who may well be supposed to consider them as the ministers of that destruction to which they think themselves devoted. In this manner, without scruple, are relations and friends separated, most of them never to see each other again. I remember in the vessel in which I was brought over, in the men's apartment, there were several brothers, who, in the sale, were sold in different lots; and it was very moving on this occasion to see and hear their cries at parting.

## THE AUTHOR IS CARRIED TO VIRGINIA

I now totally lost the small remains of comfort I had enjoyed in conversing with my countrymen; the women too, who used to wash and take care of me, were all gone different ways, and I never saw one of them afterwards.

I stayed in this island for a few days; I believe it could not be above a fortnight [two weeks]; when I and some few more slaves, that were not saleable amongst the rest, from very much fretting, were shipped off in a sloop for North America. On the passage we were better treated than when we were coming from Africa, and we had plenty of rice and fat pork.

We were landed up a river a good way from the sea, about Virginia county, where we saw few or none of our native Africans, and not one soul who could talk to me. I was a few weeks weeding grass, and gathering stones in a plantation; and at last all my companions were distributed different ways, and only myself was left.

I was now exceedingly miserable, and thought myself worse off than any of the rest of my companions; for they could talk to each other, but I had no person to speak to that I could understand. In this state I was constantly grieving and pining, and wishing for death rather than any thing else.

While I was in this plantation the gentleman, to whom I suppose the estate belonged, being unwell, I was one day sent for to his dwelling house to fan him; when I came into the room where he was I was very much affrighted at some things I saw, and the more so as I had seen a black woman slave as I came through the house, who was cooking the dinner, and the poor creature was cruelly loaded with various kinds of iron machines; she had one particularly on her head, which locked her mouth so fast that she could scarcely speak; and could not eat nor drink. I was much astonished and shocked at this contrivance, which I afterwards learned was called the iron muzzle. Soon after I had a fan put into my hand, to fan the gentleman while he slept; and so I did indeed with great fear.

While he was fast asleep I indulged myself a great deal in looking about the room, which to me appeared very fine and curious. The first object that engaged my attention was a watch which hung on the chimney, and was going. I was quite surprised at the noise it made, and was afraid it would tell the gentleman any thing I might do amiss: and when I immediately after observed a picture hanging in the room, which appeared constantly to look at me, I was still more affrighted, having never seen such things as these before. At one time I thought it was something relative to magic; and not seeing it move I thought it might be some way the whites had to keep their great men when they died, and offer them libation as we used to do to our friendly spirits.

In this state of anxiety I remained till my master awoke, when I was dismissed out of the room, to my no small satisfaction and relief; for I thought that these people were all made up of wonders.

Very soon afterward, Equiano was purchased by a British lieutenant in the Royal Navy, was renamed Gustavus Vassa (much against his will), and was taken to England; he was almost twelve years old. He spent the rest of his adolescent years traveling around the world with his new master. At the age of eighteen he was sold to the West Indies, where he slaved for three years, often aboard ships. All this time, he was earning money by various means, and eventually was able to purchase his freedom.

For many years thereafter, his life was a series of surprising and unusual adventures, many on the high seas, in almost every part of the world; he even went on an exploratory voyage to the North Pole. In 1777, at the age of thirty-two, he retired from the seafaring life, and spent the rest of his life primarily in London. There he worked as a servant to a number of high-ranking gentlemen, and even petitioned the Queen on behalf of his fellow Africans suffering as slaves in the West Indies. He died a wealthy and relatively famous man.

# MOSES ROPER

he horrifyingly violent experiences that **Moses Roper** (1816–?) related in his 1837 book, *A Narrative of the Adventures and Escape of Moses Roper, from American Slavery,* captured the attention of all of England, which is where Roper was living. The name of one of his masters, Gooch, soon became a popular symbol for the worst kind of slaveholder, and Gooch's nightmarish methods of torture became legendary. The book went through ten editions in twenty years and sold tens of thousands of copies, mostly in England, but also in the United States.

The violence of Roper's narrative began with his birth. His father was a white planter, and his mother a half-white slave.

A few months before I was born, my father married my mother's young mistress. As soon as my father's wife heard of my birth, she sent one of my mother's sisters to see whether I was white or black, and when my aunt had seen me, she returned back as soon as she could, and told her mistress that I was white, and resembled Mr. Roper very much. Mr. R.'s wife being not pleased with this report, she got a large club stick and knife, and hastened to the place in which my mother was confined. She went into my mother's room with full intention to murder me with her knife and club, but as she was going to stick the knife into me, my grandmother happening to come in, caught the knife and saved my life.

Roper was particularly concerned with the importance of telling the truth and the difficulties this could cause. So in order to impress upon people the truth of the macabre events he relates, he takes care not to describe his own feelings. Instead, he calls them "beyond description" or professes to be "unable to describe" them, and leaves them to the reader's imagination (or, in one case, draws upon an elaborate analogy). The book thus seems to consist primarily of cold, hard facts rather than impressions.

The passages below, which are not for the faint of heart, describe Roper's harsh treatment, several of his escape attempts, a surprising meeting he had during one of them, and some of the "instruments of torture" Mr. Gooch employed.

## "HERE I BEGAN TO ENTER INTO HARDSHIPS"

I was between twelve and thirteen years old at this time, and was sold to Mr. Hodge, a negro trader. Here I began to enter into hardships. After travelling several hundred miles, Mr. Hodge sold me to Mr. Gooch, the cotton planter, Kershaw county, South Carolina [not far from Columbia]; he purchased me at a town called Liberty Hill, about three miles from his home.

As soon as he got home, he immediately put me on his cotton plantation to work, and put me under overseers, gave me allowance of meat and bread with the other slaves, which was not half enough for me to live upon, and very laborious work. Here my heart was almost broke with grief at leaving my fellow slaves. Mr. Gooch did not mind my grief, for he flogged me nearly every day, and very severely.

Mr. Gooch bought me for his son-in-law, Mr. Hammans, about five miles from his residence. This man had but two slaves besides myself; he treated me very kindly for a week or two, but in summer, when cotton was ready to hoe, he gave me task work connected with this department, which I could not get done, not having worked on cotton farms before. When I failed in my task, he commenced flogging me, and set me to work without any shirt in the cotton field, in a very hot sun, in the month of July.

In August, Mr. Condell, his overseer, gave me a task at pulling fodder [hay for feeding the animals]. Having finished my task before night, I left the field; the rain came on, which soaked the fodder. On discovering this, he threatened to flog me for not getting in the fodder before the rain came. This was the first time I attempted to run away, knowing that I should get a flogging. I was then between thirteen and fourteen years of age.

I ran away to the woods half naked; I was caught by a slave-holder, who put me in Lancaster jail. When they put slaves in jail, they advertise for their masters to own them; but if the master does not claim his slave in six months from the time of imprisonment, the slave is sold for jail fees. When the slave runs away, the master always adopts a more rigorous system of flogging; this was the case in the present instance.

After this, having determined from my youth to gain my freedom, I made several attempts, was caught and got a severe flogging of one hundred lashes each time. Mr. Hammans was a very severe and cruel master, and his wife still worse; she used to tie me up and flog me while naked.

After Mr. Hammans saw that I was determined to die in the woods, and not live with him, he tried to obtain a piece of land from his father-in-law, Mr. Gooch; not having the means of purchasing it, he exchanged me for the land.

As soon as Mr. Gooch had possession of me again, knowing that I was averse to going back to him, he chained me by the neck to his chaise [two-wheeled carriage]. In this manner he took me to his home at MacDaniel's Ferry, in the county of Chester, a distance of fifteen miles. After which, he put me into a swamp, to cut trees, the heaviest work which men of twenty-five or thirty years of age have to do, I being but sixteen. Here I was on very short allowance of food, and having heavy work, was too weak to fulfil my tasks. For this I got many severe floggings; and after I had got my irons off, I made another attempt at running away. He took my irons off in the full anticipation that I could never get across the Catauba River, even when at liberty. On this I procured a small Indian canoe, which was tied to a tree, and ultimately got across the river in it. I then wandered through the wilderness for several days without any food, and but a drop of water to allay my thirst, till I became so starved, that I was obliged to go to a house to beg for something to eat, when I was captured, and again imprisoned.

Mr. Gooch, having heard of me through an advertisement, sent his son after me; he tied me up, and took me back to his father. Mr. Gooch then obtained the assistance of another slave-holder, and tied me up in his blacksmith's shop, and gave me fifty lashes with a cowhide. He then put a long chain, weighing twenty-five pounds, round my neck, and sent me into a field, into which he followed me with the cow-hide, intending to set his slaves to flog me again. Knowing this, and dreading to suffer again in this way, I gave him the slip, and got out of his sight, he having stopped to speak with the other slave-holder.

I got to a canal on the Catauba River, on the banks of which, and near to a lock, I procured a stone and a piece of iron, with which I forced the ring off my chain, and got it off, and then crossed the river, and walked about twenty miles, when I fell in with a slave-holder named Ballad, who had married the sister of Mr. Hammans. I knew that he was not so cruel as Mr. Gooch, and, therefore, begged of him to buy me. Mr. Ballad, who was one of the best planters in the neighbourhood, said, that he was not able to buy me, and stated, that he was obliged to take me back to my master, on account of the heavy fine attaching to a man harbouring a slave. Mr. Ballad proceeded to take me back. As we came in sight of Mr. Gooch's, all the treatment that I had met with there came forcibly upon my mind, the powerful influence of which is beyond description. On my knees, with tears in my eyes, with terror in my countenance, and fervency in all my features, I implored Mr. Ballad to buy me, but he again refused, and I was taken back to my dreaded and cruel master.

Having reached Mr. Gooch's, he proceeded to punish me. This he did by first tying my wrists together, and placing them over the knees; he then put a stick through, under my knees and over my arms, and having thus secured my arms, he proceeded to flog me, and gave me five hundred lashes on my bare back. This may appear incredible, but the marks which they left at present remain on my body, a standing testimony to the truth of this statement of his severity. He then chained me down in a log-pen [an enclosure for storing logs] with a 40 lb. chain, and made me lie on the damp earth all night.

In the morning after his breakfast he came to me, and without giving me any breakfast, tied me to a large heavy barrow [wheelbarrow], which is usually drawn by a horse, and made me drag it to the cotton field for the horse to use in the field. Thus, the reader will see, that it was of no possible use to my master to make me drag it to the field, and not through it; his cruelty went so far as actually to make me the slave of his horse, and thus to degrade me. He then flogged me again, and set me to work in the corn field the whole of that day, and at night chained me down in the log-pen as before.

The next morning he took me to the cotton field, and gave me a third flogging, and set me to hoe cotton. At this time I was dreadfully sore and weak with the repeated floggings and harsh treatment I had endured. He put me under a black man with orders, that if I did not keep my row up in hoeing with this man, he was to flog me. The reader must recollect here, that not being used to this kind of work, having been a domestic slave, it was quite impossible for me to keep up with him, and, therefore, I was repeatedly flogged during the day.

Mr. Gooch had a female slave about eighteen years old, who also had been a domestic slave, and through not being able to fulfil her task, had run away; which slave he was at this time punishing for that offence. On the third day, he chained me to this female slave, with a large chain of 40 lbs. weight round the neck. It was most harrowing to my feelings thus to be chained to a young female slave, for whom I would rather have suffered a hundred lashes than she should have been thus treated. He kept me chained to her during the week, and repeatedly flogged us both while thus chained together, and forced us to keep up with the other slaves, although retarded by the heavy weight of the log-chain.

Here again words are insufficient to describe the misery which possessed both body and mind whilst under this treatment, and which was most dreadfully increased by the sympathy which I felt for my poor degraded fellow sufferer. On the Friday morning, I entreated my master to set me free from my chains, and promised him to do the task which was given me, and more if possible, if he would desist from flogging me. This he refused to do until Saturday night, when he did set me free. This must rather be ascribed to his own interest in preserving me from death, as it was very evident I could no longer have survived under such treatment.

After this, though still determined in my own mind to escape, I stayed with him several months, during which he frequently flogged me, but not so severely as before related. During this time I had opportunity for recovering my health, and using means to heal my wounds.

## "TO FIND OUT MY POOR MOTHER"

I stayed with this master [Mr. Gooch] for several months, during which time we went on very well in general. In August, 1831, (this was my first acquaintance with any date,) I happened to hear a man mention this date, and, as it excited my curiosity, I asked what it meant; they told me it was the number of the year from the birth of Christ. On this date, August, 1831, some cows broke into a crib where the corn is kept, and ate a great deal. For this his slaves were tied up and received several floggings; but myself and another man, hearing the groans of those who were being flogged, stayed back in the field, and would not come up. Upon this I thought to escape punishment. On the Monday morning, however, I heard my master flogging the other man who was in the field. He could not see me, it being a field of Indian corn, which grows to a great height.

Being afraid that he would catch me, and dreading a flogging more than many others, I determined to run for it, and after travelling forty miles I arrived at the estate of Mr. Crawford, in North Carolina, Mecklinburgh county. Having formerly heard people talk about the free states, I determined upon going thither, and if possible, in my way, to find out my poor mother, who was in slavery several hundred miles from Chester; but the hope of doing the latter was very faint, and, even if I did, it was not likely that she would know me, having been separated from her when between five and six years old.

The first night I slept in a barn upon Mr. Crawford's estate, and, having overslept myself, was awoke by Mr. Crawford's overseer, upon which I was dreadfully frightened. He asked me what I was doing there? I made no reply to him then, and he making sure that he had secured a runaway slave, did not press me for an answer. On my way to his house, however, I made up the following story, which I told him in the presence of his wife:—I said, that I had been bound to a very cruel master when I was a little boy, and that having been treated very badly, I wanted to get home to see my mother. This statement may appear to some to be a direct lie, but as I understood the word *bound*, I considered it to apply to my case, having been sold to him, and thereby bound to serve him; though still, I rather hope that he would understand it, that I was bound [as an indentured servant], when a boy, till twenty-one years of age. Though I was white at the time, he would not believe my story, on account of my hair being curly and woolly, which led him to conclude I was possessed of enslaved blood. The overseer's wife, however, who seemed much interested in me, said she did not think I was of African origin, and that she had seen white men still darker than me.

Her persuasion prevailed; and, after the overseer had given me as much buttermilk as I could drink, and something to eat, which was very acceptable, having had nothing for two days, I set off for Charlotte in North Carolina, the largest town in the county. I went on very quickly the whole of that day, fearful of being pursued. The trees were very thick on each side of the road, and only a few houses at the distance of two or three miles apart. As I proceeded, I turned round in all directions to see if I was pursued, and if I caught a glimpse of any one coming along the road, I immediately rushed into the thickest part of the wood, to elude the grasp of what I was afraid might be my master. I went on in this way the whole day; at night I came up with two wagons: they had been to market. The regular road wagons do not generally put up at inns, but encamp in the roads and fields. When I came to them, I told them the same story I had told Mr. Crawford's overseer, with the assurance that the statement would meet the same success. After they had heard me, they gave me something to eat, and also a lodging in the camp with them.

I then went on with them about five miles, and they agreed to take me with them as far as they went, if I would assist them. This I promised to do. In the morning, however, I was much frightened by one of the men putting several questions to me; we were then about three miles from Charlotte. When within a mile of that town, we stopped at a brook to water the horses. While stopping here, I saw the men whispering, and fancying I overheard them say they would put me in Charlotte jail when they got there, I made my escape into the woods, pretending to be looking after something till I got out of their sight. I then ran on as fast as I could, but did not go through the town of Charlotte, as had been my intention; being a large town, I was fearful it might prove fatal to my escape. Here I was at a loss how to get on, as houses were not very distant from each other for nearly two hundred miles.

While thinking what I should do, I observed some wagons before me, which I determined to keep behind, and never go nearer to them than a quarter of a mile; in this way I travelled till I got to Salisbury. If I happened to meet any person on the road, I was afraid they would take me up; I asked them how far the wagons had got on before me, to make them suppose I belonged to the wagons. At night I slept on the ground in the woods, some little distance from the wagons, but not near enough to be seen by the men belonging to them. All this time I had but little food, principally fruit, which I found on the road.

On Thursday night, I got into Salisbury, having left Chester on the Monday morning preceding. After this, being afraid my master was in pursuit of me, I left the usual line of road, and took another direction, through Huntsville and Salem, principally through fields and woods. On my way to Caswell Courthouse [Roper was born in Caswell county, not far from the Virginia border], a distance of nearly one hundred miles from Salisbury, I was stopped by a white man, to whom I told my old story, and again succeeded in my escape. I also came up with a small cart, driven by a poor man who had been moving into some of the western territories, and was going back to Virginia to move some more of his luggage. On this, I told him I was going the same way to Hilton, thirteen miles from Caswell Court-house. He took me up in his cart, and we went to the Red House [a boardinghouse, or hotel], two miles from Hilton, the place where Mr. Mitchell [or Mr. Michael; a slave-trader] took me from when six years old, to go to the southern states. This was a very providential circumstance, for it happened that at the time I had to pass through Caswell Court-house, a fair or election was going on, which caused the place to be much crowded with people, and rendered it more dangerous for me to pass through.

At the Red House I left the cart and wandered about a long time, not knowing which way to go to find my mother. After some time, I took the road leading over to Ikeo Creek. I shortly came up with a little girl about six years old, and asked her where she was going; she said to her mother's, pointing to a house on a hill about half a mile off. She had been to the overseer's house, and was returning to her mother.

I then felt some emotions arising in my breast which I cannot describe, but will be fully explained in the sequel [shortly]. I told her that I was very thirsty, and would go with her to get something to drink. On our way, I asked her several questions, such as her name, that of her mother: she said hers was Maria, and her mother's Nancy. I inquired if her mother had any more children? She said five besides herself, and that they had been told that one had been sold when a little boy. I then asked the name of this child? She said, it was Moses.

These answers, as we approached the house, led me nearer and nearer to the finding out the object of my pursuit, and of recognising in the little girl the person of my own sister. At last I got to my mother's house! My mother was at home; I asked her if she knew me? She said, No. Her master was having a house built just by, and the men were digging a well; she supposed that I was one of the diggers. I told her I knew her very well, and thought that if she looked at me a little she would know me; but this had no effect. I then asked her if she had any sons? She said, Yes; but none so large as me.

I then waited a few minutes, and narrated some circumstances to her attending my being sold into slavery, and how she grieved at my loss. Here the mother's feelings on that dire occasion, and which a mother only can know, rushed to her mind; she saw her own son before her, for whom she had so often wept; and in an instant we were clasped in each other's arms, amidst the ardent interchange of caresses and tears of joy. Ten years had elapsed since I had seen my dear mother.

What could picture my feelings so well, as I once more beheld the mother who had brought me into the world and had nourished me, not with the anticipation of my being torn from her maternal care when only six years old, to become the prey of a mercenary and blood-stained slave-holder,—I say, what picture so vivid in description of this part of my tale, as the 7th and 8th verses of the 42d chapter of Genesis, "And Joseph saw his brethren and he knew them, but made himself strange unto them. And Joseph knew his brethren, but they knew not him." After the first emotion of the mother on recognising her first-born had somewhat subsided, could the reader not fancy the little one, my sister, as she told her simple tale of meeting with me to her mother, how she would say, while the parent listened with intense interest, "The man asked me straitly [directly] of our state and of our kindred, saying, Is your father yet alive, and have ye another brother?" Or, when at last, I could no longer refrain from making myself known, I say I was ready to burst into a frenzy of joy. How applicable the 1st, 2d, and 3d verses of the 45th chapter, "Then Joseph could not refrain himself before all them that stood by him; and he wept aloud, and said unto his brethren, I am Joseph; doth my father still live?" Then when the mother knew her son, when the brothers and sisters owned their brother; "He kissed all his brethren and wept over them, and after that his brethren talked with him," 15th verse.

At night, my mother's husband, a blacksmith, belonging to Mr. Jefferson, at the Red House, came home. He was suprised to see me with the family, not knowing who I was. He had been married to my mother when I was a babe, and had always been very fond of me. After the same tale had been told him, and the same emotions filled his soul, he again kissed the object of his early affection. The next morning I wanted to go on my journey, in order to make sure of my escape to the free states. But, as might be expected, my mother, father, brothers, and sisters, could ill part with their long lost one, and persuaded me to go into the woods in the daytime, and at night come home and sleep there. This I did for about a week. On the next Sunday night, I laid me down to sleep between my two brothers, on a pallet which my mother had prepared for me. About twelve o'clock I was suddenly awoke, and found my bed surrounded by twelve slave-holders with pistols in hand, who took me away (not allowing me to bid farewell to those I loved so dearly) to the Red House, where they confined me in a room the rest of the night, and in the morning lodged me in the jail of Caswell Courthouse.

What was the scene at home, what sorrow possessed their hearts, I am unable to describe, as I never after saw any of them more. I heard, however, that my mother, who was in the family-way when I went home, was soon after confined, and was very long before she recovered the effects of this disaster. I was told afterwards that some of those men who took me were professing Christians, but to me they did not seem to live up to what they professed. They did not seem, by their practices, at least, to recognise that God as their God, who hath said, "Thou shalt not deliver unto his master, the servant which is escaped from his master unto thee; he shall dwell with thee, even among you, in that place which he shall choose, in one of thy gates, where it liketh him best; thou shalt not oppress him." *Deut.* xxiii. 15, 16.

I was confined here in a dungeon under ground, the grating of which looked to the door of the jailer's house. His wife had a great antipathy to me. She was Mr. Roper's wife's cousin. My grandmother used to come to me nearly every day, and bring me something to eat, besides the regular jail allowance, by which my sufferings were somewhat decreased. Whenever the jailer went out, which he often did, his wife used to come to my dungeon and shut the wooden door over the grating, by which I was nearly suffocated, the place being very damp and noisome.

My master did not hear of my being in jail for thirty-one days after I had been placed there. He immediately sent his son and son-in-law, Mr. Anderson, after me. They came in a horse and chaise, took me from the jail to a blacksmith's shop, and got an iron collar fitted round my neck, with a heavy chain attached, then tied up my hands, and fastened the other end of the chain on another horse, and put me on its back. Just before we started, my grandmother came to bid me farewell; I gave her my hand as well as I could, and she having given me two or three presents, we parted. I had felt enough, far too much, for the weak state I was in; but how shall I describe my feelings upon parting with the *last* relative that I *ever saw?* The reader must judge by what would be his own feelings under similar circumstances.

## "THE INSTRUMENTS OF TORTURE"

Among the instruments of torture employed, I here describe one:

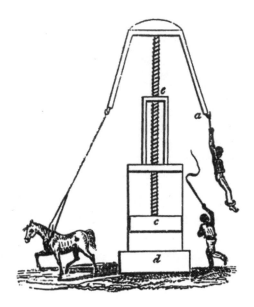

A COTTON SCREW.

This is a machine used for packing and pressing cotton. By it he hung me up by the hands at letter *a*, a horse moving round the screw *e*, and carrying it up and down, and pressing the block *c* into the box *d*, into which the cotton is put. At this time he hung me up for a quarter of an hour. I was carried up ten feet from the ground, when Mr. Gooch asked me if I was tired. He then let me rest for five minutes, then carried me round again, after which he let me down and put me into the box *d*, and shut me down in it for about ten minutes.

After this torture, I stayed with him several months, and did my work very well. It was about the beginning of 1832 when he took off my irons, and being in dread of him, he having threatened me with more punishment, I attempted again to escape from him. At this time I got into North Carolina; but a reward having been offered for me, a Mr. Robinson caught me, and chained me to a chair, upon which he sat up with me all night, and next day proceeded home with me. This was Saturday, Mr. Gooch had gone to church, several miles from his house. When he came back, the first thing he did was to pour some tar on my head, then rubbed it all over my face, took a torch, with pitch on, and set it on fire. He put it out before it did me very great injury, but the pain which I endured was most excruciating, nearly all my hair having been burnt off. On Monday he put irons on me again, weighing nearly fifty pounds. He threatened me again on the Sunday with another flogging; and on the Monday morning, before daybreak, I got away again, with my irons on, and was about three hours going a distance of two miles.

I had gone a good distance, when I met with a colored man, who got some wedges and took my irons off. However, I was caught again, and put into prison in Charlotte, where Mr. Gooch came, and took me back to Chester. He asked me how I got my irons off? They having been got off by a slave, I would not answer his question, for fear of getting the man punished.

Upon this, he put the fingers of my left hand into a vice, and squeezed all my nails off. He then had my feet put on an anvil, and ordered a man to beat my toes, till he smashed some of my nails off. The marks of this treatment still remain upon me, my nails never having grown perfect since. He inflicted this punishment, in order to get out of me how I got my irons off, but never succeeded. After this he hardly knew what to do with me, the whole stock of his cruelties seemed to be exhausted.

Mr. Gooch had now owned Moses Roper for about a year and a half. After Roper tried to escape again, Gooch, seeing that he was determined to get away, sent him to a slave dealer, who then sold him to another slave dealer, for whom Roper worked as his personal assistant for about a year. "I had to grease the faces of the blacks every morning with sweet oil, to make them shine before they are put up to sell," he wrote. He was then owned by a series of other masters, but was relatively well treated.

By 1834, when he was eighteen, he was in northeastern Florida, and when he was again sold, this time to a very harsh master, he determined to escape. He traveled by foot five hundred miles to Savannah, Georgia, narrowly escaping capture a number of times. Passing for white, he quickly obtained a position as a steward on a ship bound for New York; but before reaching there, he was almost killed by the sailors, who were mostly Southerners.

"When I arrived in the city of New York," Roper wrote, "I thought I was free; but learned I was not, and could be taken there." He went to Poughkeepsie and Albany, but found himself in terrible distress from lack of food. He couldn't find work, since he had no recommendations. He traveled a good deal more—to Vermont, New Hampshire, and Massachusetts, all the time passing for white and trying to elude the agents of his master. Finally, sixteen months after escaping, he managed to sail to England, reaching Liverpool in November 1835. There he was free at last.

After obtaining a rudimentary education, Roper gave speeches on his slave experiences, and published his narrative in 1837. Through lecturing and selling his book in more than two thousand towns and villages, he earned a living. In 1844, he moved with his wife (a white British woman) and child to West Canada, occasionally returning to England for short periods.

# LEWIS CLARKE

Lewis Clarke (1815–97) was one of the most engaging slave storytellers, as can be seen from his description, below, of his ten years under Mrs. Betsey Banton, a veritable ogre. His *Narrative of the Sufferings of Lewis Clarke, During a Captivity of More than Twenty-Five Years, Among the Algerines of Kentucky, One of the So Called Christian States of America* was published in 1845, the same year as Frederick Douglass's first slave narrative. (Clarke's reference to "Algerines" is a play on the fact that Algerians used to enslave American travelers: "Algerines" thus came to refer to slaveowners.) Clarke's and Douglass's narratives share the same flavor, combining outrage with wit. Lewis Clarke's, like his brother Milton's (published together with a reprint of Lewis's in 1846), employs biting sarcasm and broad comedy to accomplish its purpose.

Lewis and Milton Clarke didn't write their autobiographies themselves; they dictated them to Joseph C. Lovejoy, a prominent Massachusetts minister and brother of the abolitionists Owen and Elijah P. Lovejoy. We can get a sense of what Lewis was like in person from a description of one of his lectures by the abolitionist Lydia Maria Child:

> I have seldom been more entertained by any speaker. His obvious want of education was one guaranty of the truth of his story; and the uncouth awkwardness of his language had

a sort of charm, like the circuitous expression, and stammering utterance, of a foreign tongue, striving to speak our most familiar phrases. His mind was evidently full of ideas, which he was eager to express; but the medium was wanting. "I've got it in *here*," said he, laying his hand on his heart; "but I don't know how to get it out." However, in his imperfect way, I believed he conveyed much information to many minds; and that few who heard him went away without being impressed by the conviction that he was sincerely truthful, and testified of things which he did know. . . . What he *might* have been, with common advantages for education, is shown by his shrewd conclusions, and large ideas which his soul struggled so hard to utter in imperfect language.

Child wrote down a good portion of what Lewis Clarke said. Here's a sample of his own words:

Preacher Raymond didn't used to flog his slaves; he used to duck 'em. He had a little slave girl, about eight years old, that he used to duck very often. One day, the family went to meeting, and left her to take care of a young child. The child fretted, and she thought she would serve it as master served her; so she ducked it, and it slipped out of her hands, and got drowned. They put her in prison, and sentenced her to be hung; but she, poor child, didn't know nothing at all what it meant.—When they took her to the gallows, she was guarded all round by men; but she was so innocent, she didn't know what they was going to do with her. She stooped to pick up a pin, and stuck it in her frock, as she went.—The poor young thing was so glad to get out of prison, that she was as merry as if she was going to her mother's house.

It's clear from this that the homespun flavor and folksy rhetoric of Lewis Clarke's story were not just added by Lovejoy, but derive from Lewis's own mastery of the art of storytelling.

"I FELL INTO THE HANDS OF BETSEY BANTON"

The night in which I was born, I have been told, was dark and terrible—black as the night for which Job prayed, when he besought the clouds to pitch their tent round about the place of his birth ["Let the day perish wherein I was born, . . . Let darkness and the shadow of death stain it; let a cloud dwell upon it; let the blackness of the day terrify it." *Job* 3:3–5]; and my life of slavery was but too exactly prefigured by the stormy elements that hovered over the first hour of my being. It was with great difficulty that any one could be urged out for a necessary attendant for my mother. At length, one of the sons of Mr. Campbell [Samuel Campbell was Lewis's grandfather; his daughter, Letitia Campbell, was Lewis's mother, and was also Samuel Campbell's slave], William, by the promise from his mother of the child that should be born, was induced to make an effort to obtain the necessary assistance. By going five or six miles, he obtained a female professor of the couch [midwife].

William Campbell, by virtue of this title, always claimed me as his property. And well would it have been for me if this claim had been regarded. At the age of six or seven years, I fell into the hands of his sister, Mrs. Betsey Banton, whose character will be best known when I have told the horrid wrongs which she heaped upon me for ten years. If there are any *she* spirits that come up from hell, and take possession of one part of mankind, I am sure she is one of that sort.

I was consigned to her under the following circumstances: When she was married, there was given her, as part of her dower, as is common among the Algerines of Kentucky, a girl, by the name of Ruth, about fourteen or fifteen years old. In a short time, Ruth was dejected and injured, by beating and abuse of different kinds, so that she was sold, for a half-fool, to the more tender mercies of the sugar-planter in Louisiana. The amiable Mrs. Betsey obtained then, on loan from her parents, another slave, named Phillis. In six months she had suffered so severely, under the hand of this monster-woman, that she made an attempt to kill herself, and was taken home by the parents of Mrs. Banton. This produced a regular slaveholding family brawl; a regular war, of *four* years, between the *mild* and peaceable Mrs. B. and her own parents.

These wars are very common among the Algerines in Kentucky; indeed, slaveholders have not arrived at that degree of civilization that enables them to live in tolerable peace, though united by the nearest family ties. In them is fulfilled what I have heard read in the Bible— "The father is against the son, and the daughter-in-law against the mother-in-law, and their *foes* are of their own household" [*Matthew* 10:35–36]. Some of the slaveholders may have a wide house; but one of the *cat-handed*, snake-eyed, brawling women, which slavery produces, can fill it from cellar to garret. I have heard every place I could get into any way ring with their screech-owl voices. Of all the animals on the face of this earth, I am most afraid of a real mad, passionate, raving, slaveholding woman. I am sure I would sooner lie down to sleep by the side of tigers than near a raging-mad cave woman. But I must go back to *sweet* Mrs. Banton. I have been describing her in the *abstract*. I will give a full-grown portrait of her right away.

For four years after the trouble about Phillis she never came near her father's house. At the end of this period, another of the amiable sisters was to be married, and sister Betsey could not repress the tide of curiosity urging her to be present at the nuptial ceremonies. Beside, she had another motive. Either shrewdly suspecting that she might deserve less than any member of the family, or that some ungrounded partiality would be manifested toward her sister, she determined, at all hazards, to be present, and see that the scales which weighed out the children of the plantation should be held with even hand. The wedding-day was appointed; the sons and daughters of this joyful occasion were gathered together, and then came also the fair-faced, but black-hearted, Mrs. B. Satan, among the sons of God, was never less welcome than this fury among her kindred. They all knew what she came for,—to make mischief, if possible. "Well, now, if there aint Bets!" exclaimed the old lady. The father was moody and silent, knowing that she inherited largely of the disposition of her mother; but he had experienced too many of her retorts of courtesy to say as much, for dear experience had taught him the discretion of silence. The brothers smiled at the prospect of fun and frolic; the sisters trembled for fear, and word flew round among the slaves, "The old she-bear has come home! look out! look out!"

The wedding went forward. Polly, a very good sort of a girl to be raised in that region, was married, and received, as the first instalment of her dower, a *girl* and a *boy*. Now was the time for Mrs. Banton, sweet, good Mrs. Banton. "Poll has a girl and a *boy*, and I only had that fool of a girl. I reckon, if I go home without a boy too, this house won't be left standing."

This was said, too, while the sugar of the wedding-cake was yet melting upon her tongue. How the bitter words would flow when the guests had retired, all began to imagine. To arrest this whirlwind of rising passion, her mother promised any boy upon the plantation, to be taken home on her return. Now, my evil star was right in the top of the sky. Every boy was ordered in, to pass before this female sorceress, that she might select a victim for her unprovoked malice, and on whom to pour the vials of her wrath for years. I was that unlucky fellow. Mr. Campbell, my grandfather, objected, because it would divide a family, and offered her Moses, whose father and mother had been sold south. Mrs. Campbell put in for William's claim, dated *ante natum*—before I was born; but objections and claims of every kind were swept away by the wild passion and shrill-toned voice of Mrs. B. Me she would have, and none else. Mr. Campbell went out to hunt, and drive away bad thoughts; the old lady became quiet, for she was sure none of her blood run in my veins, and, if there was any of her husband's there, it was no fault of hers. Slave women are always revengeful toward the children of slaves that have any of the blood of their husbands in them.

I was too young, only seven years of age, to understand what was going on. But my poor and affectionate mother understood and appreciated it all. When she left the kitchen of the mansion-house, where she was employed as cook, and came home to her own little cottage, tear of anguish was in her eye, and the image of sorrow upon every feature of her face. She knew the female Nero [a mad emperor of Rome], whose rod was now to be over me. That night sleep departed from her eyes. With the youngest child clasped firmly to her bosom, she spent the night in walking the floor, coming ever and anon to lift up the clothes and look at me and my poor brother, who lay sleeping together. *Sleeping*, I said. Brother slept, but not I. I saw my mother when she first came to me, and I could not sleep. The vision of that night—its deep, ineffaceable impression—is now before my mind with all the distinctness of yesterday.

### "MY WEARY PILGRIMAGE OF SUFFERING WAS FAIRLY BEGUN"

In the morning, I was put into the carriage with Mrs. B. and her children, and my weary pilgrimage of suffering was fairly begun. It was her business on the road, for about twenty-five or thirty miles, to initiate her children into the art of tormenting their new victim. I was seated upon the bottom of the carriage, and these little imps were employed in pinching me, pulling my ears and hair; and they were stirred up by their mother, like a litter of young wolves, to torment me in every way possible. In the mean time, I was compelled by the old she-wolf to call them "Master," "Mistress," and bow to them, and obey them at the first call.

During that day, I had, indeed, no very agreeable foreboding of the torments to come; but, sad as were my anticipations, the reality was infinitely beyond them. Infinitely more bitter than death were the cruelties I experienced at the hand of this merciless woman. Save from one or two slaves on the plantation, during my ten years of captivity here, I scarcely heard a kind word, or saw a smile toward me from any living being. And now that I am where people look kind, and act kindly toward me, it seems like a dream. I hardly seem to be in the same world that I was then. When I first got into the free states, and saw every body look like they loved one another, sure enough, I thought, this must be the "*Heaven*" of LOVE I had heard something about.

But I must go back to what I suffered from that wicked woman. It is hard work to keep the mind upon it; I hate to think it over—but I must tell it—the world must know what is done in Kentucky. I cannot, however, tell all the ways by which she tormented me. I can only give a few instances of my suffering, as specimens of the whole. A book of a thousand pages would not be large enough to tell of all the tears I shed, and the sufferings endured, in THAT TEN YEARS OF PURGATORY.

A very trivial offence was sufficient to call forth a great burst of indignation from this woman of ungoverned passions. In my simplicity, I put my lips to the same vessel, and drank out of it, from which her children were accustomed to drink. She expressed her utter abhorrence of such an act, by throwing my head violently back, and dashing into my face two dippers of water. The shower of water was followed by a heavier shower of *kicks;* yes, delicate reader, this lady did not hesitate to *kick,* as well as cuff in a very plentiful manner; but the words, bitter and cutting, that followed, were like a storm of hail upon my young heart. "She would teach me better manners than that; she would let me know I was to be brought up to her hand; she would have one slave that knew his place; if I wanted water, go to the spring, and not drink there in the house." This was new times for me; for some days I was completely benumbed with my sorrow. I could neither eat nor sleep.

"NOR WAS OUR LIFE AN EASY ONE"

There were several children in the family, and my first main business was to wait upon them. Another young slave and myself have often been compelled to sit up by turns all night, to rock the cradle of a little, peevish scion [child] of slavery. If the cradle was stopped, the moment they awoke a dolorous [miserable] cry was sent forth to mother or father, that Lewis had gone to sleep. The reply to this call would be a direction from the mother for these petty tyrants to get up and take the whip, and give the good-for-nothing scoundrel a smart whipping. This was the midnight pastime of a child ten or twelve years old. What might you expect of the future man?

There were four house-slaves in this family, including myself; and though we had not, in all respects, so hard work as the field hands, yet in many things our condition was much worse. We were constantly exposed to the whims and passions of every member of the family; from the least to the greatest their anger was wreaked upon us. Nor was our life an easy one, in the hours of our toil or in the amount of labor performed. We were always required to sit up until all the family had retired; then we must be up at early dawn in summer, and before day in winter. If we failed, through weariness or for any other reason, to appear at the first morning summons, we were sure to have our hearing quickened by a severe chastisement. Such horror has seized me, lest I might not hear the first shrill call, that I have often in dreams fancied I heard that unwelcome voice, and have leaped from my couch, and walked through the house and out of it before I awoke. I have gone and called the other slaves, in my sleep, and asked them if they did not hear master call. Never, while I live, will the remembrance of those long, bitter nights of fear pass from my mind.

But I want to give you a few specimens of the abuse which I received. During the ten years that I lived with Mrs. Banton, I do not think there were as many days, when she was at home, that I, or some other slave, did not receive some kind of beating or abuse at her hands. It seemed as though she could not live nor sleep unless some poor back was smarting, some head beating with pain, or some eye filled with tears, around her. Her tender mercies were indeed cruel. She brought up her children to imitate her example. Two of them manifested some dislike to the cruelties taught them by their mother, but they never stood high in favor with her; indeed, any thing like humanity or kindness to a slave, was looked upon by her as a great offence.

Her instruments of torture were ordinarily the raw hide, or a bunch of hickory-sprouts seasoned in the fire and tied together. But if these were not at hand, nothing came amiss. She could relish a beating with a chair, the broom, tongs, shovel, shears, knife-handle, the heavy heel of her slipper, or a bunch of keys; her zeal was so active in these barbarous inflictions, that her invention was wonderfully quick, and some way of inflicting the requisite torture was soon found out.

One instrument of torture is worthy of particular description. *This was an oak club, a foot and a half in length and an inch and a half square.* With this delicate weapon she would beat us upon the hands and upon the feet until they were blistered. This instrument was carefully preserved for a period of four years. Every day, for that time, I was compelled to see that hated tool of cruelty lying in the chair by my side. The least degree of delinquency either in not doing all the appointed work, or in look or behavior, was visited with a beating from this oak club. That club will always be a prominent object in the picture of horrors of my life of more than twenty years of bitter bondage.

When about nine years old, I was sent in the evening to catch and kill a turkey. They were securely sleeping in a tree—their accustomed resting-place for the night. I approached as cautiously as possible, and selected the victim I was directed to catch; but, just as I grasped him in my hand, my foot slipped, and he made his escape from the tree, and fled beyond my reach. I returned with a heavy heart to my mistress with the story of my misfortune. She was enraged beyond measure. She determined, at once, that I should have a whipping of the worst kind, and she was bent upon adding all the aggravations possible.

Master had gone to bed drunk, and was now as fast asleep as drunkards ever are. At any rate, he was filling the house with the noise of his snoring and with the perfume of his breath. I was ordered to go and call him—wake him up—and ask him to be *kind* enough to give me fifty good smart lashes. To be *whipped* is bad enough—to *ask* for it is worse—to ask a drunken man to whip you is too bad. I would sooner have gone to a nest of rattlesnakes, than to the bed of this drunkard. But go I must. Softly I crept along, and gently shaking his arm, said, with a trembling voice, "Master, master, mistress wants you to wake up." This did not go to the extent of her command, and in a great fury she called out, "What, you wont ask him to whip you, will you?" I then added, "Mistress wants you to give me fifty lashes." A bear at the smell of a lamb was never roused quicker. "Yes, yes, that I will; I'll give you such a whipping as you will never want again." And, sure enough, so he did. He sprang from the bed, seized me by the hair, lashed me with a handful of switches, threw me my whole length upon the floor; beat, kicked, and cuffed me worse than he would a dog, and then threw me, with all his strength, out of the door, more dead than alive. There I lay for a long time, scarcely able and not daring to move, till I could hear no sound of the furies within, and then crept to my couch, longing for death to put an end to my misery. I had no friend in the world to whom I could utter one word of complaint, or to whom I could look for protection.

Mr. Banton owned a blacksmith's shop, in which he spent some of his time, though he was not a very efficient hand at the forge. One day, mistress told me to go over to the shop and let master give me a flogging. I knew the mode of punishing there too well. I would rather die than go. The poor fellow who worked in the shop, a very skilful workman, one day came to the determination that he would work no more, unless he could be paid for his labor. The enraged master put a handful of nail-rods into the fire, and when they were *red-hot*, took them out, and *cooled* one after another of them in the blood and flesh of the poor slave's back. I knew this was the shop mode of punishment. I would not go; and Mr. Banton came home, and his amiable lady told him the story of my refusal. He broke forth in a great rage, and gave me a most unmerciful beating; adding that, if I had come, he would have burned the hot nail-rods into my back.

Mrs. Banton, as is common among slaveholding women, seemed to hate and abuse me all the more, because I had some of the blood of her father in my veins. There are no slaves that are so badly abused, as those that are related to some of the women, or the children of their own husband; it seems as though they never could hate these quite bad enough. My sisters were as white and good-looking as any of the young ladies in Kentucky. It happened once of a time, that a young man called at the house of Mr. Campbell, to see a sister of Mrs. Banton. Seeing one of my sisters in the house, and pretty well dressed, with a strong family look, he thought it was Miss Campbell; and, with that supposition, addressed some conversation to her which he had intended for the private ear of Miss C. The mistake was noised [talked about] abroad, and occasioned some amusement to young people. Mrs. Banton heard of it, and it made her caldron of wrath sizzling hot; every thing that diverted and amused other people seemed to enrage her. There are hot-springs in Kentucky; she was just like one of them, only brimful of boiling poison.

She must wreak her vengeance, for this innocent mistake of the young man, upon me. "She would fix me, so that nobody should ever think I was white." Accordingly, in a burning hot day, she *made me take off every rag of clothes, go out into the garden,* and pick herbs for hours, in order to *burn* me black. When I went out, she threw cold water on me, so that the sun might take effect upon me; when I came in, she gave me a severe beating on my blistered back.

After I had lived with Mrs. B. three or four years, I was put to spinning hemp, flax, and tow, on an old-fashioned foot-wheel. There were four or five slaves at this business, a good part of the time. We were kept at our work from daylight to dark in summer, from long before day to nine or ten o'clock in the evening in winter. Mrs. Banton, for the most part, was near, or kept continually passing in and out, to see that each of us performed as much work as she thought we ought to do. Being young, and sick at heart all the time, it was very hard work to go through the day and evening and not suffer exceedingly for want of more sleep. Very often, too, I was compelled to work beyond the ordinary hour, to finish the appointed task of the day. Sometimes I found it impossible not to drop asleep at the wheel.

On these occasions, Mrs. B. had her peculiar contrivances for keeping us awake. She would sometimes sit, by the hour, with a dipper of vinegar and salt, and throw it in my eyes to keep them open. My hair was pulled till there was no longer any pain from that source. *And I can now suffer myself to be lifted by the hair of the head, without experiencing the least pain.*

She very often kept me from getting water to satisfy my thirst, and in one instance kept me for two entire days without a particle of food. This she did, in order that I might make up for lost time. But, of course, I lost rather than gained upon my task. Every meal taken from me made me less able to work. It finally ended in a terrible beating.

But all my severe labor, and bitter and cruel punishments, for these ten years of captivity with this worse than Arab family, all these were as nothing to the sufferings I experienced by being separated from my mother, brothers, and sisters; the same things, with them near to sympathize with me, to hear my story of sorrow, would have been comparatively tolerable.

They were distant only about thirty miles; and yet, in ten long, lonely years of childhood, I was only permitted to see them three times.

My mother occasionally found an opportunity to send me some token of remembrance and affection, a sugar-plum or an apple; but I scarcely ever ate them; they were laid up, and handled and wept over till they wasted away in my hand.

My thoughts continually by day, and my dreams by night, were of mother and home; and the horror experienced in the morning, when I awoke and behold it was a dream, is beyond the power of language to describe.

At the age of sixteen or seventeen, Clarke was hired out to work on a tobacco plantation for four or five years. Then in 1841, about to be sold to Louisiana, he made his escape (he was twenty-six years old). Passing for white, he traveled on a pony through Kentucky and crossed the Ohio River, eventually reaching Canada—and freedom. He didn't stay there long, however: he journeyed to Oberlin, Ohio, to visit his brother Milton, who had escaped a year before Lewis. From there he went back to Kentucky to rescue his youngest brother, Cyrus—a terribly hazardous undertaking indeed, and one that left his friends aghast at his foolhardiness. Against all odds, however, he succeeded.

Here is Lewis's description of what Cyrus did once he had crossed the Ohio:

> When we were fairly landed upon the northern bank, and had gone a few steps, Cyrus stopped suddenly, on seeing the water gush out at the side of the hill. Said he, "Lewis, give me that tin cup." "What in the world do you want of a tin cup now? We have not time to stop." The cup he would have. Then he went up to the spring, dipped and drank, and dipped and drank; then he would look round, and drink again. "What in the world," said I, "are you fooling there for?" "O," said he, "this is the first time I ever had a chance to drink water that ran out of the *free* dirt." Then we went a little further, and he sat down on a log. I urged him forward. "O," said he, "I must sit on this free timber a little while."
>
> A short distance further on, we saw a man, who seemed to watch us very closely. I asked him which was the best way to go, *over* the hill before us, or *around* it. I did this, to appear to know something about the location. He went off, without offering any obstacles to our journey. In going up the hill, Cyrus would stop, and lay down and roll over. "What in the world are you about, Cyrus? Don't you see Kentucky is over there?" He still continued to roll and kiss the ground; said it was a game horse that could roll clear over. Then he would put face to the ground, and roll over and over. "First time," he said, "he ever rolled on *free* grass."

Lewis Clarke spent several years traveling around New England telling his story, lecturing on slavery, and helping other runaway slaves. Harriet Beecher Stowe, who interviewed Clarke many times in her home, based the character of George Harris in *Uncle Tom's Cabin* on him. He eventually settled in Windsor, Ontario, but returned with his children to Oberlin in 1875, where he is buried.

# FREDERICK DOUGLASS

**F** **rederick Douglass** (1818–1895)—slave, orator, auto-
biographer, editor, activist, and statesman—was the
most famous African American of the nineteenth century.
More than any other black man, he was responsible for the
downfall of slavery, for the enlistment of black troops in the
Union army, and, in the last few years of his life, for the
awakening of the American people to the realization that
Southern blacks had lost almost every gain they had made
during the Civil War and Reconstruction.

His first book, the 1845 *Narrative of the Life of Frederick
Douglass, an American Slave*, has become the most widely
studied slave narrative. His second, the 1855 *My Bondage
and My Freedom*, is an equally militant and far longer, more
sophisticated, and playful autobiography. The following
account of Douglass's youth draws from both narratives—
the first forceful and heroic, the second intimate and
often humorous.

The 1845 *Narrative* was written, in part, to prove to
doubters that he really had been a slave. It had been seven
years since his escape, and four years since his first speech;
listeners were now openly questioning whether he was telling
the truth about his life. He spoke too well, his English was too
pure, he looked too elegant and self-confident, and he
refused to tell anyone his slave name (for fear of recapture)

or the means of his escape (for fear of closing off similar opportunities to other slaves). Douglass, who had probably read several slave narratives by this time, decided to write his own, as evidence that the skeptics were wrong.

The book was enormously popular, selling out its first printing of five-thousand copies in four months. By 1850 approximately thirty thousand copies had been sold. Reviewers were ecstatic: one newspaper called it "the most thrilling work which the American press ever issued—and the most important."

The *Narrative* is, in a sense, all about a slave becoming a master: a master of language (through learning to read and write), a master of his self (through self-recognition and through freedom from slavery), a master of the incidents of his life (through retelling and shaping them). Its climax comes not when Douglass escapes—he refuses to tell us about that—but when he masters his identity by assuming a new one.

But that identity was bound to the abolitionist cause. The two most prominent white abolitionists of his day, William Lloyd Garrison and Wendell Phillips, contributed to his narrative, and he closes it with an account of an antislavery meeting. Everything in the book is viewed through abolitionist lenses: the slaves and everything antislavery are light and good, and everything that smacks of slavery or ownership is dark and bad. Although Douglass is very careful in sticking to the facts, he presents them along abolitionist lines: in the *Narrative*, he is a heroic figure alone in the hell of slavery, almost completely isolated from the African American community. As Henry Louis Gates Jr. has made clear, "Douglass's rhetorical power convinces us that he is 'the' black slave, that he embodies the structures of thoughts and feelings of all black slaves, that he is the resplendent, articulate part that stands for the whole, for the collective black slave community."

In *My Bondage and My Freedom*, Douglass, who had by this time broken with Garrison and his followers while continuing his abolitionist work in a more political framework, presented a much more rounded view of his experience, and paid tribute to the real black slave community that, in fact, had nurtured and surrounded him. In the *Narrative*, Douglass never mentioned his grandmother, and one is left to imagine that he was brought up solely by cruel masters; never does the comfort of family make an appearance—all in slavery is bleak and harsh. *My Bondage and My Freedom* displays, as did the *Narrative*, Douglass's extraordinary skill with language and his unflagging militancy—in *My Bondage* he even goes so far as to condone killing one's master. But here he mixes it with a warm, human, and complex portrait of himself, his family, his friends, and even his oppressors. The emphasis in the *Narrative* on liberation is here replaced by an emphasis on brotherhood and community.

## FIRST KNOWLEDGE OF BEING A SLAVE
[from *My Bondage and My Freedom*]

Living with my dear old grandmother and grandfather, it was a long time before I knew myself to be *a slave*. I knew many other things before I knew that. Grandmother and grandfather were the greatest people in the world to me; and being with them so snugly in their own little cabin—I supposed it be their own—knowing no higher authority over me or the other children than the authority of grandmamma, for a time there was nothing to disturb me; but, as I grew larger and older, I learned by degrees the sad fact, that the "little hut," and the lot on which it stood, belonged not to my dear old grandparents, but to some person who lived a great distance off, and who was called, by grandmother, "OLD MASTER." I further learned the sadder fact, that not only the house and lot, but that grandmother herself, (grandfather was free,) and all the little children around her, belonged to this mysterious personage, called by grandmother, with every mark of reverence, "Old Master." Thus early did clouds and shadows begin to fall upon my path.

Once on the track—troubles never come singly—I was not long in finding out another fact, still more grievous to my childish heart. I was told that this "old master," whose name seemed ever to be mentioned with fear and shuddering, only allowed the children to live with grandmother for a limited time, and that in fact as soon as they were big enough, they were promptly taken away, to live with the said "old master." These were distressing revelations indeed; and though I was quite too young to comprehend the full import of the intelligence [news], and mostly spent my childhood days in gleesome [fun] sports with the other children, a shade of disquiet rested upon me.

The absolute power of this distant "old master" had touched my young spirit with but the point of its cold, cruel iron, and left me something to brood over after the play and in moments of repose. Grandmammy was, indeed, at that time, all the world to me; and the thought of being separated from her, in any considerable time, was more than an unwelcome intruder. It was intolerable.

But the sorrows of childhood, like the pleasures of after life, are transient. It is not even within the power of slavery to write *indelible* [permanent] sorrow, at a single dash, over the heart of a child. There is, after all, but little difference in the measure of contentment felt by the slave-child neglected and the slaveholder's child cared for and petted. The spirit of the All Just mercifully holds the balance for the young.

The slaveholder, having nothing to fear from impotent childhood, easily affords to refrain from cruel inflictions; and if cold and hunger do not pierce the tender frame, the first seven or eight years of the slave-boy's life are about as full of sweet content as those of the most favored and petted *white* children of the slaveholder. The slave-boy escapes many troubles which befall and vex his white brother. He seldom has to listen to lectures on propriety of behavior, or on anything else. He is never chided for handling his little knife and fork improperly or awkwardly, for he uses none. He is never reprimanded for soiling the table-cloth, for he takes his meals on the clay floor. He never has the misfortune, in his games or sports, of soiling or tearing his clothes, for he has almost none to soil or tear. He is never expected to act like a nice little gentleman, for he is only a rude little slave. Thus, freed from all restraint, the slave-boy can be, in his life and conduct, a genuine boy, doing whatever his boyish nature suggests; enacting, by turns, all the strange antics and freaks of horses, dogs, pigs, and barn-door fowls, without in any manner compromising his dignity, or incurring reproach of any sort. He literally runs wild; has no pretty little verses to learn in the nursery; no nice little speeches to make for aunts, uncles, or cousins, to show how smart he is; and, if he can only manage to keep out of the way of the heavy feet and fists of the older slave boys, he may trot on, in his joyous and roguish tricks, as happy as any little heathen under the palm trees of Africa. To be sure, he is occasionally reminded, when he stumbles in the path of his master—and this he early learns to avoid—that he is eating his *"white bread,"* and that he will be made to *"see sights"* by-and-by. The threat is soon forgotten; the shadow soon passes, and our sable [dark] boy continues to roll in the dust, or play in the mud, as best suits him, and in the veriest freedom. If he feels uncomfortable, from mud or from dust, the coast is clear; he can plunge into the river or the pond, without the ceremony of undressing, or the fear of wetting his clothes; his little tow[coarse]-linen shirt—for that is all he has on—is easily dried; and it needed ablution [washing] as much as did his skin. His food is of the coarsest kind, consisting for the most part of cornmeal mush, which often finds it way from the wooden tray to his mouth in an oyster shell. His days, when the weather is warm, are spent in the pure, open air, and in the bright sunshine. He always sleeps in airy apartments; he seldom has to take powders [ground-up medicines], or to be paid to swallow pretty little sugar-coated pills, to cleanse his blood, or to quicken his appetite. He eats no candies; gets no lumps of loaf sugar; always relishes his food; cries but little, for nobody cares for his crying; learns to esteem his bruises but slight, because others so esteem them [see them that way]. In a word, he is, for the most part of the first eight years of his life, a spirited, joyous, uproarious, and happy boy, upon whom troubles fall only like water on a duck's back. And such a boy, so far as I can now remember, was the boy whose life in slavery I am now narrating.

## THE AUTHOR REMOVED FROM HIS FIRST HOME
[from *My Bondage and My Freedom*]

When the time of my departure was decided upon, my grandmother, knowing my fears, and in pity for them, kindly kept me ignorant of the dreaded event about to transpire. Up to the morning (a beautiful summer morning) when we were to start, and, indeed, during the whole journey—a journey which, child as I was, I remember as well as if it were yesterday—she kept the sad fact hidden from me. This reserve was necessary; for, could I have known all, I should have given grandmother some trouble in getting me started. As it was, I was helpless, and she—dear woman!—led me along by the hand, resisting, with the reserve and solemnity of a priestess, all my inquiring looks to the last.

The distance from Tuckahoe to Wye river—where my old master lived—was full twelve miles, and the walk was quite a severe test of the endurance of my young legs. The journey would have proved too severe for me, but that my dear old grandmother—blessings on her memory!— afforded occasional relief by "toting" me (as Marylanders have it) on her shoulder. My grandmother, though advanced in years—as was evident from more than one gray hair, which peeped from between the ample and graceful folds of her newly-ironed bandana turban—was yet a woman of power and spirit. She was marvelously straight in figure, elastic, and muscular. I seemed hardly to be a burden to her. She would have "toted" me farther, but that I felt myself too much of a man to allow it, and insisted on walking.

As the day advanced the heat increased; and it was not until the afternoon that we reached the much dreaded end of the journey. I found myself in the midst of a group of children of many colors; black, brown, copper colored, and nearly white. I had not seen so many children before. Great houses loomed up in different directions, and a great many men and women were at work in the fields. All this hurry, noise, and singing was very different from the stillness of Tuckahoe. As a new comer, I was an object of special interest; and, after laughing and yelling around me, and playing all sorts of wild tricks, they (the children) asked me to go out and play with them. This I refused to do, preferring to stay with grandmamma. I could not help feeling that our being there boded no good to me. Grandmamma looked sad. She was soon to lose another object of affection, as she had lost many before. I knew she was unhappy, and the shadow fell from her brow on me, though I knew not the cause.

All suspense, however, must have an end; and the end of mine, in this instance, was at hand. Affectionately patting me on the head, and exhorting me to be a good boy, grandmamma told me to go and play with the little children. "They are kin to you," said she; "go and play with them." Among a number of cousins were Phil, Tom, Steve, and Jerry, Nance and Betty.

Grandmother pointed out my brother PERRY, my sister SARAH, and my sister ELIZA, who stood in the group. I had never seen my brother nor my sisters before; and, though I had sometimes heard of them, and felt a curious interest in them, I really did not understand what they were to me, or I to them. We were brothers and sisters, but what of that? Why should they be attached to me, or I to them? Brothers and sisters were by blood; but *slavery* had made us strangers.

I really wanted to play with my brother and sisters, but they were strangers to me, and I was full of fear that grandmother might leave without taking me with her. Entreated to do so, however, and that, too, by my dear grandmother, I went to the back part of the house, to play with them and the other children. *Play*, however, I did not, but stood with my back against the wall, witnessing the playing of the others. At last, while standing there, one of the children, who had been in the kitchen, ran up to me, in a sort of roguish glee, exclaiming, "Fed, Fed! grandmammy gone! grandmammy gone!" I could not believe it; yet, fearing the worst, I ran into the kitchen, to see for myself, and found it even so. Grandmammy had indeed gone, and was now far away, "clean" out of sight.

I need not tell all that happened now. Almost heart-broken at the discovery, I fell upon the ground, and wept a boy's bitter tears, refusing to be comforted. My brother and sisters came around me, and said, "Don't cry," and gave me peaches and pears, but I flung them away, and refused all their kindly advances. I had never been deceived before; and I felt not only grieved at parting—as I supposed forever—with my grandmother, but indignant that a trick had been played upon me in a matter so serious.

It was now late in the afternoon. The day had been an exciting and wearisome one, and I knew not how or where, but I suppose I sobbed myself to sleep. There is a healing in the angel wing of sleep, even for the slave-boy; and its balm was never more welcome to any wounded soul than it was to mine, the first night I spent at the domicile of old master. The reader may be surprised that I narrate so minutely an incident apparently so trivial, and which must have occurred when I was not more than seven years old; but as I wish to give a faithful history of my experience in slavery, I cannot withhold a circumstance which, at the time, affected me so deeply. Besides, this was, in fact, my first introduction to the realities of slavery.

MY MOTHER [from *My Bondage and My Freedom*]

My mother was hired out to a Mr. Stewart, who lived about twelve miles from old master's, and, being a field hand, she seldom had leisure, by day, for the performance of the journey. The nights and the distance were both obstacles to her visits. She was obliged to walk, unless chance flung into her way an opportunity to ride; and the latter was sometimes her good luck. But she always had to walk one way or the other.

One of the visits of my mother to me, while at Col. Lloyd's, I remember very vividly, as affording a bright gleam of a mother's love, and the earnestness of a mother's care.

I had on that day offended "Aunt Katy," (called "Aunt" by way of respect,) the cook of old master's establishment. I do not now remember the nature of my offense in this instance, for my offenses were numerous in that quarter, greatly depending, however, upon the mood of Aunt Katy, as to their heinousness; but she had adopted, that day, her favorite mode of punishing me, namely, making me go without food all day—that is, from after breakfast. The first hour or two after dinner, I succeeded pretty well in keeping up my spirits; but though I made an excellent stand against the foe, and fought bravely during the afternoon, I knew I must be conquered at last, unless I got the accustomed reënforcement of a slice of corn bread, at sundown. Sundown came, but *no bread,* and, in its stead, there came the threat, with a scowl well suited to its terrible import, that she "meant to *starve the life out of me!*" Brandishing her knife, she chopped off the heavy slices for the other children, and put the loaf away, muttering, all the while, her savage designs upon myself. Against this disappointment, for I was expecting that her heart would relent at last, I made an extra effort to maintain my dignity; but when I saw all the other children around me with merry and satisfied faces, I could stand it no longer. I went out behind the house, and cried like a fine fellow! When tired of this, I returned to the kitchen, sat by the fire, and brooded over my hard lot. I was too hungry to sleep.

While I sat in the corner, I caught sight of an ear of Indian corn on an upper shelf of the kitchen. I watched my chance, and got it, and, shelling off a few grains, I put it back again. The grains in my hand, I quickly put in some ashes, and covered them with embers, to roast them. All this I did at the risk of getting a brutal thumping, for Aunt Katy could beat, as well as starve me. My corn was not long in roasting, and, with my keen appetite, it did not matter even if the grains were not exactly done. I eagerly pulled them out, and placed them on my stool, in a clever little pile. Just as I began to help myself to my very dry meal, in came my dear mother.

And now, dear reader, a scene occurred which was altogether worth beholding, and to me it was instructive as well as interesting. The friendless and hungry boy, in his extremest need—and when he did not dare to look for succor—found himself in the strong, protecting arms of a mother; a mother who was, at the moment (being endowed with high powers of manner as well as matter) more than a match for all his enemies. I shall never forget the indescribable expression of her countenance, when I told her that I had had no food since morning; and that Aunt Katy said she "meant to starve the life out of me." There was pity in her glance at me, and a fiery indignation at Aunt Katy at the same time; and, while she took the corn from me, and gave me a large ginger cake, in its stead, she read Aunt Katy a lecture which she never forgot. My mother threatened her with complaining to old master in my behalf; for the latter, though harsh and cruel himself, at times, did not sanction the meanness, injustice, partiality and oppressions enacted by Aunt Katy in the kitchen. That night I learned the fact, that I was not only a child, but *somebody's* child. The "sweet cake" my mother gave me was in the shape of a heart, with a rich, dark ring glazed upon the edge of it. I was victorious, and well off for the moment; prouder, on my mother's knee, than a king upon his throne. But my triumph was short. I dropped off to sleep, and waked in the morning only to find my mother gone, and myself left at the mercy of the sable virago [loud, threatening woman], dominant in my old master's kitchen, whose fiery wrath was my constant dread.

I do not remember to have seen my mother after this occurrence. Death soon ended the little communication that had existed between us; and with it, I believe, a life—judging from her weary, sad, downcast countenance and mute demeanor—full of heart-felt sorrow. I was not allowed to visit her during any part of her long illness; nor did I see her for a long time before she was taken ill and died.

My mother died when I could not have been more than eight or nine years old, on one of old master's farms in Tuckahoe, in the neighborhood of Hillsborough. Her grave is, as the grave of the dead at sea, unmarked, and without stone or stake.

## SUFFERING FROM COLD—HOW WE TOOK OUR MEALS

[from *Narrative of the Life of Frederick Douglass*]

I was seldom whipped by my old master, and suffered little from any thing else than hunger and cold. I suffered much from hunger, but much more from cold. In hottest summer and coldest winter, I was kept almost naked—no shoes, no stockings, no jacket, no trousers, nothing on but a coarse tow linen shirt, reaching only to my knees. I had no bed. I must have perished with cold, but that, the coldest nights, I used to steal a bag which was used for carrying corn to the mill. I would crawl into this bag, and there sleep on the cold, damp, clay floor, with my head in and feet out. My feet have been so cracked with the frost, that the pen with which I am writing might be laid in the gashes.

We were not regularly allowanced. Our food was coarse corn meal boiled. This was called *mush*. It was put into a large wooden tray or trough, and set down upon the ground. The children were then called, like so many pigs, and like so many pigs they would come and devour the mush; some with oyster-shells, others with pieces of shingle, some with naked hands, and none with spoons. He that ate fastest got most; he that was strongest secured the best place; and few left the trough satisfied.

## A TURNING POINT IN MY HISTORY

[from *Narrative of the Life of Frederick Douglass*]

I was probably between seven and eight years old when I left Colonel Lloyd's plantation. I left it with joy. I shall never forget the ecstasy with which I received the intelligence that my old master (Anthony) had determined to let me go to Baltimore, to live with Mr. Hugh Auld, brother to my old master's son-in-law, Captain Thomas Auld. We arrived at Baltimore early on Sunday morning, landing at Smith's Wharf, not far from Bowley's Wharf. We had on board the sloop a large flock of sheep; and after aiding in driving them to the slaughterhouse of Mr. Curtis on Louden Slater's Hill, I was conducted by Rich, one of the hands belonging on board of the sloop, to my new home in Alliciana Street, near Mr. Gardner's ship-yard, on Fells Point.

Mr. and Mrs. Auld were both at home, and met me at the door with their little son Thomas, to take care of whom I had been given. And here I saw what I had never seen before; it was a white face beaming with the most kindly emotions; it was the face of my new mistress, Sophia Auld. I wish I could describe the rapture that flashed through my soul as I beheld it. It was a new and strange sight to me, brightening up my pathway with the light of happiness. Little Thomas was told, there was his Freddy,—and I was told to take care of little Thomas; and thus I entered upon the duties of my new home with the most cheering prospect ahead.

My new mistress proved to be all she appeared when I first met her at the door,—a woman of the kindest heart and finest feelings. She had never had a slave under her control previously to myself, and prior to her marriage she had been dependent upon her own industry for a living. She was by trade a weaver; and by constant application to her business, she had been in a good degree preserved from the blighting and dehumanizing effects of slavery. I was utterly astonished at her goodness. I scarcely knew how to behave towards her. She was entirely unlike any other white woman I had ever seen. I could not approach her as I was accustomed to approach other white ladies. My early instruction was all out of place. The crouching servility, usually so acceptable a quality in a slave, did not answer when manifested toward her. Her favor was not gained by it; she seemed to be disturbed by it. She did not deem it impudent or unmannerly for a slave to look her in the face. The meanest slave was put fully at ease in her presence, and none left without feeling better for having seen her. Her face was made of heavenly smiles, and her voice of tranquil music.

But, alas! this kind heart had but a short time to remain such. The fatal poison of irresponsible power was already in her hands, and soon commenced its infernal work. That cheerful eye, under the influence of slavery, soon became red with rage; that voice, made all of sweet accord, changed to one of harsh and horrid discord; and that angelic face gave place to that of a demon.

## COMMENCEMENT OF LEARNING TO READ—WHY DISCONTINUED
[from *Narrative of the Life of Frederick Douglass*]

Very soon after I went to live with Mr. and Mrs. Auld, she very kindly commenced to teach me the A, B, C. After I had learned this, she assisted me in learning to spell words of three or four letters.

Just at this point of my progress, Mr. Auld found out what was going on, and at once forbade Mrs. Auld to instruct me further, telling her, among other things, that it was unlawful, as well as unsafe, to teach a slave to read. To use his own words, further, he said, "If you give a nigger an inch, he will take an ell. A nigger should know nothing but to obey his master—to do as he is told to do. Learning would *spoil* the best nigger in the world. Now," said he, "if you teach that nigger (speaking of myself) how to read, there would be no keeping him. It would forever unfit him to be a slave. He would at once become unmanageable, and of no value to his master. As to himself, it could do him no good, but a great deal of harm. It would make him discontented and unhappy."

These words sank deep into my heart, stirred up sentiments within that lay slumbering, and called into existence an entirely new train of thought. It was a new and special revelation, explaining dark and mysterious things, with which my youthful understanding had struggled, but struggled in vain. I now understood what had been to me a most perplexing difficulty—to wit, the white man's power to enslave the black man. It was a grand achievement, and I prized it highly. From that moment, I understood the pathway from slavery to freedom. It was just what I wanted, and I got it at a time when I the least expected it. Whilst I was saddened by the thought of losing the aid of my kind mistress, I was gladdened by the invaluable instruction which, by the merest accident, I had gained from my master. Though conscious of the difficulty of learning without a teacher, I set out with high hope, and a fixed purpose, at whatever cost of trouble, to learn how to read. The very decided manner with which he spoke, and strove to impress his wife with the evil consequences of giving me instruction, served to convince me that he was deeply sensible of the truths he was uttering. It gave me the best assurance that I might rely with the utmost confidence on the results which, he said, would flow from teaching me to read. What he most dreaded, that I most desired. What he most loved, that I most hated. That which to him was a great evil, to be carefully shunned, was to me a great good, to be diligently sought; and the argument which he so warmly urged, against my learning to read, only served to inspire me with a desire and determination to learn. In learning to read, I owe almost as much to the bitter opposition of my master, as to the kindly aid of my mistress. I acknowledge the benefit of both.

## "A CHANGE CAME O'ER THE SPIRIT OF MY DREAM"
[from *Narrative of the Life of Frederick Douglass*]

I lived in Master Hugh's family about seven years. During this time, I succeeded in learning to read and write. In accomplishing this, I was compelled to resort to various stratagems. I had no regular teacher. My mistress, who had kindly commenced to instruct me, had, in compliance with the advice and direction of her husband, not only ceased to instruct, but had set her face against my being instructed by any one else. It is due, however, to my mistress to say of her, that she did not adopt this course of treatment immediately. She at first lacked the depravity indispensable to shutting me up in mental darkness. It was at least necessary for her to have some training in the exercise of irresponsible power, to make her equal to the task of treating me as though I were a brute.

My mistress was, as I have said, a kind and tender-hearted woman; and in the simplicity of her soul she commenced, when I first went to live with her, to treat me as she supposed one human being ought to treat another. In entering upon the duties of a slaveholder, she did not seem to perceive that I sustained to her the relation of a mere chattel [piece of movable property], and that for her to treat me as a human being was not only wrong, but dangerously so. Slavery proved as injurious to her as it did to me. When I went there, she was a pious, warm, and tender-hearted woman. There was no sorrow or suffering for which she had not a tear. She had bread for the hungry, clothes for the naked, and comfort for every mourner that came within her reach. Slavery soon proved its ability to divest her of these heavenly qualities. Under its influence, the tender heart became stone, and the lamblike disposition gave way to one of tiger-like fierceness. The first step in her downward course was in her ceasing to instruct me. She now commenced to practise her husband's precepts. She finally became even more violent in her opposition than her husband himself. She was not satisfied with simply doing as well as he had commanded; she seemed anxious to do better. Nothing seemed to make her more angry than to see me with a newspaper. She seemed to think that here lay the danger. I have had her rush at me with a face made all up of fury, and snatch from me a newspaper, in a manner that fully revealed her apprehension. She was an apt woman; and a little experience soon demonstrated, to her satisfaction, that education and slavery were incompatible with each other.

From this time I was most narrowly watched. If I was in a separate room any considerable length of time, I was sure to be suspected of having a book, and was at once called to give an account of myself. All this, however, was too late. The first step had been taken. Mistress, in teaching me the alphabet, had given me the *inch*, and no precaution could prevent me from taking the *ell* [45 inches].

The plan which I adopted, and the one by which I was most successful, was that of making friends of all the little white boys whom I met in the street. As many of these as I could, I converted into teachers. With their kindly aid, obtained at different times and in different places, I finally succeeded in learning to read. When I was sent of errands, I always took my book with me, and by going one part of my errand quickly, I found time to get a lesson before my return. I used also to carry bread with me, enough of which was always in the house, and to which I was always welcome; for I was much better off in this regard than many of the poor white children in our neighborhood. This bread I used to bestow upon the hungry little urchins, who, in return, would give me that more valuable bread of knowledge. I am strongly tempted to give the names of two or three of those little boys, as a testimonial of the gratitude and affection I bear them; but prudence forbids;—not that it would injure me, but it might embarrass them; for it is almost an unpardonable offence to teach slaves to read in this Christian country. It is enough to say of the dear little fellows, that they lived on Philpot Street, very near Durgin and Bailey's shipyard. I used to talk this matter of slavery over with them. I would sometimes say to them, I wished I could be as free as they would be when they got to be men. "You will be free as soon as you are twenty-one, *but I am a slave for life!* Have not I as good a right to be free as you have?" These words used to trouble them; they would express for me the liveliest sympathy, and console me with the hope that something would occur by which I might be free.

## DIFFERENCES WITH MASTER THOMAS

[from *My Bondage and My Freedom*]

Not long after his marriage, Master Thomas [Douglass's new owner, following the death of Captain Anthony] had a misunderstanding with Master Hugh, and, as a means of punishing his brother, he ordered him to send me home.

It was now more than seven years since I had lived with Master Thomas Auld, in the family of my old master, on Col. Lloyd's plantation. We were almost entire strangers to each other; for, when I knew him at the house of my old master, it was not as a *master*, but simply as "Captain Auld," who had married old master's daughter. All my lessons concerning his temper and disposition, and the best methods of pleasing him, were yet to be learnt. Slaveholders, however, are not very ceremonious in approaching a slave; and my ignorance of the new material in the shape of a master was but transient.

In Baltimore, I could, occasionally, get into a Sabbath school, among the free children, and receive lessons, with the rest; but, having already learned both to read and to write, I was more of a teacher than a pupil, even there. When, however, I went back to the Eastern Shore, and was at the house of Master Thomas, I was neither allowed to teach, nor to be taught. The whole community—with but a single exception, among the whites—frowned upon everything like imparting instruction either to slaves or to free colored persons. That single exception, a pious young man, named Wilson, asked me, one day, if I would like to assist him in teaching a little Sabbath school, at the house of a free colored man in St. Michael's, named James Mitchell. The idea was to me a delightful one, and I told him I would gladly devote as much of my Sabbaths as I could command, to that most laudable [praiseworthy] work. Mr. Wilson soon mustered up a dozen old spelling books, and a few testaments; and we commenced operations, with some twenty scholars, in our Sunday school. Here, thought I, is something worth living for; here is an excellent chance for usefulness;

and I shall soon have a company of young friends, lovers of knowledge, like some of my Baltimore friends, from whom I now felt parted forever.

Our first Sabbath passed delightfully, and I spent the week after very joyously. I could not go to Baltimore, but I could make a little Baltimore here. At our second meeting, I learned that there was some objection to the existence of the Sabbath school; and, sure enough, we had scarcely got at work—*good work*, simply teaching a few colored children how to read the gospel of the Son of God—when in rushed a mob, headed by Mr. Wright Fairbanks and Mr. Garrison West—two class-leaders—and Master Thomas; who, armed with sticks and other missiles, drove us off, and commanded us never to meet for such a purpose again. One of this pious crew told me, that as for my part, I wanted to be another Nat Turner [leader of a famous slave revolt]; and if I did not look out, I should get as many balls into me, as Nat did into him. Thus ended the infant Sabbath school, in the town of St. Michael's. The reader will not be surprised when I say, that the breaking up of my Sabbath school, by these class-leaders, and professedly holy men, did not serve to strengthen my religious convictions. The cloud over my St. Michael's home grew heavier and blacker than ever.

Bad as my condition was when I lived with Master Thomas, I was soon to experience a life far more goading and bitter. The many differences springing up between myself and Master Thomas, owing to the clear perception I had of his character, and the boldness with which I defended myself against his capricious complaints, led him to declare that I was unsuited to his wants; that my city life had affected me perniciously; that, in fact, it had almost ruined me for every good purpose, and had fitted me for everything that was bad. One of my greatest faults, or offenses, was that of letting his horse get away, and go down to the farm belonging to his father-in-law. The animal had a liking for that farm, with which I fully sympathized. Whenever I let it out, it would go dashing down the road to Mr. Hamilton's, as if going on a grand frolic. My horse gone, of course I must go after it. The explanation of our mutual attachment to the place is the same; the horse found there good pasturage, and I found there plenty of bread. Mr. Hamilton had his faults, but starving his slaves was not among them. He gave food, in abundance, and that, too, of an excellent quality. In Mr. Hamilton's cook—Aunt Mary—I found a most generous and considerate friend. She never allowed me to go there without giving me bread enough to make good the deficiencies of a day or two. Master Thomas at last resolved to endure my behavior no longer; he could neither keep me, nor his horse, we liked so well to be at his father-in-law's farm. I had now lived with him nearly nine months, and he had given me a number of severe whippings, without any visible improvement in my character, or my conduct; and now he was resolved to put me out—as he said—"to be broken."

## COVEY, THE NEGRO-BREAKER
[from *My Bondage and My Freedom*]

There was, in the Bay Side, very near the camp ground, where my master got his religious impressions, a man named Edward Covey, who enjoyed the execrated reputation, of being a first rate hand at breaking young negroes. This Covey was a poor man, a farm renter; and this reputation, (hateful as it was to the slaves and to all good men,) was, at the same time, of immense advantage to him. It enabled him to get his farm tilled with very little expense, compared with what it would have cost him without this most extraordinary reputation. Some slaveholders thought it an advantage to let Mr. Covey have the government of their slaves a year or two, almost free of charge, for the sake of the excellent training such slaves got under his happy management! Like some horse breakers, noted for their skill, who ride the best horses in the country without expense, Mr. Covey could have under him, the most fiery bloods of the neighborhood, for the simple reward of returning them to their owners, *well broken.* Added to the natural fitness of Mr. Covey for the duties of his profession, he was said to "enjoy religion," and was as strict in the cultivation of piety, as he was in the cultivation of his farm. I was made aware of his character by some who had been under his hand; and while I could not look forward to going to him with any pleasure, I was glad to get away from St. Michael's. I was sure of getting enough to eat at Covey's, even if I suffered in other respects. *This*, to a hungry man, is not a prospect to be regarded with indifference.

The family consisted of Mr. and Mrs. Covey; Miss Kemp, (a broken-backed woman,) a sister of Mrs. Covey; William Hughes, cousin to Edward Covey; Caroline, the cook; Bill Smith, a hired man; and myself. Bill Smith, Bill Hughes, and myself, were the working force of the farm, which consisted of three or four hundred acres. I was now, for the first time in my life, to be a field hand; and in my new employment I found myself even more awkward than a green country boy may be supposed to be, upon his first entrance into the bewildering scenes of city life; and my awkwardness gave me much trouble. Strange and unnatural as it may seem, I had been at my new home but three days, before Mr. Covey, (my brother in the Methodist church,) gave me a bitter fore-taste of what was in reserve for me. I presume he thought, that since he had but a single year in which to complete his work, the sooner he began, the better. Perhaps he thought that, by coming to blows at once, we should mutually better understand our relations. But to whatever motive, direct or indirect, the cause may be referred, I had not been in his possession three whole days, before he subjected me to a most brutal chastisement. Under his heavy blows, blood flowed freely, and welts were left on my back as large as my little finger. The sores on my back, from this flogging, continued for weeks, for they were kept open by the rough and coarse cloth which I wore for shirting.

Covey was not a large man; he was only about five feet ten inches in height, I should think; short necked, round shoulders; of quick and wiry motion, of thin and wolfish visage; with a pair of small, greenish-gray eyes, set well back under a forehead without dignity, and constantly in motion, and floating his passions, rather than his thoughts, in sight, but denying them utterance in words. The creature presented an appearance altogether ferocious and sinister, disagreeable and forbidding, in the extreme. When he spoke, it was from the corner of his mouth, and in a sort of light growl, like a dog, when an attempt is made to take a bone from him.

I remained with Mr. Covey one year, (I cannot say I *lived* with him,) and during the first six months that I was there, I was whipped, either with sticks or cowskins, every week. Aching bones and a sore back were my constant companions. Frequent as the lash was used, Mr. Covey thought less of it, as a means of breaking down my spirit, than that of hard and long continued labor. He worked me steadily, up to the point of my powers of endurance. From the dawn of day in the morning, till the darkness was complete in the evening, I was kept at hard work, in the field or the woods. At certain seasons of the year, we were all kept in the field till eleven and twelve o'clock at night. At these times, Covey would attend us in the field, and urge us on with words or blows, as it seemed best to him. He had, in his life, been an overseer, and he well understood the business of slave driving. There was no deceiving him. He knew just what a man or boy could do, and he held both to strict account. When he pleased, he would work himself, like a very Turk, making everything fly before him. It was, however, scarcely necessary for Mr. Covey to be really present in the field, to have his work go on industriously. He had the faculty of making us feel that he was always present. By a series of adroitly managed surprises, which he practiced, I was prepared to expect him at any moment. His plan was, never to approach the spot where his hands were at work, in an open, manly and direct manner. No thief was ever more artful in his devices than this man Covey. He would creep and crawl, in ditches and gullies; hide behind stumps and bushes, and practice so much of the cunning of the serpent, that Bill Smith and I—between ourselves—never called him by any other name than *"the snake."* We fancied that in his eyes and his gait we could see a snakish resemblance. One half of his proficiency in the art of negro breaking, consisted, I should think, in this species of cunning. We were never secure. He could see or hear us nearly all the time. He was, to us, behind every stump, tree, bush and fence on the plantation. He carried this kind of trickery so far, that he would sometimes mount his horse, and make believe he was going to St. Michael's; and, in thirty minutes afterward, you might find his horse tied in the woods, and the snake-like Covey lying flat in the ditch, with his head lifted above its edge, or in a fence corner, watching every movement of the slaves! I have known him walk up to us and give us special orders, as to our work, in advance, as if he were leaving home with a view to being absent several days; and before he got half way to the house, he would avail himself of our inattention to his movements, to turn short on his heels, conceal himself behind a fence corner or a tree, and watch us until the going down of the sun. Mean and contemptible as is all this, it is in keeping with the character which the life of a slaveholder is calculated to produce. There is no earthly inducement, in the slave's condition, to incite him to labor faithfully. The fear of punishment is the sole motive for any sort of industry, with him. Knowing this fact, as the slaveholder does, and judging the slave by himself, he naturally concludes the slave will be idle whenever the cause for this fear is absent. Hence, all sorts of petty deceptions are practiced, to inspire this fear.

## THE AUTHOR BROKEN DOWN

[from *Narrative of the Life of Frederick Douglass*]

If at any one time of my life, more than another, I was made to drink the bitterest dregs of slavery, that time was during the first six months of my stay with Mr. Covey. We were worked all weathers. It was never too hot or too cold; it could never rain, blow, snow, or hail too hard for us to work in the field. Work, work, work, was scarcely more the order of the day than of the night. The longest days were too short for him, and the shortest nights were too long for him. I was somewhat unmanageable when I first went there; but a few months of this discipline tamed me. Mr. Covey succeeded in breaking me. I was broken in body, soul and spirit. My natural elasticity was crushed; my intellect languished; the disposition to read departed; the cheerful spark that lingered about my eye died; the dark night of slavery closed in upon me; and behold a man transformed into a brute!

Sunday was my only leisure time. I spent this in a sort of beast-like stupor, between sleep and wake, under some large tree. At times, I would rise up, a flash of energetic freedom would dart through my soul, accompanied with a faint beam of hope, that flickered for a moment, and then vanished. I sank down again, mourning over my wretched condition. I was sometimes prompted to take my life, and that of Covey, but was prevented by a combination of hope and fear. My sufferings on this plantation seem now like a dream rather than a stern reality.

## ANOTHER PRESSURE OF THE TYRANT'S VICE

[from *Narrative of the Life of Frederick Douglass*]

I have already intimated that my condition was much worse, during the first six months of my stay at Mr. Covey's, than in the last six. The circumstances leading to the change in Mr. Covey's course toward me form an epoch in my humble history. You have seen how a man was made a slave; you shall see how a slave was made a man.

On one of the hottest days of the month of August, 1833, Bill Smith, William Hughes, a slave named Eli, and myself, were engaged in fanning [separating the chaff from the grain] wheat. Hughes was clearing the fanned wheat from before the fan. Eli was turning, Smith was feeding, and I was carrying wheat to the fan. The work was simple, requiring strength rather than intellect; yet, to one entirely unused to such work, it came very hard. About three o'clock of that day, I broke down; my strength failed me; I was seized with a violent aching of the head, attended with extreme dizziness; I trembled in every limb. Finding what was coming, I nerved myself up, feeling it would never do to stop work. I stood as long as I could stagger to the hopper with grain. When I could stand no longer, I fell, and felt as if held down by an immense weight. The fan of course stopped; every one had his own work to do; and no one could do the work of the other, and have his own go on at the same time.

Mr. Covey was at the house, about one hundred yards from the treading-yard where we were fanning. On hearing the fan stop, he left immediately, and came to the spot where we were. He hastily inquired what the matter was. Bill answered that I was sick, and there was no one to bring wheat to the fan. I had by this time crawled away under the side of the post and rail-fence by which the yard was enclosed, hoping to find relief by getting out of the sun. He then asked where I was. He was told by one of the hands. He came to the spot, and, after looking at me awhile, asked me what was the matter. I told him as well as I could, for I scarce had strength to speak. He then gave me a savage kick in the side, and told me to get up. I tried to do so, but fell back in the attempt. He gave me another kick, and again told me to rise. I again tried, and succeeded in gaining my feet; but, stooping to get the tub with which I was feeding the fan, I again staggered and fell.

While [I was] down in this situation, Mr. Covey took up the hickory slat with which Hughes had been striking off the half-bushel measure, and with it gave me a heavy blow upon the head, making a large wound, and the blood ran freely; and with this again told me to get up. I made no effort to comply, having now made up my mind to let him do his worst.

In a short time after receiving this blow, my head grew better. Mr. Covey had now left me to my fate. At this moment I resolved, for the first time, to go to my master, enter a complaint, and ask his protection. In order to this, I must that afternoon walk seven miles; and this, under the circumstances, was truly a severe undertaking. I was exceedingly feeble; made so as much by the kicks and blows which I received, as by the severe fit of sickness to which I had been subjected. I, however, watched my chance, while Covey was looking in an opposite direction, and started for St. Michael's.

I succeeded in getting a considerable distance on my way to the woods, when Covey discovered me, and called after me to come back, threatening what he would do if I did not come. I disregarded both his calls and his threats, and made my way to the woods as fast as my feeble state would allow; and thinking I might be overhauled by him if I kept the road, I walked through the woods, keeping far enough from the road to avoid detection, and near enough to prevent losing my way. I had not gone far before my little strength again failed me. I could go no farther. I fell down, and lay for a considerable time. The blood was yet oozing from the wound on my head. For a time I thought I should bleed to death; and think now that I should have done so, but that the blood so matted my hair as to stop the wound. After lying there about three quarters of an hour, I nerved myself up again, and started on my way, through bogs and briers, barefooted and bareheaded, tearing my feet sometimes at nearly every step; and after a journey of about seven miles, occupying some five hours to perform it, I arrived at master's store.

I then presented an appearance enough to affect any but a heart of iron. From the crown of my head to my feet, I was covered with blood. My hair was all clotted with dust and blood; my shirt was stiff with blood. I suppose I looked like a man who had escaped a den of wild beasts, and barely escaped them. In this state I appeared before my master, humbly entreating him to interpose his authority for my protection. I told him all the circumstances as well as I could, and it seemed, as I spoke, at times to affect him. He would then walk the floor, and seek to justify Covey by saying he expected I deserved it. He asked me what I wanted. I told him, to let me get a new home; that as sure as I lived with Mr. Covey again, I should live with but to die with him; that Covey would surely kill me; he was in a fair way for it. Master

Thomas ridiculed the idea that there was any danger of Mr. Covey's killing me, and said that he knew Mr. Covey; that he was a good man, and that he could not think of taking me from him; that, should he do so, he would lose the whole year's wages; that I belonged to Mr. Covey for one year, and that I must go back to him, come what might; and that I must not trouble him with any more stories, or that he would himself *get hold of me.*

After threatening me thus, he gave me a very large dose of [epsom] salts [magnesium sulfate, a strong medicine], telling me that I might remain in St. Michael's that night, (it being quite late,) but that I must be off back to Mr. Covey's early in the morning; and that if I did not, he would *get hold of me,* which meant that he would whip me. I remained all night, and, according to his orders, I started off to Covey's in the morning, (Saturday morning,) wearied in body and broken in spirit. I got no supper that night, or breakfast that morning.

## THE LAST FLOGGING

[from *Narrative of the Life of Frederick Douglass*]

I reached Covey's about nine o'clock; and just as I was getting over the fence that divided Mrs. Kemp's fields from ours, out ran Covey with his cowskin, to give me another whipping. Before he could reach me, I succeeded in getting to the cornfield; and as the corn was very high, it afforded me the means of hiding. He seemed very angry, and searched for me a long time. My behavior was altogether unaccountable. He finally gave up the chase, thinking, I suppose, that I must come home for something to eat; he would give himself no further trouble in looking for me.

I spent that day mostly in the woods, having the alternative before me,—to go home and be whipped to death, or stay in the woods and be starved to death. That night, I fell in with Sandy Jenkins, a slave with whom I was somewhat acquainted. Sandy had a free wife who lived about four miles from Mr. Covey's; and it being Saturday, he was on his way to see her. I told him my circumstances, and he very kindly invited me to go home with him.

I went home with him, and talked this whole matter over, and got his advice as to what course it was best for me to pursue. I found Sandy an old adviser. He told me, with great solemnity, I must go back to Covey; but that before I went, I must go with him into another part of the woods, where there was a certain *root*, which, if I would take some of it with me, carrying it *always on my right side*, would render it impossible for Mr. Covey, or any other white man, to whip me. He said he had carried it for years; and since he had done so, he had never received a blow, and never expected to while he carried it. I at first rejected the idea, that the simple carrying of a root in my pocket would have any such effect as he had said, and was not disposed to take it; but Sandy impressed the necessity with much earnestness, telling me it could do no harm, if it did no good. To please him, I at length took the root, and, according to his direction, carried it upon my right side.

This was Sunday morning. I immediately started for home; and upon entering the yard gate, out came Mr. Covey on his way to meeting. He spoke to me very kindly, bade me drive the pigs from a lot near by, and passed on towards the church. Now, this singular conduct of Mr. Covey really made me begin to think that there was something in the *root* which Sandy had given me; and had it been on any other day than Sunday, I could have attributed the conduct to no other cause than the influence of that root; and as it was, I was half inclined to think the *root* to be something more than I at first had taken it to be.

All went well till Monday morning. On this morning, the virtue of the *root* was fully tested. Long before daylight, I was called to go and rub, curry [clean with a comb], and feed, the horses. I obeyed, and was glad to obey. But whilst thus engaged, whilst in the act of throwing down some blades from the loft, Mr. Covey entered the stable with a long rope; and just as I was half out of the loft, he caught hold of my legs, and was about tying me. As soon as I found what he was up to,

I gave a sudden spring, and as I did so, he holding to my legs, I was brought sprawling on the stable floor. Mr. Covey seemed now to think he had me, and could do what he pleased; but at this moment—from whence came the spirit I don't know—I resolved to fight; and, suiting my action to the resolution, I seized Covey hard by the throat; and as I did so, I rose. He held on to me, and I to him. My resistance was so entirely unexpected that Covey seemed taken all aback. He trembled like a leaf. This gave me assurance, and I held him uneasy, causing the blood to run where I touched him with the ends of my fingers.

Mr. Covey soon called out to Hughes for help. Hughes came, and, while Covey held me, attempted to tie my right hand. While he was in the act of doing so, I watched my chance, and gave him a heavy kick close under the ribs. This kick fairly sickened Hughes, so that he left me in the hands of Mr. Covey. This kick had the effect of not only weakening Hughes, but Covey also. When he saw Hughes bending over with pain, his courage quailed. He asked me if I meant to persist in my resistance. I told him I did, come what might; that he had used me like a brute for six months, and that I was determined to be used so no longer. With that, he strove to drag me to a stick that was lying just out of the stable door. He meant to knock me down. But just as he was leaning over to get the stick, I seized him with both hands by his collar, and brought him by a sudden snatch to the ground.

By this time, Bill came. Covey called upon him for assistance. Bill wanted to know what he could do. Covey said, "Take hold of him, take hold of him!" Bill said his master hired him out to work, and not to help to whip me; so he left Covey and myself to fight our own battle out.

We were at it for nearly two hours. Covey at length let me go, puffing and blowing at a great rate, saying that if I had not resisted, he would not have whipped me half so much. The truth was, that he had not whipped me at all. I considered him as getting entirely the worst end of the bargain; for he had drawn no blood from me, but I had from him. The whole six months afterwards, that I spent with Mr. Covey, he

never laid the weight of his finger upon me in anger. He would occasionally say, he didn't want to get hold of me again. "No," thought I, "you need not; for you will come off worse than you did before."

This battle with Mr. Covey was the turning-point in my career as a slave. It rekindled the few expiring embers of freedom, and revived within me a sense of my own manhood. It recalled the departed self-confidence, and inspired me again with a determination to be free. The gratification afforded by the triumph was a full compensation for whatever else might follow, even death itself. He only can understand the deep satisfaction which I experienced, who has himself repelled by force the bloody arm of slavery. I felt as I never felt before. It was a glorious resurrection, from the tomb of slavery, to the heaven of freedom. My long-crushed spirit rose, cowardice departed, bold defiance took its place; and I now resolved that, however long I might remain a slave in form, the day had passed forever when I could be a slave in fact. I did not hesitate to let it be known of me, that the white man who expected to succeed in whipping, must also succeed in killing me.

From this time I was never again what might be called fairly whipped, though I remained a slave four years afterwards. I had several fights, but was never whipped.

It was for a long time a matter of surprise to me why Mr. Covey did not immediately have me taken by the constable to the whipping-post, and there regularly whipped for the crime of raising my hand against a white man in defence of myself. And the only explanation I can now think of does not entirely satisfy me; but such as it is, I will give it. Mr. Covey enjoyed the most unbounded reputation for being a first-rate overseer and negro-breaker. It was of considerable importance to him. That reputation was at stake; and had he sent me—a boy about sixteen years old—to the public whipping-post, his reputation would have been lost; so, to save his reputation, he suffered me to go unpunished.

* * *

After his year's service with Covey was over, Douglass worked for a Mr. Freeland, a comparatively mild master, as a hired hand. Once again, Douglass set up a Sabbath school, teaching slaves to read. He devised an escape plan with several of his fellow slaves, but was betrayed, and sent back to Baltimore. There he worked in a shipyard for eight months, but got into a terrible fight with some white workers who didn't want to work with blacks.

Hugh Auld soon allowed Douglass to hire his own time, so long as Douglass paid him six dollars a week. But Douglass proved increasingly unmanageable, and finally made his escape in September 1838, at the age of twenty, by disguising himself as a free black sailor and taking trains to New York. There his intended wife, Anna, a free black woman, joined him; they married and moved to New Bedford, Massachusetts, where Douglass was introduced to abolitionism via *The Liberator*, an abolitionist newspaper.

In 1845, Douglass published his *Narrative*, and was well on his way to becoming famous. But now that he had proved that he was indeed a fugitive slave, it was no longer safe for him to remain in the United States, so he reluctantly left for Britain. In 1846, friends purchased his freedom from Hugh Auld, and he returned to the States a few months later. For the next sixteen years, he edited his own publication, based primarily in Rochester, New York. He was also involved in the national Negro convention movement, various black conferences, and the women's suffrage movement.

During the Civil War, Douglass was on close terms with President Lincoln, and urged him to enlist black troops in the Union army. He was now the preeminent spokesman for the black race. In the 1870s and 1880s he held various government jobs, continued making speeches and fighting for equal rights, and in 1881 published a third autobiography, *The Life and Times of Frederick Douglass*. Throughout his life, he tried to transcend issues of race, claiming allegiance only to the human race.

Just as Douglass, in his *Narrative*, transformed his story into the story of all slaves by making himself the prime example of the slaves, so, in his life, he transformed his concern for his people into a concern for all America. By making the "Negro question" into an "American question," he was perhaps the most significant motivator of America's long (and as yet unfinished) transformation from a land of oppression into the land of the free.

# WILLIAM WELLS BROWN

**illiam Wells Brown** (1814–84) was the first African American novelist, playwright, travel writer, and military historian, the most versatile and prolific black writer of the nineteenth century. His 1847 *Narrative of William W. Brown, a Fugitive Slave* was his first book. It was so remarkably original and effective that it became the second-bestselling slave narrative of the 1840s (after the *Narrative of the Life of Frederick Douglass*).

Brown was one of the few slave writers to spend most of his enslaved life west of the Mississippi: his master moved to the Missouri Territory in 1816, and Brown lived in the St. Louis area until his escape in 1834. Hired out as an assistant to a brutal slave trader, Brown shuttled up and down the Mississippi River between St. Louis and New Orleans, meeting hundreds of slaves, witnessing horrific abuses of power, and gaining an unbeatable education in how slavery worked.

Brown's writing may appear plain at first, but he was a master of understatement and irony. Each word is poised to spring out upon careful reading rather than at first glance. The first paragraph of the book, for example, supplies us with a series of unexpected statements, each one quietly undermining the standard opening of a nineteenth-century autobiography. "I was born in Lexington, Ky. The man who stole me as soon as I was born, recorded the births of all the infants which he claimed to be born his property, in a book which he kept for that purpose." Although his words seem straightforward, he here implies that he was born free, not a slave, that he was not his master's property, and that he was stolen. At the same time he contrasts his own book to his master's record book. He then lists, in imitation of "the man who stole him," the seven children of his mother, but without revealing his own name (which his master changed from William to Sandford, and which he changed back to William during his escape from slavery). Rather than stating outright how slavery forces slave women to submit to sexual manipulation, he simply writes, "No two of us were children of the same father." And while a white person might take some pride in the fact that his father was "connected with some of the first families in Kentucky," coming from a slave the phrase becomes ironic, especially since Brown had no real "family" himself.

Brown here is essentially "signifying" (an African American term meaning to say without really saying, to criticize without really criticizing). He does this throughout his book, even signifying to his master in conversations that imply that the master has no authority over his slave. This signifying goes hand-in-hand with how Brown presents himself: he's not a bold, heroic resister, like Frederick Douglass; instead, he's a sly trickster, like the heroes of African folktales.

"IT WAS NOT YET DAYLIGHT"

I was born in Lexington, Ky. The man who stole me as soon as I was born, recorded the births of all the infants which he claimed to be born his property, in a book which he kept for that purpose. My mother's name was Elizabeth. She had seven children, viz: Solomon, Leander, Benjamin, Joseph, Millford, Elizabeth, and myself. No two of us were children of the same father. My father's name, as I learned from my mother, was George Higgins. He was a white man, a relative [a cousin] of my master, and connected with some of the first families in Kentucky.

My master [Dr. Benjamin Young] owned about forty slaves, twenty-five of whom were field hands. He removed from Kentucky to Missouri [at this time (1816) Missouri was not yet a state], when I was quite young [about two years old], and settled thirty or forty miles above St. Charles, on the Missouri [River], where, in addition to his practice as a physician, he carried on milling, merchandizing and farming. He had a large farm, the principal productions of which were tobacco and hemp. The slave cabins were situated on the back part of the farm, with the house of the overseer, whose name was Grove Cook, in their midst. He had the entire charge of the farm, and having no family, was allowed a woman to keep house for him, whose business it was to deal out the provisions for the hands.

A woman was also kept at the quarters to do the cooking for the field hands, who were summoned to their unrequited toil every morning at four o'clock, by the ringing of a bell, hung on a post near the house of the overseer. They were allowed half an hour to eat their breakfast, and get to the field. At half past four, a horn was blown by the overseer, which was the signal to commence work; and every one that was not on the spot at the time, had to receive ten lashes from the negro-whip, with which the overseer always went armed. The handle was about three feet long, with the butt-end filled with lead, and the lash six or seven feet in length, made of cowhide, with platted [braided] wire on the end of it. This whip was put in requisition [demand] very frequently and freely, and a small offence on the part of a slave furnished an occasion for its use. During the time that Mr. Cook was overseer, I was a house servant—a situation preferable to that of a field hand, as I was better fed, better clothed, and not obliged to rise at the ringing of the bell, but about half an hour after. I have often laid and heard the crack of the whip, and the screams of the slave.

My mother was a field hand, and one morning was ten or fifteen minutes behind the others in getting into the field. As soon as she reached the spot where they were at work, the overseer commenced whipping her. She cried, "Oh! pray—Oh! pray—Oh! pray"—these are generally the words of slaves, when imploring mercy at the hands of their oppressors. I heard her voice, and knew it, and jumped out of my bunk, and went to the door. Though the field was some distance from the house, I could hear every crack of the whip, and every groan and cry of my poor mother. I remained at the door, not daring to venture any further. The cold chills ran over me, and I wept aloud. After giving her ten lashes, the sound of the whip ceased, and I returned to my bed, and found no consolation but in my tears. It was not yet daylight.

## "VIRGINIA PLAY"

My mother was hired out in the city, and I was also hired out there to Major Freeland, who kept a public house. He was formerly from Virginia, and was a horse-racer, cock-fighter, gambler, and withal [besides] an inveterate [habitual] drunkard. There were ten or twelve servants in the house, and when he was present, it was cut and slash— knock down and drag out. In his fits of anger, he would take up a chair, and throw it at a servant; and in his more rational moments, when he wished to chastise [punish] one, he would tie them up in the smoke-house, and whip them; after which, he would cause a fire to be made of tobacco stems, and smoke them. This he called *"Virginia play."*

I complained to my master of the treatment which I received from Major Freeland; but it made no difference. He cared nothing about it, so long as he received the money for my labor. After living with Major Freeland five or six months, I ran away, and went into the woods back of the city; and when night came on, I made my way to my master's farm, but was afraid to be seen, knowing that if Mr. Haskell, the overseer, should discover me, I should be again carried back to Major Freeland; so I kept in the woods. One day, while in the woods, I heard the barking and howling of dogs, and in a short time they came so near, that I knew them to be the bloodhounds of Major Benjamin O'Fallon. He kept five or six, to hunt runaway slaves with.

As soon as I was convinced that it was them, I knew there was no chance of escape. I took refuge in the top of a tree, and the hounds were soon at its base, and there remained until the hunters came up in a half or three quarters of an hour afterwards. There were two men with the dogs, who, as soon as they came up, ordered me to descend. I came down, was tied, and taken to St. Louis jail. Major Freeland soon made his appearance, and took me out, and ordered me to follow him, which I did. After we returned home, I was tied up in the smokehouse, and was very severely whipped. After the Major had flogged me to his satisfaction, he sent out his son Robert, a young man eighteen or twenty years of age, to see that I was well smoked. He made a fire of tobacco stems, which soon set me to coughing and sneezing. This, Robert told me, was the way his father used to do to his slaves in Virginia. After giving me what they conceived to be a decent smoking, I was untied and again set to work.

## "I LOST THE SITUATION"

I was soon hired to Elijah P. Lovejoy [later an important abolitionist, he was killed by an angry mob in 1837], who was at that time publisher and editor of the "St. Louis Observer." My work, while with him, was mainly in the printing office, waiting on the hands, working the press, &c. Mr. Lovejoy was a very good man, and decidedly the best master that I had ever had. I am chiefly indebted to him, and to my employment in the printing office, for what little learning I obtained while in slavery.

While living with Mr. Lovejoy, I was often sent on errands to the office of the "Missouri Republican," published by Mr. Edward Charles. Once, while returning to the office with type, I was attacked by several large boys, sons of slave-holders, who pelted me with snow-balls. Having the heavy form of type in my hands, I could not make my escape by running; so I laid down the type and gave them battle. They gathered around me, pelting me with stones and sticks, until they overpowered me, and would have captured me, if I had not resorted to my heels. Upon my retreat, they took possession of the type; and what to do to regain it I could not devise. Knowing Mr. Lovejoy to be a very humane man, I went to the office, and laid the case before him. He told me to remain in the office. He took one of the apprentices with him, and went after the type, and soon returned with it; but on his return informed me that Samuel McKinney had told him that he would whip me, because I had hurt his boy. Soon after, McKinney was seen making his way to the office by one of the printers, who informed me of the fact, and I made my escape through the back door.

McKinney not being able to find me on his arrival, left the office in a great rage, swearing that he would whip me to death. A few days after, as I was walking along Main Street, he seized me by the collar, and struck me over the head five or six times with a large cane, which caused the blood to gush from my nose and ears in such a manner that my clothes were completely saturated with blood. After beating me to his satisfaction, he let me go, and I returned to the office so weak from the loss of blood, that Mr. Lovejoy sent me home to my master. It was five weeks before I was able to walk again. During this time, it was necessary to have some one to supply my place at the office, and I lost the situation.

## "I BESEECH YOU NOT TO LET US HINDER YOU"

After my recovery, I was hired to Capt. Otis Reynolds, as a waiter on board the steamboat Enterprize, owned by Messrs. John and Edward Walsh, commission merchants at St. Louis. This boat was then running on the upper Mississippi. My employment on board was to wait on gentlemen, and the captain being a good man, the situation was a pleasant one to me;—but in passing from place to place, and seeing new faces every day, and knowing that they could go where they pleased, I soon became unhappy, and several times thought of leaving the boat at some landing place, and trying to make my escape to

Canada, which I had heard much about as a place where the slave might live, be free, and be protected.

But whenever such thoughts would come into my mind, my resolution would soon be shaken by the remembrance that my dear mother was a slave in St. Louis, and I could not bear the idea of leaving her in that condition. She had often taken me upon her knee, and told me how she had carried me upon her back to the field when I was an infant—how often she had been whipped for leaving her work to nurse me—and how happy I would appear when she would take me into her arms. When these thoughts came over me, I would resolve never to leave the land of slavery without my mother. I thought that to leave her in slavery, after she had undergone and suffered so much for me, would be proving recreant [unfaithful] to the duty which I owed to her. Besides this, I had three brothers and a sister there,—two of my brothers having died.

My mother, my brothers Joseph and Millford, and my sister Elizabeth, belonged to Mr. Isaac Mansfield, formerly from one of the Free States, (Massachusetts, I believe.) He was a tinner by trade, and carried on a large manufacturing establishment. Of all my relatives, mother was first, and sister next. One evening, while visiting them, I made some allusion to a proposed journey to Canada, and sister took her seat by my side, and taking my hand in hers, said, with tears in her eyes,—

"Brother, you are not going to leave mother and your dear sister here without a friend, are you?"

I looked into her face, as the tears coursed swiftly down her cheeks, and bursting into tears myself, said—

"No, I will never desert you and mother."

She clasped my hand in hers, and said—

"Brother, you have often declared that you would not end your days in slavery. I see no possible way in which you can escape with us; and now, brother, you are on a steamboat where there is some chance for you to escape to a land of liberty. I beseech you not to let us hinder you. If we cannot get our liberty, we do not wish to be the means of keeping you from a land of freedom."

I could restrain my feelings no longer, and an outburst of my own feelings, caused her to cease speaking upon that subject. In opposition to their wishes, I pledged myself not to leave them in the hand of the oppressor. I took leave of them, and returned to the boat, and laid down in my bunk; but "sleep departed from my eyes, and slumber from my eyelids" [adapted from *Proverbs* 6:4, *Psalms* 132:4].

### "HIRED TO A 'SOUL-DRIVER'"

Soon after this, I was hired out to Mr. Walker [a slave trader]. Seeing me in the capacity of steward on the boat, and thinking that I would make a good hand to take care of slaves, he determined to have me for that purpose; and finding that my master would not sell me, he hired me for the term of one year.

When I learned the fact of my having been hired to a negro speculator, or a "soul-driver" as they are generally called among slaves, no one can tell my emotions. Mr. Walker had offered a high price for me, as I afterwards learned, but I suppose my master was restrained from selling me by the fact that I was a near relative of his. On entering the service of Mr. Walker, I found that my opportunity of getting to a land of liberty was gone, at least for the time being. He had a gang of slaves in readiness to start for New Orleans, and in a few days we were on our journey. I am at a loss for language to express my feelings on that occasion. Although my master had told me that he had not sold me, and Mr. Walker had told me that he had not purchased me, I did not believe them; and not until I had been to New Orleans, and was on my return, did I believe that I was not sold.

There was on the boat a large room on the lower deck, in which the slaves were kept, men and women, promiscuously [indiscriminately]— all chained two and two, and a strict watch kept that they did not get loose; for cases have occurred in which slaves have got off their chains, and made their escape at landing-places, while the boats were taking in wood;—and with all our care, we lost one woman who had been taken from her husband and children, and having no desire to live without them, in the agony of her soul jumped overboard, and drowned herself. She was not chained.

It was almost impossible to keep that part of the boat clean.

On landing at Natchez, the slaves were all carried to the slave-pen, and there kept one week, during which time, several of them were sold. Mr. Walker fed his slaves well. We took on board, at St. Louis, several hundred pounds of bacon (smoked meat) and corn-meal, and his slaves were better fed than slaves generally were in Natchez, so far as my observation extended.

At the end of a week, we left for New Orleans, the place of our final destination, which we reached in two days. Here the slaves were placed in a negro-pen, where those who wished to purchase could call and examine them. The negro-pen is a small yard, surrounded by buildings, from fifteen to twenty feet wide, with the exception of a large gate with iron bars. The slaves are kept in the buildings during the night, and turned out into the yard during the day. After the best of the stock was sold at private sale at the pen, the balance were taken to the Exchange Coffee House Auction Rooms, kept by Isaac L. McCoy, and sold at public auction. After the sale of this lot of slaves, we left New Orleans for St. Louis.

On our arrival at St. Louis, I went to Dr. Young [William's master], and told him that I did not wish to live with Mr. Walker any longer. I was heart-sick at seeing my fellow-creatures bought and sold. But the Dr. had hired me for the year, and stay I must. Mr. Walker again commenced purchasing another gang of slaves.

In the course of eight or nine weeks Mr. Walker had his cargo of human flesh made up. There was in this lot a number of old men and women, some of them with gray locks. We left St. Louis in the steamboat Carlton, Captain Swan, bound for New Orleans. On our way down, and before we reached Rodney [in Mississippi], the place where we made our first stop, I had to prepare the old slaves for market. I was ordered to have the old men's whiskers shaved off, and the grey hairs plucked out, where they were not too numerous, in which case he had a preparation of blacking to color it, and with a blacking-brush we would put it on. This was new business to me, and was performed in a room where the passengers could not see us. These slaves were also taught how old they were by Mr. Walker, and after going through the blacking process, they looked ten or fifteen years younger; and I am sure that some of those who purchased slaves of Mr. Walker, were dreadfully cheated, especially in the ages of the slaves which they bought.

We landed at Rodney, and the slaves were driven to the pen in the back part of the village. Several were sold at this place, during our stay of four or five days, when we proceeded to Natchez. There we landed at night, and the gang were put in the warehouse until morning, when they were driven to the pen. As soon as the slaves are put in these pens, swarms of planters may be seen in and about them. They knew when Walker was expected, as he always had the time advertised beforehand when he would be in Rodney, Natchez, and New Orleans. These were the principal places where he offered his slaves for sale.

When at Natchez the second time, I saw a slave very cruelly whipped. He belonged to a Mr. Broadwell, a merchant who kept a store on the wharf. The slave's name was Lewis. I had known him several years, as he was formerly from St. Louis. We were expecting a steam-boat down the river, in which we were to take passage for New Orleans. Mr. Walker sent me to the landing to watch for the boat, ordering me to inform him on its arrival. While there, I went into the store to see Lewis. I saw a slave in the store, and asked him where Lewis was. Said he, "They have got Lewis hanging between the heavens and the earth." I asked him what he meant by that. He told me to go into the warehouse and see. I went in, and found Lewis there. He was tied up to a beam, with his toes just touching the floor. As there was no one in the warehouse but himself, I inquired the reason of his being in that situation. He said Mr. Broadwell had sold his wife to a planter six miles from the city, and that he had been to visit her,—that he went in the night, expecting to return before daylight, and went without his master's permission. The patrol had taken him up before he reached his wife. He was put in jail, and his master had to pay for his catching and keeping, and that was what he was tied up for.

Just as he finished his story, Mr. Broadwell came in, and inquired what I was doing there. I knew not what to say, and while I was thinking what reply to make, he struck me over the head with the cowhide, the end of which struck me over my right eye, sinking deep into the flesh, leaving a scar which I carry to this day. Before I visited Lewis, he had received fifty lashes. Mr. Broadwell gave him fifty lashes more after I came out, as I was afterwards informed by Lewis himself.

The next day we proceeded to New Orleans, and put the gang in the same negro-pen which we occupied before. In a short time, the planters came flocking to the pen to purchase slaves. Before the slaves were exhibited for sale, they were dressed and driven out into the yard. Some were set to dancing, some to jumping, some to singing, and some to playing cards. This was done to make them appear cheerful and happy. My business was to see that they were placed in those situations before the arrival of the purchasers, and I have often set them to dancing when their cheeks were wet with tears. As slaves were in good demand at that time, they were all soon disposed of, and we again set out for St. Louis.

## "I WAS DETERMINED NOT TO BE WHIPPED"

Mr. Walker, though not a good master, had not flogged a slave since I had been with him, though he had threatened me. The slaves were kept in the pen, and he always put up at the best hotel, and kept his wines in his room, for the accommodation of those who called to negotiate with him for the purchase of slaves. One day while we were at Vicksburg, several gentlemen came to see him for this purpose, and as usual the wine was called for. I took the tray and started around with it, and having accidentally filled some of the glasses too full, the gentlemen spilled the wine on their clothes as they went to drink. Mr. Walker apologized to them for my carelessness, but looked at me as though he would see me again on this subject.

After the gentlemen had left the room, he asked me what I meant by my carelessness, and said that he would attend to me. The next morning, he gave me a note to carry to the jailer, and a dollar in money to give to him. I suspected that all was not right, so I went down near the landing where I met with a sailor, and walking up to him, asked him if he would be so kind as to read the note for me. He read it over, and then looked at me. I asked him to tell me what was in it. Said he,

"They are going to give you hell."

"Why?" said I.

He said, "This is a note to have you whipped, and says that you have a dollar to pay for it."

He handed me back the note, and off I started. I knew not what to do, but was determined not to be whipped. I went up to the jail—took a look at it, and walked off again. As Mr. Walker was acquainted with the jailer, I feared that I should be found out if I did not go, and be treated in consequence of it still worse.

While I was meditating on the subject, I saw a colored man about my size walk up, and the thought struck me in a moment to send him with my note. I walked up to him, and asked him who he belonged to. He said he was a free man, and had been in the city but a short time. I told him I had a note to go into the jail, and get a trunk to carry to one of the steamboats; but was so busily engaged that I could not do it, although I had a dollar to pay for it. He asked me if I would not give him the job. I handed him the note and the dollar, and off he started for the jail.

I watched to see that he went in, and as soon as I saw the door close behind him, I walked around the corner, and took my station, intending to see how my friend looked when he came out. I had been there but a short time, when a colored man came around the corner, and said to another colored man with whom he was acquainted—

"They are giving a nigger scissors in the jail."

"What for?" said the other. The man continued,

"A nigger came into the jail, and asked for the jailer. The jailer came out, and he handed him a note, and said he wanted to get a trunk. The jailer told him to go with him, and he would give him the trunk. So he took him into the room, and told the nigger to give up the dollar. He said a man had given him the dollar to pay for getting the trunk. But that lie would not answer. So they made him strip himself, and then they tied him down, and are now whipping him."

I stood by all the while listening to their talk, and soon found out that the person alluded to was my customer. I went into the street opposite the jail, and concealed myself in such a manner that I could not be seen by any one coming out. I had been there but a short time, when the young man made his appearance, and looked around for me. I, unobserved, came forth from my hiding-place, behind a pile of brick, and he pretty soon saw me and came up to me complaining bitterly, saying that I had played a trick upon him. I denied any knowledge of what the note contained, and asked him what they had done to him. He told me in substance what I heard the man tell who had come out of the jail.

"Yes," said he, "they whipped me and took my dollar, and gave me this note."

He showed me the note which the jailer had given him, telling him to give it to his master. I told him I would give him fifty cents for it,—

that being all the money I had. He gave it to me, and took his money. He had received twenty lashes on his bare back, with the negro-whip.

I took the note and started for the hotel where I had left Mr. Walker. Upon reaching the hotel, I handed it to a stranger whom I had not seen before, and requested him to read it to me. As near as I can recollect, it was as follows:—

"DEAR SIR:—By your direction, I have given your boy twenty lashes. He is a very saucy boy, and tried to make me believe that he did not belong to you, and I put it on to him well for lying to me.

    I remain,
    Your obedient servant."

It is true that in most of the slave-holding cities, when a gentleman wishes his servants whipped, he can send him to the jail and have it done. Before I went in where Mr. Walker was, I wet my cheeks a little, as though I had been crying. He looked at me, and inquired what was the matter. I told him that I had never had such a whipping in my life, and handed him the note. He looked at it and laughed;—"and so you told him that you did not belong to me." "Yes, sir," said I. "I did not know that there was any harm in that." He told me I must behave myself, if I did not want to be whipped again.

This incident shows how it is that slavery makes its victims lying and mean; for which vices it afterwards reproaches them, and uses them as arguments to prove that they deserve no better fate. I have often, since my escape, deeply regretted the deception I practiced upon this poor fellow; and I heartily desire that it may be, at some time or other, in my power to make him amends for his vicarious sufferings in my behalf.

## "FIND YOU A GOOD MASTER"

My time was up with Mr. Walker. I had served him one year, and it was the longest year I ever lived.

I was sent home, and was glad enough to leave the service of one who was tearing the husband from the wife, the child from the mother, and the sister from the brother,—but a trial more severe and heartrending than any which I had yet met with awaited me. My dear sister had been sold to a man who was going to Natchez, and was lying in jail awaiting the hour of his departure. She had expressed her determination to die, rather than go to the far south, and she was put in jail for safe keeping. I went to the jail the same day that I arrived, but as the jailor was not in, I could not see her.

I went home to my master, in the country, and the first day after my return, he came where I was at work, and spoke to me very politely. I knew from his appearance that something was the matter. After talking about my several journeys to New Orleans with Mr. Walker, he told me that he was hard pressed for money, and as he had sold my mother and all her children except me, he thought it would be better to sell me than any other one, and that as I had been used to living in the city, he thought it probable that I would prefer it to a country life. I raised up my head, and looked him full in the face. When my eyes caught his, he immediately looked to the ground. After a short pause, I said,

"Master, mother has often told me that you are a near relative of mine, and I have often heard you admit the fact; and after you have hired me out, and received, as I once heard you say, nine hundred dollars for my services,—after receiving this large sum, will you sell me to be carried to New Orleans or some other place?"

"No," said he, "I do not intend to sell you to a negro trader. If I had wished to have done that, I might have sold you to Mr. Walker for a large sum, but I would not sell you to a negro trader. You may go to the city, and find you a good master."

"But," said I, "I cannot find a good master in the whole city of St. Louis."

"Why?" said he.

"Because there are no good masters in the State."

"Do you not call me a good master?"

"If you were, you would not sell me."

"Now I will give you one week to find a master in, and surely you can do it in that time."

The price set by my evangelical master upon my soul and body was the trifling sum of five hundred dollars. I tried to enter into some arrangement by which I might purchase my freedom; but he would enter into no such arrangement.

## "THE ATTEMPT TO REACH A LAND OF LIBERTY"

I set out for the city with the understanding that I was to return in a week with some one to become my new master. Soon after reaching the city, I went to the jail, to learn if I could once more see my sister; but could not gain admission. I then went to mother, and learned from her that the owner of my sister intended to start for Natchez in a few days.

I went to the jail again the next day, and Mr. Simonds, the keeper, allowed me to see my sister for the last time. I cannot give a just description of the scene at that parting interview. Never, never can be erased from my heart the occurrences of that day! When I entered the room where she was, she was seated in one corner, alone. There were four other women in the same room, belonging to the same man. He had purchased them, he said, for his own use. She was seated with her face towards the door where I entered, yet she did not look up until I walked up to her. As soon as she observed me, she sprung up, threw her arms around my neck, leaned her head upon my breast, and, without uttering a word, burst into tears. As soon as she recovered herself sufficiently to speak, she advised me to take mother, and try to get out of slavery. She said there was no hope for herself,—that she must live and die a slave. After giving her some advice, and taking from my finger a ring and placing it upon hers, I bade her farewell forever, and returned to my mother, and then and there made up my mind to leave for Canada as soon as possible.

I had been in the city nearly two days, and as I was to be absent only a week, I thought best to get on my journey as soon as possible. In conversing with mother, I found her unwilling to make the attempt to reach a land of liberty, but she counselled me to get my liberty if I could. She said, as all her children were in slavery, she did not wish to leave them. I could not bear the idea of leaving her among those pirates, when there was a prospect of being able to get away from them. After much persuasion, I succeeded in inducing her to make the attempt to get away.

The time fixed for our departure was the next night. I had with me a little money that I had received, from time to time, from gentlemen for whom I had done errands. I took my scanty means and purchased some dried beef, crackers and cheese, which I carried to mother, who had provided herself with a bag to carry it in. I occasionally thought of my old master, and of my mission to the city to find a new one. I waited with the most intense anxiety for the appointed time to leave the land of slavery, in search of a land of liberty.

The time at length arrived, and we left the city just as the clock struck nine. We proceeded to the upper part of the city, where I had been two or three times during the day, and selected a skiff to carry us across the river. The boat was not mine, nor did I know to whom it did belong; neither did I care. The boat was fastened with a small pole, which, with the aid of a rail, I soon loosened from its moorings. After hunting round and finding a board to use as an oar, I turned to the city, and bidding it a long farewell, pushed off my boat. The current running very swift, we had not reached the middle of the stream before we were directly opposite the city.

We were soon upon the Illinois shore, and, leaping from the boat, turned it adrift, and the last I saw of it, it was going down the river at good speed. We took the main road to Alton, and passed through just at daylight, when we made for the woods, where we remained during the day. Our reason for going into the woods was, that we expected that Mr. Mansfield (the man who owned my mother) would start in pursuit of her as soon as he discovered that she was missing. He also knew that I had been in the city looking for a new master, and we thought probably he would go out to my master's to see if he could find my mother, and in so doing, Dr. Young might be led to suspect that I had gone to Canada to find a purchaser.

We remained in the woods during the day, and as soon as darkness overshadowed the earth, we started again on our gloomy way, having no guide but the NORTH STAR. We continued to travel by night, and secrete ourselves in woods by day; and every night, before emerging from our hiding-place, we would anxiously look for our friend and leader,—the NORTH STAR.

## "FLEEING FROM A LAND OF OPPRESSION"

As we travelled towards a land of liberty, my heart would at times leap for joy. At other times, being, as I was, almost constantly on my feet, I felt as though I could travel no further. But when I thought of slavery with its Democratic whips—its Republican chains—its evangelical blood-hounds, and its religious slave-holders—when I thought of all this paraphernalia of American Democracy and Religion behind me, and the prospect of liberty before me, I was encouraged to press forward, my heart was strengthened, and I forgot that I was tired or hungry.

On the eighth day of our journey, we had a very heavy rain, and in a few hours after it commenced, we had not a dry thread upon our bodies. This made our journey still more unpleasant. On the tenth day, we found ourselves entirely destitute of provisions, and how to obtain any we could not tell. We finally resolved to stop at some farmhouse, and try to get something to eat. We had no sooner determined to do this, than we went to a house, and asked them for some food. We were

treated with great kindness, and they not only gave us something to eat, but gave us provisions to carry with us. They advised us to travel by day, and lie by at night. Finding ourselves about one hundred and fifty miles from St. Louis, we concluded that it would be safe to travel by daylight, and did not leave the house until the next morning. We travelled on that day through a thickly settled country, and through one small village. Though we were fleeing from a land of oppression, our hearts were still there. My dear sister and two beloved brothers were behind us, and the idea of giving them up, and leaving them forever, made us feel sad. But with all this depression of heart, the thought that I should one day be free, and call my body my own, buoyed me up, and made my heart leap for joy. I had just been telling mother how I should try to get employment as soon as we reached Canada, and how I intended to purchase us a little farm, and how I would earn money enough to buy sister and brothers, and how happy we would be in our own FREE HOME,—when three men came up on horseback, and ordered us to stop.

I turned to the one who appeared to be the principal man, and asked him what he wanted. He said he had a warrant to take us up. The three immediately dismounted, and one took from his pocket a handbill, advertising us as runaways, and offering a reward of two hundred dollars for our apprehension, and delivery in the city of St. Louis. The advertisement had been put out by Isaac Mansfield and John Young.

While they were reading the advertisement, mother looked me in the face, and burst into tears. A cold chill ran over me, and such a sensation I never experienced before, and I hope never to again. They took out a rope and tied me, and we were taken back about six miles, to the house of the individual who appeared to be the leader. We reached there about seven o'clock in the evening, had supper, and were separated for the night. Two men remained in the room during the night. Before the family retired to rest, they were all called together to attend prayers.

The man who but a few hours before had bound my hands together with a strong cord, read a chapter from the Bible, and then offered up prayer, just as though God sanctioned the act he had just committed upon a poor panting, fugitive slave.

The next morning, a blacksmith came in, and put a pair of hand-cuffs on me, and we started on our journey back to the land of whips, chains and Bibles. Mother was not tied, but was closely watched at night. We were carried back in a wagon, and after four days travel, we came in sight of St. Louis. I cannot describe my feelings upon approaching the city.

As we were crossing the ferry, Mr. Wiggins, the owner of the ferry, came up to me, and inquired what I had been doing that I was in chains. He had not heard that I had run away. In a few minutes, we were on the Missouri side, and were taken directly to the jail. On the way thither, I saw several of my friends, who gave me a nod of recognition as I passed them. After reaching the jail, we were locked up in different apartments.

I had been in jail but a short time when I heard that my master was sick, and nothing brought more joy to my heart than that intelligence. I prayed fervently for him—not for his recovery, but for his death. I knew he would be exasperated at having to pay for my apprehension, and knowing his cruelty, I feared him. While in jail, I learned that my sister Elizabeth, who was in prison when we left the city, had been carried off four days before our arrival.

I had been in jail but a few hours when three negro-traders, learning that I was secured thus for running away, came to my prison-house and looked at me, expecting that I would be offered for sale. Mr. Mansfield, the man who owned mother, came into the jail as soon as Mr. Jones, the man who arrested us, informed him that he had brought her back. He told her that he would not whip her, but would sell her to a negro-trader, or take her to New Orleans himself. After being in jail about one week, master sent a man to take me out of jail, and send me home. I was taken out and carried home, and the old man was well enough to sit up. He had me brought into the room where he was, and as I entered, he asked me where I had been? I told him I had acted according to his orders. He had told me to look for a master, and I had been to look for one. He answered that he did not tell me to go to Canada to look for a master. I told him that as I had served him faithfully, and had been the means of putting a number of hundreds of dollars into his pocket, I thought I had a right to my liberty. He said he had promised my father that I should not be sold to supply the New Orleans market, or he would sell me to a negro-trader.

\* \* \*

William was sold to a merchant tailor, who hired him out to work on a Mississippi River steamer once more. His mother was sold to New Orleans, and he never saw her again. He was then sold to Captain Enoch Price, a St. Louis steamboat owner, for whom he worked as a carriage driver. Mrs. Price arranged for William to be engaged to marry another of her slaves, Eliza, and William pretended to go along with it. Telling his owner that "nothing but death should part" him from Eliza, he persuaded the Prices to allow him to travel with them to Cincinnati. On New Year's Day, 1834, at the age of nineteen, he ran away from the boat onto free soil.

On his journey to Canada, he decided to change his name from Sandford back to William, and after he was rescued from cold and hunger by an Ohio Quaker named Wells Brown, he adopted those two names as his own. He settled in Cleveland, working aboard a steamboat once more. In the year 1842 alone, he carried sixty-nine slaves across Lake Erie to Canada.

After publishing his narrative in 1847, he continued to lecture against slavery until the end of the Civil War, both in the United States and in England, where in one five-year period he delivered over a thousand lectures. He also continued to write: a book of anti-slavery songs; two accounts of his European travels; *Clotel*, the first African American novel; a history of Haiti; two plays; another memoir; two books on African American achievement; a history of blacks in the Revolutionary War; and a book on the South and its people.

# THOMAS H. JONES

**homas H. Jones** (1806-?) first published his autobiography in 1855, and it remained popular even after the Civil War: it was reprinted in 1857, 1862, 1868, 1871, 1880, and in a much-expanded edition in 1885, making it one of the nineteenth-century slave narratives with the longest life. Its first edition was entitled *Experience and Personal Narrative of Uncle Tom Jones; Who Was for Forty Years a Slave,* despite the fact that Jones had nothing in common with the fictional Uncle Tom (of Harriet Beecher Stowe's *Uncle Tom's Cabin*) besides being a slave named Tom. Subsequent editions were entitled *The Experience of Thomas H. Jones* [or *Rev. Thomas H. Jones*], *Who Was a Slave for Forty-Three Years.* The reason for the narrative's enduring appeal was likely Jones's fascinating account of how he learned to read and write, one of the fullest in any slave narrative.

## "AN INTENSE, BURNING DESIRE TO LEARN TO READ"

My mistress complained of me at length, that I was not so obedient as I ought to be, and so I was taken from the house into the store [Jones was probably eleven or twelve years old at the time]. My business there was to open and sweep out the store in the morning, and get all the things ready for the accommodation of customers who might come in during the day. Then I had to bring out and deliver all heavy articles that might be called for such as salt, large quantities of which were sold in the store; ship stores, grain, etc., etc. I had also to hold myself ready to run on any errand my master or his clerk, David Cogdell, might wish to send me on.

While Cogdell remained in the store, I enjoyed a *gleam* of happiness. He was very kind to me, never giving me a cross word or a sour look; always ready to show me how to do anything which I did not understand, and to perform little acts of kindness to me. But his kindness and generosity to the poor slaves was very offensive to my master and to other slave-holders; and so, at length, Mr. Jones turned him off, though he was compelled to acknowledge, at the same time, that he was the most trustworthy and valuable assistant he had ever had in his store.

After my master dismissed Mr. C., he tried to get along with me alone in the store. He kept the books and waited upon the most genteel of his customers, leaving me to do the rest of the work. This went on six months, when he declared that he could not bear this confinement any longer; and so he got a white boy to come and enter as clerk, to stay till he was of age.

James Dixon was a poor boy, about my own age, and when he came into the store, could hardly read or write. He was accordingly engaged a part of each day with his books and writing. I saw him studying, and asked him to let me see his book. When he felt in a good humor, James was very kind and obliging. The great trouble with him was, that his fits of ill-humor were much more frequent than his times of good feeling. It happened, however, that he was on good terms with himself when I asked him to show me his book, and so he let me take it, and look at it, and he answered very kindly many questions which I asked him about books and schools and learning. He told me that he was trying to get learning enough to fit him to do a good business for himself after he should get through with Mr. Jones. He told me that a man who had learning would always find friends, and get along very well in the world without having to work hard, while those who had no learning would have no friends, and be compelled to work very hard for a poor living all their days.

This was all new to me, and furnished me topics for wondering thought for days afterwards. The result of my meditations was, that an intense, burning desire to learn to read and write took possession of my mind, occupying me wholly in waking hours, and stirring up earnest thoughts in my soul even when I slept. The question, which then took hold of my whole consciousness was, how can I get a book to begin? James told me that, a spelling-book was the first one necessary in getting learning. So I contrived how I might obtain a spelling-book.

At length, after much study, I hit upon this plan: I cleaned the boots of Mr. David Smith, Jr., who carried on the printing business, in Wilmington, and edited the Cape Fear *Recorder*. He had always appeared to me to be a very kind man. I thought I would get him to aid me in procuring a spelling-book. So I went one morning, with a beating heart, into his office, and asked him to sell me a spelling-book. He looked at me in silence, and with close attention, for some time, and asked me what I wanted it for? I told him I wanted to learn to read. He shook his head, and replied, "No, Thomas; it would not answer for me to sell you a book to learn out of; you will only get yourself into trouble if you attempt it; and I advise you to get that foolish notion out of your head as quickly as you can."

David's brother, Peter Smith, kept a book and stationery store under the printing-office, and I next applied to him for a book, determined to persevere till I obtained this coveted treasure. He asked me the same question that his brother David had done, and with the same searching, suspicious look. By my previous repulse I had discovered that I could not get a spelling-book, if I told what I wanted to do with it, and so I told a lie, in order to get it. I answered, that I wanted it for a white boy, naming one that lived at my master's, and that he had given me the money to get it with, and had asked me to call at the store and buy it. The book was then handed out to me, the money taken in return, and I left, feeling very rich with my long desired treasure. I got out of the store, and, looking round to see that no one observed me, I hid my book in my bosom, and hurried on to my work, conscious that a new era in my life was opening upon me through the possession of this book.

That consciousness at once awakened new thoughts, purposes and hopes, a new life, in fact, in my experience. My mind was excited. The words spoken by James Dixon of the great advantages of learning, made me intensely anxious to learn. I was a slave, and I knew that the whole community was in league to keep the poor slave in ignorance and chains. Yet I longed to be free, and to be able to move the minds, of other men by my thoughts. It seemed to me now, that, if I could learn to read and write, this learning might—nay, I really thought it would, point out to me the way to freedom, influence, and real, secure happiness.

So, I hurried on to my master's store, and, watching my opportunity to do it, safe from curious eyes, I hid my book with the utmost care, under some liquor barrels in the smokehouse. The first opportunity I improved [took advantage of] to examine it. I looked it over with the most intense eagerness, turned over its leaves, and tried to discover what the new and strange characters which I saw in its pages might mean. But I found it a vain endeavor. I could understand a picture, and from it make out a story of immediate interest to my mind. But I could not associate any thought or fact with these crooked letters with which my primer was filled.

So the next day I sought a favorable moment, and asked James to tell me where a scholar must begin in order to learn to read, and how. He laughed at my ignorance, and, taking his spelling-book, showed me the alphabet in large and small letters on the same page. I asked him the name of the first letter, pointing it out, he told me A; so of the next, and so on through the alphabet. I managed to remember A and B, and I studied and looked out the same letters in many other parts of the book. And so I fixed in a tenacious memory the names of the two first letters of the alphabet. But I found I could not get on without help, and so I applied to James again to show me the letters and tell me their names. This time he suspected me of trying to learn to read myself, and he plied me with questions till he ascertained that I was, in good earnest, entering upon an effort to get knowledge. At this discovery, he manifested a good deal of indignation. He told me, in scorn, that it was not for such as *me* to try to improve, that I was a *slave*, and that it was not proper for *me* to learn to read. He threatened to tell my master, and at length, by his hard language, my anger was fully aroused, and I answered taunt with taunt. He called me a poor, miserable nigger; and I called him a poor, ignorant servant boy.

While we were engaged in loud and angry words, of mutual defiance and scorn, my master came into the store. Mr. Jones had never given me a whipping since the time I have already described, during my first year of toil, want and suffering in his service. But he had now caught me in the unpardonable offence of giving saucy language to a white boy, and one, too, who was in his employ. Without stopping to make any inquiries, he took down the cow-hide, and gave me a severe whipping. He told me never to talk back to a white man on pain of flogging. I suppose this law or custom is universal at the south. And I suppose it is thought necessary to enforce this habit of obsequious submission on the parts of the colored people to the whites, in order to maintain their supremacy over the poor, outraged slaves.

"MY BEST, MY CONSTANT FRIEND"

I was now repulsed by James, so that I could hope for no assistance from him in learning to read. But I could not go on alone. I must get some one to aid me in starting, or give up the effort to learn. This I could not bear to do. I thought of a little boy, Hiram Bricket, ten years old, or about that age, who came along by the store one day, on his way home from school, while my master was gone home to dinner, and James was in the front part of the store. I beckoned to Hiram to come round to the back door; and with him I made a bargain to meet me each day at noon, when I was allowed a little while to get my dinner, and to give me instruction in reading. I was to give him six cents a week. I met him the next day at his father's stable, the place agreed upon for our daily meeting; and, going into one of the stables, the noble little fellow gave me a thorough lesson in the alphabet. I learned it nearly all at that time, with what study I could give it by stealth during the day and night. And then again I felt lifted up and happy.

I was permitted to enjoy these advantages, however, but a short time. A black boy, belonging to Hiram's father, one day discovered our meeting and what we were doing. He told his master of it, and Hiram was at once forbidden this employment. I had then got along so that I was reading and spelling in words of two syllables.

After I was deprived of my kind little teacher, I plodded on the best way I could by myself, and in this way I got into words of five syllables. I got some little time to study by daylight in the morning, before any of my master's family had risen. I got a moment's opportunity also at noon, and sometimes at night. During the day I was in the back store a good deal, and whenever I thought I could have a few minutes to myself, I would take my book and try to learn a little in reading and spelling. If I heard James, or master Jones, or any customer coming in, I would drop my book among the barrels, and pretended to be very busy shoveling the salt or doing some other work. Several times I came very near being detected. My master suspected something, because I was so still in the back room, and a number of times he came very slyly to see what I was about. But at such times I was always so fortunate as to hear his tread or to see his shadow on the wall in time to hide away my book.

When I had got along to words of five syllables, I went to see a free colored friend, Ned Cowen, whom I knew I could trust, and told him that I was trying to learn to read, and asked him to help me a little. He told me I had got along far enough to get another book, in which I could learn to write the letters, as well as to read. He told me where and how to procure this book. I followed his directions, and obtained another spelling book at Worcester's store in Wilmington. Jacob showed me a little about writing. He set me a copy, first of straight marks. I now got me a box, which I could hide under my bed, some ink, pens, and a bit of candle. So, when I went to bed, I pulled my box out from under my cot, turned it up on end, and began my first attempt at writing. I worked away till my candle was burned out, and then lay down to sleep. Jacob next set me a copy, which he called pot-hooks; then, the letters of the alphabet. These letters were also in my new spelling-book, and according to Jacob's directions, I set them before me for a copy, and wrote on these exercises till I could form all the letters and call them by name. One evening, I wrote out my name in large letters, — THOMAS JONES. This I carried to Jacob, in a great excitement of happiness, and he warmly commended me for my perseverance and diligence.

About this time, I was at the store early one morning, and thinking I was safe from all danger for a few minutes, had seated myself in the back store, on one of the barrels, to study in my precious spelling-book. While I was absorbed in this happy enterprise, my master came in, much earlier than usual, and I did not hear him. He came directly into the back store. I saw his shadow on the wall, just in time to throw my book over in among the barrels, before he could see what it was, although he saw that I had thrown something quickly away. His suspicion was aroused. He said that I had been stealing something out of the store, and he fiercely ordered me to get what I threw away just as he was coming in at the door.

Without a moment's hesitation, I determined to save my precious book and my future opportunities to learn out of it. I knew if my book was discovered, that all was lost, and I felt prepared for any hazard or suffering rather than give up my book and my hopes of improvement. So I replied at once to his question, that I had not thrown anything away; that I had not stolen anything from the store; that I did not have anything in my hands which I could throw away when he came in.

My master declared, in high passion, that I was lying, and ordered me to begin and roll away the barrels. This I did; but managed to keep the book slipping along so that he could not see it, as he stood in the door-way. He charged me again with stealing and throwing something away, and I again denied the charge. In a great rage, he then got down his long, heavy cow-hide, and ordered me to strip off my jacket and shirt, saying, with an oath, "I will make you tell me what it was you had when I came in." I stripped myself, and came forward, according to his directions, the same time denying his charge with great earnestness of tone, and look, and manner.

He cut me on my naked back, perhaps thirty times, with great severity, making the blood flow freely. He then stopped, and asked me what I had thrown away as he came in. I answered again that I had thrown nothing away. He swore terribly; said he was certain I was lying, and declared that he would kill me, if I did not tell him the truth. He whipped me the second time with greater severity, and at greater length than before. He then repeated his question, and I answered again as before. I was determined to die, if I could possibly bear the pain, rather than give up my dear book. He whipped me the third time, with the same result as before, and then, seizing hold of my shoulders, turned me round, as though he would inflict on my quivering flesh still another scourging; but he saw the deep gashes he had already made, and the blood already flowing under his cruel infliction; and his stern purpose failed him. He said, "Why, Tom, I didn't think I had cut you so bad," and, saying that, he stopped, and told me to put on my shirt again. I did as he bade me, although my coarse shirt touching my raw

back put me to a cruel pain. He then went out, and I got my book and hid it safely away before he came in again.

When I went to the house, my wounds had dried and I was in an agony of pain. My mistress told the servant girl, Rachel, to help me off with my shirt, and to wash my wounds for me, and to put on to them some sweet oil. The shirt was dried to my back, so that it could not be got off without tearing off some of the skin with it. The pain, upon doing this, was greater even than I had endured from my cruel whipping. After Rachel had got my shirt off, my mistress asked me what I had done for which my master had whipped me so severely. I told her he had accused me of stealing when I had not, and then had whipped me to make me own it.

While Rachel was putting on the sweet oil, my master came in, and I could hear mistress scolding him for giving me such an inhuman beating, when I had done nothing. He said in reply, that Tom was an obstinate liar, and that was the reason why he had whipped me.

But I got well of my mangled back, and my book was as still left. This was my best, my constant friend. With great eagerness, I snatched every moment I could get, morning, noon, and night, for study. I had begun to read; and, Oh, how I loved to study, and to dwell on the thoughts which I gained from my reading.

## "I COULD NOT STOP PRAYING"

About this time, I read a piece in my book about God. It said that "God, who sees and knows all our thoughts, loves the good and makes them happy; while he is angry with the bad, and will punish them for all their sins." This made me feel very unhappy, because I was sure that I was not good in the sight of God. I thought about this, and couldn't get it out of my mind a single hour.

So I went to James Galley, a colored man, who exhorted the slaves sometimes on Sunday, and told him my trouble, asking, "what shall I do?" He told me about Jesus, and told me I must pray the Lord to forgive me and help me to be good and happy. So I went home, and went down cellar and prayed, but I found no relief, no comfort for my unhappy mind. I felt so bad, that I could not even study my book.

My master saw that I looked very unhappy, and he asked me what ailed me. I did not dare now to tell a lie, for I wanted to be good, that I might be happy. So I told master just how it was with me; and then he swore terribly at me, and said he would whip me if I did not give over praying. He said there was no heaven and no hell, and that Christians were all hypocrites, and that there was nothing, after this life, and that he would not permit me to go moping round, praying and going to the meetings. I told him I could not help praying; and then he cursed me in a great passion, and declared that he would whip me if he knew of my going on any more in that foolish way.

The next night I was to a meeting, which was led by Jack Cammon, a free colored man, and a class leader in the Methodist Church. I was so much overcome by my feelings, that I staid very late. They prayed for me, but I did not yet find any relief; I was still very unhappy. The next morning, my master came in, and asked me if I went the night before to the meeting. I told him the truth. He said, "Didn't I tell you I would whip you if you went nigh these meetings, and didn't I tell you to stop this foolish praying." I told him he did, and if he would, why, he might whip me, but still I could not stop praying, because I wanted to be good, that I might be happy and go to heaven.

This reply made my master very angry. With many bitter oaths, he said he had promised me a whipping, and now he should be as good as his word. And so he was. He whipped me, and then forbade, with bitter threatenings, my praying any more, and especially my going again to meeting. This was Friday morning.

I continued to pray for comfort and peace. The next Sunday I went to meeting. The minister preached a sermon on being born again, from the words of Jesus to Nicodemus. All this only deepened my trouble of mind. I returned home very unhappy. Collins, a free man of color, was at the meeting, and told my master that I was there. So, on Monday morning my master whipped me again, and once more forbade my going to meetings and praying.

The next Sunday there was a class meeting, led by Binney Pennison, a colored free man. I asked my master, towards night, if I might go out. I told him I did not feel well. I wanted to go to the class meeting. Without asking me where I was going, he said I might go. I went to the class. I staid very late, and was so overcome by my feelings, that I could not go home that night. So they carried me to Joseph Jones's cabin, a slave of Mr. Jones. Joseph talked and prayed with me nearly all night. In the morning I went home as soon as it was light, and, for fear of master, I asked Nancy, one of the slaves, to go up into mistress's room and get the store key for me, that I might go and open the store. My master told her to go back and tell me to come up. I obeyed with many fears. My master asked me where I had been the night before. I told him the whole truth. He cursed me again, and said he should whip me for my obstinate disobedience; and he declared that he would kill me if I did not promise to obey him. He refused to listen to my mistress who was a professor [believer], and who tried to intercede for me. And, just as soon as he had finished threatening me with what he would do, he ordered me to take the key and go and open the store.

When he came into the store that morning, two of his neighbors, Julius Dumbiven, and MacCauslin, came in too. He called me up, and asked me again where I staid last night. I told him with his boy, Joseph. He said he knew that was a lie; and he immediately sent off for Joseph to confirm his suspicions. He ordered me to strip off my clothes, and, as I did so, he took down the cow hide heavy and stiff with blood which he had before drawn from my body with that cruel weapon, and which was congealed upon it. Dumbiven professed to be a Christian, and he now came forward and earnestly interceded for me, but to no purpose, and then he left. McCauslin asked my master, if he did not know, that a slave was worth more money after he became pious than he was before. And why then, he said, should you forbid Tom going to meetings and praying? He replied, that religion was all a damned mockery, and he was not going to have any of his slaves praying and whining round about their souls. McCauslin then left. Joseph came and told the same story about the night before that I had done, and then began to beg master not to whip me. He cursed him and drove him off. He then whipped me with great severity, inflicting terrible pain at every blow upon my quivering body which was still very tender from recent lacerations. My suffering was so great, that it seemed to me that I should die. He paused at length, and asked me would I mind him and stop praying. I told him I could not promise him not to pray any more, for I felt that I must and should pray as long as I lived. "Well, then, Tom," he said, "I swear that I will whip you to death." I told him I could not help myself, if he was determined to kill me, but that I must pray while I lived. He then began to whip me the second time, but soon stopped, threw down the bloody cow-hide, and told me to go wash myself in the river, just back of the store, and then dress myself, and if I was determined to be a fool, why I must be one.

My mistress now interceded earnestly for me with my cruel master. The next Sabbath was love feast, and I felt very anxious to join in that feast. This I could not do without a paper from my master, and so I asked mistress to help me. She advised me to be patient, and said she would help me all she could. Master refused to give any paper, and so I could not join the loving feast the next day.

On the next Friday evening, I went to the prayer meeting. Jack Cammon was there, and opened the meeting with prayer. Then Binney Pennison gave out the sweet hymn, which begins in these words:

"Come ye sinners poor and needy,
Weak and wounded, sick and sore."

I felt that it all applied most sweetly to my condition, and I said in my heart, I will come now to Jesus, and trust in him. So when those who felt anxious were requested to come forward and kneel within the altar for prayer, I came and knelt down. While Jacob Cammon was praying for me, and for those who knelt by my side, my burden of sorrow, which had so long weighed me down, was removed. I felt the glory of God's love warming my heart, and making me very happy, I shouted aloud for joy, and tried to tell all my poor slave brothers and sisters, who were in the house, what a dear Saviour I had found, and how happy I felt in his precious love. Binney Pennison asked me if I could forgive my master. I told him I could, and did, and that I could pray God to forgive him, too, and make him a good man. He asked me if I could tell my master of the change in my feelings. I told him I should tell him in the morning. "And what," he asked, "will you do if he whips you still for praying and going to meeting?" I said I will ask Jesus to help me bear the pain, and to forgive my master for being so wicked. He then said, "Well, then, Brother Jones, I believe that you are a Christian."

A good many of us went from the meeting to a brother's cabin, where we began to express our joy in happy songs. The palace of General Dudley was only a little way off, and he soon sent over a slave with orders to stop our noise, or he would send the patrolers upon us. We then stopped our singing, and spent the remainder of the night in talking, rejoicing, and praying. It was a night of very great happiness to me. The contrast between my feelings then, and for many weeks previous, was very great. Now all was bright and joyous in my relations towards my precious Saviour. I felt certain that Jesus was my Saviour, and in this blessed assurance, a flood of glory and joy filled my happy soul.

But this sweet night passed away, and, as the morning came, I felt that I must go home, and bear the slave's heavy cross. I went and told my mistress the blessed change in my feelings. She promised me what aid she could give with my master, and enjoined upon me to be patient and very faithful to his interest, and, in this way, I should at length wear out his opposition to my praying and going to meeting.

I went down to the store in a very happy state of mind. I told James my feelings. He called me a fool, and said master would be sure to whip me. I told him I hoped I should be able to bear it, and to forgive master for his cruelty to me. Master came down, talked with me a while, and told me that he should whip me because I had disobeyed him in staying out all night. He had told me he should whip me if ever I did so, and he should make every promise good. So I began to take off my clothes. He called me a crazy fool, and told me to keep my clothes on, till he told me to take them off. He whipped me over my jacket; but I enjoyed so much peace of mind, that I scarcely felt the cow-hide. This was the last whipping that Mr. Jones inflicted upon me.

I was then nearly eighteen years old. I waited and begged for a paper to join the Church six months before I could get it. But all this time I was cheerful, as far as a slave can be, and very earnest to do all I could for my master and mistress. I was resolved to convince them that I was happier and better for being a Christian, and my master at last acknowledged that he could not find any fault with my conduct, and that it was impossible to find a more faithful slave than I was to him. And so, at last he gave a paper to Ben English, the leader of the colored members, and I joined the love feast, and was taken into the Church on trial for six months. I was put into Billy Cochran's class. At the expiration of six months, I was received into the Church in full fellowship, Quaker Davis' class. I remained there three years.

My master was much kinder after this time than he had formerly been, and I was allowed some more time to myself than I had been before. I pursued my studies as far as I could, but I soon found the utter impossibility of carrying on my studies as I wished to do. I was a slave, and all avenues to real improvement I found guarded with jealous care and cruel tenacity against the despised and desolate bondman.

At a young age, Jones married and had three children; both wife and children were sold, however, and he never saw them again. In 1829, when Jones was twenty-three, his master died and he was sold to Owen Holmes, a Wilmington, North Carolina, attorney, who hired him out to do dockwork. Jones remarried and purchased his wife so that his children with her could be free; he was also able to free his mother and father in their old age. But in 1848, he received word that "some white men were plotting to enslave my wife and children again," so he sent them to New York. The following year he made his escape by stowing aboard a ship bound for New York, where he was reunited with his family.

In 1850, following the passage of the Fugitive Slave Law, Jones moved to Canada, where he preached in various places for four years; in 1854, he returned to the United States to preach and give abolitionist lectures in Boston, where he spent the rest of his long life.

# HARRIET JACOBS
## (LINDA BRENT)

**H**arriet Jacobs (1813–97) was the first female slave to write her own autobiography (previous narratives of female slaves had been written by others based on the slave's spoken account). Published shortly before the Civil War under a pseudonym (Linda Brent), her book, *Incidents in the Life of a Slave Girl*, is perhaps the most intimate and emotionally compelling slave narrative of all.

She wrote the book in darkness. While she was writing it, she was employed to take care of the children of a prominent New York writer, Nathaniel Parker Willis, and it was in his home that she wrote her memoirs; but because Willis was proslavery, Jacobs kept her writing secret, working only at night. When it was almost finished, she wrote to her confidante, Amy Post, a Quaker reformer with whom Jacobs lived for nine months: "I have . . . Striven faithfully to give a true and just account of my own life in Slavery . . . there are some things that I might have made plainer I know—Woman can whisper—her cool wrongs into the ear of a very dear friend—much easier than she can record them for the world to read."

For several years she tried to get her book published, but in vain. So she sent it to Lydia Maria Child, one of the most famous writers in the country and a prominent abolitionist, who arranged for the book's publication by a Boston publisher. Unfortunately that publisher went bankrupt, so Jacobs bought the plates and published it herself. It finally appeared in early February 1861, only two months before the Civil War began, and because of that bad timing, few people read it.

For Jacobs, slavery wasn't so much a political fact as a poison, a disease. Her master had been a doctor whose "treatment" of her was absolutely repulsive. From her point of view, all of society under slavery was sick.

In her struggles, Jacobs frequently received support from her family, from the black community, and from a number of black and white women. Unlike male slaves, who often represented themselves as solitary figures in a wilderness, Jacobs rarely acted alone, but relied on her family and friends, forming a kind of sisterhood in the process. But all the while she was often overpowered by loneliness and deprivation, and by the demand for secrecy. Not even the most horrifying Gothic novels of the time describe conditions more oppressive than those that Jacobs suffered during her years in the South.

*Incidents* is a narrative that reverses most of our expectations. This starts with the title: by calling the book *Incidents in the Life of a Slave Girl* instead of *Narrative of the Life of a Slave Girl*, Jacobs tells us that she is going to tell an *incomplete* story—one that has to be incomplete since she can't fully reveal her sexual history due to what people were allowed to write at the time. In most slave narratives, even the most gruesome, excruciating details are spelled out in full; but in this book Jacobs concentrates on the psychological rather than the physical effects of oppression. These departures from the slave narrative tradition—which Jacobs was well aware of by this time, having run a bookstore in Frederick Douglass's building in Rochester, New York—show that Jacobs was shaping her book to read more like a novel.

For, like novels, this book is full of dialogue—it has more in it than in any other black autobiography written before the Civil War. This allows Jacobs to describe the verbal battles she had with her master, in which she says things she's forbidden to say, and twists her master's words in her favor. But more important than what is said is what goes unsaid. Jacobs's world is one of secrets, and secrets are everywhere in her book—in its pseudonyms, elisions, deceptions, and subterfuges. It is the secretive method that leads to deliverance for Jacobs.

In the conventional woman's novel of the nineteenth century, the heroine, a genteel young lady, is virtuous but helpless; she falls prey to an unscrupulous man and yields to him; and she dies. Jacobs will have none of this. She challenges the sexual roles she has been given and uses her sexuality as a weapon. No wonder that her book wasn't popular until over one hundred years after its publication. It was at first neglected, then called fiction, and it wasn't finally reprinted until 1973.

Below are several excerpts dealing with Jacobs's early life. Although there is nothing explicitly sexual in them, readers who wish to avoid discussions of sexual manipulation might want to skip this narrative.

## CHILDHOOD

I was born a slave; but I never knew it till six years of happy childhood had passed away.

In complexion my parents were a light shade of brownish yellow, and were termed mulattoes. They lived together in a comfortable home; and, though we were all slaves, I was so fondly shielded that I never dreamed I was a piece of merchandise, trusted to them for safe keeping, and liable to be demanded of them at any moment.

I had one brother, William, who was two years younger than myself—a bright, affectionate child. I had also a great treasure in my maternal grandmother, who was a remarkable woman in many respects. To this good grandmother I was indebted for many comforts. My brother Willie and I often received portions of the crackers, cakes, and preserves, she made to sell; and after we ceased to be children we were indebted to her for many more important services.

Such were the unusually fortunate circumstances of my early childhood. When I was six years old, my mother died; and then, for the first time, I learned, by the talk around me, that I was a slave. My mother's mistress was the daughter of my grandmother's mistress. She was the foster sister of my mother; they were both nourished at my grandmother's breast. In fact, my mother had been weaned at three months old, that the babe of the mistress might obtain sufficient food. They played together as children; and, when they became women, my mother was a most faithful servant to her whiter foster sister. On her death-bed her mistress promised that her children should never suffer for any thing; and during her lifetime she kept her word. They all spoke kindly of my dead mother, who had been a slave merely in name, but in nature was noble and womanly. I grieved for her, and my young mind was troubled with the thought who would now take care of me and my little brother.

I was told that my home was now to be with her mistress; and I found it a happy one. No toilsome or disagreeable duties were imposed upon me. My mistress was so kind to me that I was always glad to do her bidding, and proud to labor for her as much as my young years would permit. I would sit by her side for hours, sewing diligently, with a heart as free from care as that of any free-born white child. When she thought I was tired, she would send me out to run and jump; and away I bounded, to gather berries or flowers to decorate her room. Those were happy days—too happy to last. The slave child had no thought for the morrow; but there came that blight, which too surely waits on every human being born to be a chattel.

When I was nearly twelve years old, my kind mistress sickened and died. As I saw the cheek grow paler, and the eye more glassy, how earnestly I prayed in my heart that she might live! I loved her; for she had been almost like a mother to me. My prayers were not answered.

She died, and they buried her in the little churchyard, where, day after day, my tears fell upon her grave.

I was sent to spend a week with my grandmother. I was now old enough to begin to think of the future; and again and again I asked myself what they would do with me. I felt sure I should never find another mistress so kind as the one who was gone. She had promised my dying mother that her children should never suffer for any thing; and when I remembered that, and recalled her many proofs of attachment to me, I could not help having some hopes that she had left me free. My friends were almost certain it would be so. They thought she would be sure to do it, on account of my mother's love and faithful service. But, alas! we all know that the memory of a faithful slave does not avail much to save her children from the auction block.

After a brief period of suspense, the will of my mistress was read, and we learned that she had bequeathed me to her sister's daughter, a child of five years old. So vanished our hopes. My mistress had taught me the precepts of God's Word: "Thou shalt love thy neighbor as thyself" [*Mark* 12:31]. "Whatsoever ye would that men should do unto you, do ye even so unto them" [*Matthew* 7:12]. But I was her slave, and I suppose she did not recognize me as her neighbor. I would give much to blot out from my memory that one great wrong. As a child, I loved my mistress; and, looking back on the happy days I spent with her, I try to think with less bitterness of this act of injustice. While I was with her, she taught me to read and spell; and for this privilege, which so rarely falls to the lot of a slave, I bless her memory.

She possessed but few slaves; and at her death those were all distributed among her relatives. Five of them were my grandmother's children, and had shared the same milk that nourished her mother's children. Notwithstanding my grandmother's long and faithful service to her owners, not one of her children escaped the auction block. These God-breathing machines are no more, in the sight of their masters, than the cotton they plant, or the horses they tend.

## THE NEW MASTER AND MISTRESS

Dr. Flint, a physician in the neighborhood, had married the sister of my mistress, and I was now the property of their little daughter. Grandmother tried to cheer us with hopeful words, and they found an echo in the credulous hearts of youth.

When we entered our new home we encountered cold looks, cold words, and cold treatment. We were glad when the night came. On my narrow bed I moaned and wept, I felt so desolate and alone.

I had been there nearly a year, when a dear little friend of mine was buried. I heard her mother sob, as the clods fell on the coffin of her only child, and I turned away from the grave, feeling thankful that I still had something left to love. I met my grandmother, who said, "Come with me, Linda;" and from her tone I knew that something sad had happened. She led me apart from the people, and then said, "My child, your father is dead." Dead! How could I believe it? He had died so suddenly I had not even heard that he was sick.

I went home with my grandmother. My heart rebelled against God, who had taken from me mother, father, mistress, and friend. The good grandmother tried to comfort me. "Who knows the ways of God?" said she. "Perhaps they have been kindly taken from the evil days to come." Years afterwards I often thought of this. She promised to be a mother to her grandchildren, so far as she might be permitted to do so; and strengthened by her love, I returned to my master's. I thought I should be allowed to go to my father's house the next morning; but I was ordered to go for flowers, that my mistress's house might be decorated for an evening party. I spent the day gathering flowers and weaving them into festoons, while the dead body of my father was lying within a mile of me. What cared my owners for that? he was merely a piece of property. Moreover, they thought he had spoiled his children, by teaching them to feel that they were human beings. This was blasphemous doctrine for a slave to teach; presumptuous in him, and dangerous to the masters.

The next day I followed his remains to a humble grave beside that of my dear mother. There were those who knew my father's worth, and respected his memory.

My home now seemed more dreary than ever. The laugh of the little slave-children sounded harsh and cruel. It was selfish to feel so about the joy of others. My brother moved about with a very grave face. I tried to comfort him, by saying, "Take courage, Willie; brighter days will come by and by."

"You don't know any thing about it, Linda," he replied. "We shall have to stay here all our days; we shall never be free."

I argued that we were growing older and stronger, and that perhaps we might, before long, be allowed to hire our own time, and then we could earn money to buy our freedom. William declared this was much easier to say than to do; moreover, he did not intend to buy his freedom. We held daily controversies upon this subject.

Little attention was paid to the slaves' meals in Dr. Flint's house. If they could catch a bit of food while it was going, well and good. I gave myself no trouble on that score, for on my various errands I passed my grandmother's house, where there was always something to spare for me. I was frequently threatened with punishment if I stopped there; and my grandmother, to avoid detaining me, often stood at the gate with something for my breakfast or dinner. I was indebted to her for all my comforts, spiritual or temporal. It was *her* labor that supplied my scanty wardrobe. I have a vivid recollection of the linsey-woolsey [coarse fabric made of wool and linen or cotton] dress given me every winter by Mrs. Flint. How I hated it! It was one of the badges of slavery.

I remember the first time I was punished. It was in the month of February. My grandmother had taken my old shoes, and replaced them with a new pair. I needed them; for several inches of snow had fallen, and it still continued to fall. When I walked through Mrs. Flint's room, their creaking grated harshly on her refined nerves. She called me to her, and asked what I had about me that made such a horrid noise.

I told her it was my new shoes. "Take them off," said she; "and if you put them on again, I'll throw them into the fire."

I took them off, and my stockings also. She then sent me a long distance, on an errand. As I went through the snow, my bare feet tingled. That night I was very hoarse; and I went to bed thinking the next day would find me sick, perhaps dead. What was my grief on waking to find myself quite well!

I had imagined if I died, or was laid up for some time, that my mistress would feel a twinge of remorse that she had so hated "the little imp," as she styled me. It was my ignorance of that mistress that gave rise to such extravagant imaginings.

Dr. Flint occasionally had high prices offered for me; but he always said, "She don't belong to me. She is my daughter's property, and I have no right to sell her." Good, honest man! My young mistress was still a child, and I could look for no protection from her. I loved her, and she returned my affection. I once heard her father allude to her attachment to me; and his wife promptly replied that it proceeded from fear. This put unpleasant doubts into my mind. Did the child feign what she did not feel? or was her mother jealous of the mite of love she bestowed on me? I concluded it must be the latter. I said to myself, "Surely, little children are true."

## THE TRIALS OF GIRLHOOD

During the first years of my service in Dr. Flint's family, I was accustomed to share some indulgences with the children of my mistress. Though this seemed to me no more than right, I was grateful for it, and tried to merit the kindness by the faithful discharge of my duties. But I now entered on my fifteenth year—a sad epoch in the life of a slave girl. My master began to whisper foul words in my ear. Young as I was, I could not remain ignorant of their import. I tried to treat them with indifference or contempt. The master's age, my extreme youth, and the

fear that his conduct would be reported to my grandmother, made him bear this treatment for many months. He was a crafty man, and resorted to many means to accomplish his purposes. Sometimes he had stormy, terrific ways, that made his victims tremble; sometimes he assumed a gentleness that he thought must surely subdue. Of the two, I preferred his stormy moods, although they left me trembling. He tried his utmost to corrupt the pure principles my grandmother had instilled. He peopled my young mind with unclean images, such as only a vile monster could think of. I turned from him with disgust and hatred. But he was my master. I was compelled to live under the same roof with him—where I saw a man forty years my senior daily violating the most sacred commandments of nature. He told me I was his property; that I must be subject to his will in all things. My soul revolted against the mean tyranny. But where could I turn for protection? No matter whether the slave girl be as black as ebony or as fair as her mistress. In either case, there is no shadow of law to protect her from insult, from violence, or even from death; all these are inflicted by fiends who bear the shape of men. The mistress, who ought to protect the helpless victim, has no other feelings towards her but those of jealousy and rage. The degradation, the wrongs, the vices, that grow out of slavery, are more than I can describe. They are greater than you would willingly believe. Surely, if you credited one half the truths that are told you concerning the helpless millions suffering in this cruel bondage, you at the north would not help to tighten the yoke. You surely would refuse to do for the master, on your own soil, the mean and cruel work which trained bloodhounds and the lowest class of whites do for him at the south.

Every where the years bring to all enough of sin and sorrow; but in slavery the very dawn of life is darkened by these shadows. Even the little child, who is accustomed to wait on her mistress and her children, will learn, before she is twelve years old, why it is that her mistress hates such and such a one among the slaves. Perhaps the child's own mother is among those hated ones. She listens to violent outbreaks of jealous passion, and cannot help understanding what is the cause. She will become prematurely knowing in evil things. Soon she will learn to tremble when she hears her master's footfall. She will be compelled to realize that she is no longer a child. If God has bestowed beauty upon her, it will prove her greatest curse. That which commands admiration in the white woman only hastens the degradation of the female slave. I know that some are too much brutalized by slavery to feel the humiliation of their position; but many slaves feel it most acutely, and shrink from the memory of it. I cannot tell how much I suffered in the presence of these wrongs, nor how I am still pained by the retrospect [memory]. My master met me at every turn, reminding me that I belonged to him, and swearing by heaven and earth that he would compel me to submit to him. If I went out for a breath of fresh air, after a day of unwearied toil, his footsteps dogged me. If I knelt by my mother's grave, his dark shadow fell on me even there. The light heart which nature had given me became heavy with sad forebodings. The other slaves in my master's house noticed the change. Many of them pitied me; but none dared to ask the cause. They had no need to inquire. They knew too well the guilty practices under that roof; and they were aware that to speak of them was an offence that never went unpunished.

I longed for some one to confide in. I would have given the world to have laid my head on my grandmother's faithful bosom, and told her all my troubles. But Dr. Flint swore he would kill me, if I was not as silent as the grave. Then, although my grandmother was all in all to me, I feared her as well as loved her. I had been accustomed to look up to her with a respect bordering upon awe. I was very young, and felt shamefaced about telling her such impure things, especially as I knew her to be very strict on such subjects. Moreover, she was a woman of a high spirit. She was usually very quiet in her demeanor; but if her indignation was once roused, it was not very easily quelled. I had been told that she once chased a white gentleman with a loaded pistol, because he insulted one of her daughters. I dreaded the consequences of a violent outbreak; and both pride and fear kept me silent. But though I did not confide in my grandmother, and even evaded her vigilant watchfulness and inquiry, her presence in the neighborhood was some protection to me. Though she had been a slave, Dr. Flint was afraid of her. He dreaded her scorching rebukes. Moreover, she was known and patronized by many people; and he did not wish to have his villainy made public. It was lucky for me that I did not live on a distant plantation, but in a town not so large that the inhabitants were ignorant of each other's affairs. Bad as are the laws and customs in a slaveholding community, the doctor, as a professional man, deemed it prudent to keep up some outward show of decency.

O, what days and nights of fear and sorrow that man caused me! Reader, it is not to awaken sympathy for myself that I am telling you truthfully what I suffered in slavery. I do it to kindle a flame of compassion in your hearts for my sisters who are still in bondage, suffering as I once suffered.

### THE JEALOUS MISTRESS

Mrs. Flint possessed the key to her husband's character before I was born. She might have used this knowledge to counsel and to screen the young and the innocent among her slaves; but for them she had no sympathy. They were the objects of her constant suspicion and malevolence. She watched her husband with unceasing vigilance; but he was well practiced in means to evade it. What he could not find opportunity to say in words he manifested in signs. He invented more than were ever thought of in a deaf and dumb asylum. I let them pass, as if I did not understand what he meant; and many were the curses and threats bestowed on me for my stupidity.

One day he caught me teaching myself to write. He frowned, as if he was not well pleased; but I suppose he came to the conclusion that such an accomplishment might help to advance his favorite scheme. Before long, notes were often slipped into my hand. I would return them, saying, "I can't read them, sir." "Can't you?" he replied; "then I must read them to you." He always finished the reading by asking, "Do you understand?"

Sometimes he would complain of the heat of the tea room, and order his supper to be placed on a small table in the piazza. He would seat himself there with a well-satisfied smile, and tell me to stand by and brush away the flies. He would eat very slowly, pausing between the mouthfuls. These intervals were employed in describing the happiness I was so foolishly throwing away, and in threatening me with the penalty that finally awaited my stubborn disobedience. He boasted much of the forbearance he had exercised towards me, and reminded me that there was a limit to his patience.

When I succeeded in avoiding opportunities for him to talk to me at home, I was ordered to come to his office, to do some errand. When there, I was obliged to stand and listen to such language as he saw fit to address to me. Sometimes I so openly expressed my contempt for him that he would become violently enraged, and I wondered why he did not strike me. Circumstanced as he was, he probably thought it was better policy to be forbearing [patient]. But the state of things grew worse and worse daily. In desperation I told him that I must and would apply to my grandmother for protection. He threatened me with death, and worse than death, if I made any complaint to her. Strange to say, I did not despair. I was naturally of a buoyant disposition, and always I had a hope of somehow getting out of his clutches. Like many a poor, simple slave before me, I trusted that some threads of joy would yet be woven into my dark destiny.

I had entered my sixteenth year, and every day it became more apparent that my presence was intolerable to Mrs. Flint. Angry words frequently passed between her and her husband. He had never punished me himself, and he would not allow any body else to punish me. In that respect, she was never satisfied; but, in her angry moods, no terms were too vile for her to bestow upon me. Yet I, whom she detested so bitterly, had far more pity for her than he had, whose duty it was to make her life happy. I never wronged her, or wished to wrong her; and one word of kindness from her would have brought me to her feet.

After repeated quarrels between the doctor and his wife, he announced his intention to take his youngest daughter, then four years old, to sleep in his apartment. It was necessary that a servant should sleep in the same room, to be on hand if the child stirred. I was selected for that office, and informed for what purpose that arrangement had been made. By managing to keep within sight of people, as much as possible, during the day time, I had hitherto succeeded in eluding my master, though a razor was often held to my throat to force me to change this line of policy. At night I slept by the side of my great aunt, where I felt safe. He was too prudent to come into her room. She was an old woman, and had been in the family many years. Moreover, as a married man, and a professional man, he deemed it necessary to save appearances in some degree. But he resolved to remove the obstacle in the way of his scheme; and he thought he had planned it so that he should evade suspicion. He was well aware how much I prized my refuge by the side of my old aunt, and he determined to dispossess me of it. The first night the doctor had the little child in his room alone. The next morning, I was ordered to take my station as nurse the following night. A kind Providence interposed in my favor. During the day Mrs. Flint heard of this new arrangement, and a storm followed. I rejoiced to hear it rage.

After a while my mistress sent for me to come to her room. Her first question was, "Did you know you were to sleep in the doctor's room?"

"Yes, ma'am."

"Who told you?"

"My master."

"Will you answer truly all the questions I ask?"

"Yes, ma'am."

"Tell me, then, as you hope to be forgiven, are you innocent of what I have accused you?"

"I am."

She handed me a Bible, and said, "Lay your hand on your heart, kiss this holy book, and swear before God that you tell me the truth."

I took the oath she required, and I did it with a clear conscience.

"You have taken God's holy word to testify your innocence," said she. "If you have deceived me, beware! Now take this stool, sit down, look me directly in the face, and tell me all that has passed between your master and you."

I did as she ordered. As I went on with my account her color changed frequently, she wept, and sometimes groaned. She spoke in tones so sad, that I was touched by her grief. The tears came to my eyes; but I was soon convinced that her emotions arose from anger and wounded pride. She felt that her marriage vows were desecrated, her dignity insulted; but she had no compassion for the poor victim of her husband's perfidy. She pitied herself as a martyr; but she was incapable of feeling for the condition of shame and misery in which her unfortunate, helpless slave was placed.

Yet perhaps she had some touch of feeling for me; for when the conference was ended, she spoke kindly, and promised to protect me. I should have been much comforted by this assurance if I could have had confidence in it; but my experiences in slavery had filled me with distrust. She was not a very refined woman, and had not much control over her passions. I was an object of her jealousy, and, consequently, of her hatred; and I knew I could not expect kindness or confidence from her under the circumstances in which I was placed. I could not blame her. Slaveholders' wives feel as other women would under similar circumstances. The fire of her temper kindled from small sparks, and now the flame became so intense that the doctor was obliged to give up his intended arrangement.

I knew I had ignited the torch, and I expected to suffer for it afterwards; but I felt too thankful to my mistress for the timely aid she rendered me to care much about that. She now took me to sleep in a room adjoining her own. There I was an object of her especial care, though not of her especial comfort, for she spent many a sleepless night to watch over me. Sometimes I woke up, and found her bending over me. At other times she whispered in my ear, as though it was her husband who was speaking to me, and listened to hear what I would answer. If she startled me, on such occasions, she would glide stealthily away; and the next morning she would tell me I had been talking in my sleep, and ask who I was talking to. At last, I began to be fearful for my life. It had been often threatened; and you can imagine, better than I can describe, what an unpleasant sensation it must produce to wake up in the dead of night and find a jealous woman bending over you. Terrible as this experience was, I had fears that it would give place to one more terrible.

My mistress grew weary of her vigils; they did not prove satisfactory. She changed her tactics. She now tried the trick of accusing my master of crime, in my presence, and gave my name as the author of the accusation. To my utter astonishment, he replied, "I don't believe it; but if she did acknowledge it, you tortured her into exposing me." Tortured into exposing him! Truly, Satan had no difficulty in distinguishing the color of his soul! I understood his object in making this false representation. It was to show me that I gained nothing by seeking the protection of my mistress; that the power was still all in his own hands.

I pitied Mrs. Flint. She was a second wife, many years the junior of her husband; and the hoary-headed [gray-haired] miscreant [vicious person] was enough to try the patience of a wiser and better woman. She was completely foiled, and knew not how to proceed. She would gladly have had me flogged for my supposed false oath; but, as I have already stated, the doctor never allowed any one to whip me. The old sinner was politic. The application of the lash might have led to remarks that would have exposed him in the eyes of his children and grandchildren. How often did I rejoice that I lived in a town where all the inhabitants knew each other! If I had been on a remote plantation, or lost among the multitude of a crowded city, I should not be a living woman at this day.

The secrets of slavery are concealed like those of the Inquisition. My master was, to my knowledge, the father of eleven slaves. But did the mothers dare to tell who was the father of their children? Did the other slaves dare to allude to it, except in whispers among themselves? No, indeed! They knew too well the terrible consequences.

My grandmother could not avoid seeing things which excited her suspicions. She was uneasy about me, and tried various ways to buy me; but the never-changing answer was always repeated: "Linda does not belong to *me*. She is my daughter's property, and I have no legal right to sell her." The conscientious man! He was too scrupulous to *sell* me; but he had no scruples whatever about committing a much greater wrong against the helpless young girl placed under his guardianship, as his daughter's property. Sometimes my persecutor would ask me whether I would like to be sold. I told him I would rather be sold to any body than to lead such a life as I did. On such occasions he would assume the air of a very injured individual, and reproach me for my ingratitude. "Did I not take you into the house, and make you the companion of my own children?" he would say. "Have I ever treated you like a negro? I have never allowed you to be punished, not even to please your mistress. And this is the recompense I get, you ungrateful girl!" I answered that he had reasons of his own for screening me from punishment, and that the course he pursued made my mistress hate me and persecute me. If I wept, he would say, "Poor child! Don't cry! don't cry! I will make peace for you with your mistress. Only let me arrange matters in my own way. Poor, foolish girl! you don't know what is for your own good. I would cherish you. I would make a lady of you. Now go, and think of all I have promised you."

I did think of it.

## THE LOVER

Why does the slave ever love? Why allow the tendrils of the heart to twine around objects which may at any moment be wrenched away by the hand of violence? When separations come by the hand of death, the pious soul can bow in resignation, and say, "Not my will, but thine be done, O Lord!" But when the ruthless hand of man strikes the blow, regardless of the misery he causes, it is hard to be submissive. I did not reason thus when I was a young girl. Youth will be youth. I loved, and I indulged the hope that the dark clouds around me would turn out a bright lining. I forgot that in the land of my birth the shadows are too dense for light to penetrate.

There was in the neighborhood a young colored carpenter; a free born man. We had been well acquainted in childhood, and frequently met together afterwards. We became mutually attached, and he proposed to marry me. I loved him with all the ardor of a young girl's first love. But when I reflected that I was a slave, and that the laws gave no sanction to the marriage of such, my heart sank within me. My lover wanted to buy me; but I knew that Dr. Flint was too wilful and arbitrary a man to consent to that arrangement. From him, I was sure of experiencing all sorts of opposition, and I had nothing to hope from my mistress. She would have been delighted to have got rid of me, but not in that way. It would have relieved her mind of a burden if she could have seen me sold to some distant state, but if I was married near home I should be just as much in her husband's power as I had previously been,—for the husband of a slave has no power to protect her. Moreover, my mistress, like many others, seemed to think that slaves had no right to any family ties of their own; that they were created merely to wait upon the family of the mistress. I once heard her abuse a young slave girl, who told her that a colored man wanted to make her his wife. "I will have you peeled and pickled [whipped and washed in brine], my lady," said she, "if I ever hear you mention that subject again. Do you suppose that I will have you tending my children with the children of that nigger?" The girl to whom she said this had a mulatto child, of course not acknowledged by its father. The poor black man who loved her would have been proud to acknowledge his helpless offspring.

Many and anxious were the thoughts I revolved in my mind. I was at a loss what to do. Above all things, I was desirous to spare my lover the insults that had cut so deeply into my own soul. I talked with my grandmother about it, and partly told her my fears. I did not dare to tell her the worst. She had long suspected all was not right, and if I confirmed her suspicions I knew a storm would rise that would prove the overthrow of all my hopes.

This love-dream had been my support through many trials; and I could not bear to run the risk of having it suddenly dissipated. There was a lady in the neighborhood, a particular friend of Dr. Flint's, who often visited the house. I had a great respect for her, and she had always manifested a friendly interest in me. Grandmother thought she would have great influence with the doctor. I went to this lady, and told her my story. I told her I was aware that my lover's being a free-born man would prove a great objection; but he wanted to buy me; and if Dr. Flint would consent to that arrangement, I felt sure he would be willing to pay any reasonable price. She knew that Mrs. Flint disliked me; therefore, I ventured to suggest that perhaps my mistress would approve of my being sold, as that would rid her of me. The lady listened with kindly sympathy, and promised to do her utmost to promote my wishes. She had an interview with the doctor, and I believe she pleaded my cause earnestly; but it was all to no purpose.

How I dreaded my master now! Every minute I expected to be summoned to his presence; but the day passed, and I heard nothing from him. The next morning, a message was brought to me: "Master wants you in his study." I found the door ajar, and I stood a moment gazing at the hateful man who claimed a right to rule me, body and soul. I entered, and tried to appear calm. I did not want him to know how my heart was bleeding. He looked fixedly at me, with an expression which seemed to say, "I have half a mind to kill you on the spot." At last he broke the silence, and that was a relief to both of us.

"So you want to be married, do you?" said he, "and to a free nigger."

"Yes, sir."

"Well, I'll soon convince you whether I am your master, or the nigger fellow you honor so highly. If you must have a husband, you may take up with one of my slaves."

What a situation I should be in, as the wife of one of *his* slaves, even if my heart had been interested!

I replied, "Don't you suppose, sir, that a slave can have some preference about marrying? Do you suppose that all men are alike to her?"

"Do you love this nigger?" said he, abruptly.

"Yes, sir."

"How dare you tell me so!" he exclaimed, in great wrath. After a slight pause, he added, "I supposed you thought more of yourself; that you felt above the insults of such puppies."

I replied, "If he is a puppy I am a puppy, for we are both of the negro race. It is right and honorable for us to love each other. The man you call a puppy never insulted me, sir; and he would not love me if he did not believe me to be a virtuous woman."

He sprang upon me like a tiger, and gave me a stunning blow. It was the first time he had ever struck me; and fear did not enable me to control my anger. When I had recovered a little from the effects, I exclaimed, "You have struck me for answering you honestly. How I despise you!"

There was silence for some minutes. Perhaps he was deciding what should be my punishment; or, perhaps, he wanted to give me time to reflect on what I had said, and to whom I had said it. Finally, he asked, "Do you know what you have said?"

"Yes, sir; but your treatment drove me to it."

"Do you know that I have a right to do as I like with you,—that I can kill you, if I please?"

"You have tried to kill me, and I wish you had; but you have no right to do as you like with me."

"Silence!" he exclaimed, in a thundering voice. "By heavens, girl, you forget yourself too far! Are you mad? If you are, I will soon bring you to your senses. Do you think any other master would bear what I have borne from you this morning? Many masters would have killed you on the spot. How would you like to be sent to jail for your insolence?"

"I know I have been disrespectful, sir," I replied; "but you drove me to it; I couldn't help it. As for the jail, there would be more peace for me there than there is here."

"You deserve to go there," said he, "and to be under such treatment, that you would forget the meaning of the word *peace*. It would do you good. It would take some of your high notions out of you. But I am not ready to send you there yet, notwithstanding your ingratitude for all my kindness and forbearance. You have been the plague of my life. I have wanted to make you happy, and I have been repaid with the basest ingratitude; but though you have proved yourself incapable of appreciating my kindness, I will be lenient towards you, Linda. I will give you one more chance to redeem your character. If you behave yourself and do as I require, I will forgive you and treat you as I always have done; but if you disobey me, I will punish you as I would the meanest slave on my plantation. Never let me hear that fellow's name mentioned again. If I ever know of your speaking to him, I will cowhide you both; and if I catch him lurking about my premises, I will shoot him as soon as I would a dog. Do you hear what I say? I'll teach you a lesson about marriage and free niggers! Now go, and let this be the last time I have occasion to speak to you on this subject."

Reader, did you ever hate? I hope not. I never did but once; and I trust I never shall again. Somebody has called it "the atmosphere of hell;" and I believe it is so.

For a fortnight the doctor did not speak to me. He thought to mortify me; to make me feel that I had disgraced myself by receiving the honorable addresses of a respectable colored man, in preference to the base proposals of a white man. But though his lips disdained to address me, his eyes were very loquacious. No animal ever watched its prey more narrowly than he watched me. He knew that I could write, though he had failed to make me read his letters; and he was now troubled lest I should exchange letters with another man. After a while he became weary of silence; and I was sorry for it. One morning, as he passed through the hall, to leave the house, he contrived to thrust a note into my hand. I thought I had better read it, and spare myself the vexation of having him read it to me. It expressed regret for the blow he had given me, and reminded me that I myself was wholly to blame for it. He hoped I had become convinced of the injury I was doing myself by incurring his displeasure. He wrote that he had made up his mind to go to Louisiana; that he should take several slaves with him, and intended I should be one of the number. My mistress would remain where she was; therefore I should have nothing to fear from that quarter. If I merited kindness from him, he assured me that it would be lavishly bestowed. He begged me to think over the matter, and answer the following day.

The next morning I was called to carry a pair of scissors to his room. I laid them on the table, with the letter beside them. He thought it was my answer, and did not call me back. I went as usual to attend my young mistress to and from school. He met me in the street, and ordered me to stop at his office on my way back. When I entered, he showed me his letter, and asked me why I had not answered it. I replied, "I am your daughter's property, and it is in your power to send me, or take me, wherever you please." He said he was very glad to find me so willing to go, and that we should start early in the autumn. He had a large practice in the town, and I rather thought he had made up the story merely to frighten me. However that might be, I was determined that I would never go to Louisiana with him.

Summer passed away, and early in the autumn Dr. Flint's eldest son was sent to Louisiana to examine the country, with a view to emigrating. That news did not disturb me. I knew very well that I should not be sent with him. That I had not been taken to the plantation before this time, was owing to the fact that his son was there. He was jealous of his son; and jealousy of the overseer had kept him from punishing me by sending me into the fields to work. Is it strange that I was not proud of these protectors? As for the overseer, he was a man for whom I had less respect than I had for a bloodhound.

Young Mr. Flint did not bring back a favorable report of Louisiana, and I heard no more of that scheme. Soon after this, my lover met me at the corner of the street, and I stopped to speak to him. Looking up, I saw my master watching us from his window. I hurried home, trembling with fear. I was sent for, immediately, to go to his room. He met me with a blow. "When is mistress to be married?" said he, in a sneering tone. A shower of oaths and imprecations followed. How thankful I was that my lover was a free man! that my tyrant had no power to dog him for speaking to me in the street!

Again and again I revolved in my mind how all this would end. There was no hope that the doctor would consent to sell me on any terms. He had an iron will, and was determined to keep me, and to conquer me. My lover was an intelligent and religious man. Even if he could have obtained permission to marry me while I was a slave, the marriage would give him no power to protect me from my master. It would have made him miserable to witness the insults I should have been subjected to. And then, if we had children, I knew they must "follow the condition of the mother." [Under the laws of U.S. slavery, children would be free if their mother was free and slaves if their mother was a slave.] What a terrible blight that would be on the heart of a free, intelligent father! For *his* sake, I felt that I ought not to link his fate with my own unhappy destiny. He was going to Savannah to see about a little property left him by an uncle; and hard as it was to bring my feelings to it, I earnestly entreated him not to come back. I advised him to go to the Free States, where his tongue would not be tied, and where his intelligence would be of more avail to him. He left me, still hoping the day would come when I could be bought. With me the lamp of hope had gone out. The dream of my girlhood was over. I felt lonely and desolate.

Still I was not stripped of all. I still had my good grandmother, and my affectionate brother. When he put his arms round my neck, and looked into my eyes, as if to read there the troubles I dared not tell, I felt that I still had something to love. But even that pleasant emotion was chilled by the reflection that he might be torn from me at any moment, by some sudden freak of my master. If he had known how we loved each other, I think he would have exulted in separating us. We often planned together how we could get to the north. But, as William remarked, such things are easier said than done. My movements were very closely watched, and we had no means of getting any money to defray our expenses. As for grandmother, she was strongly opposed to her children's undertaking any such project. She had not forgotten poor Benjamin's sufferings [Harriet's brother Benjamin had managed to escape, but not before undergoing severe trials], and she was afraid that if another child tried to escape, he would have a similar or a worse fate. To me, nothing seemed more dreadful than my present life. I said to myself, "William *must* be free. He shall go to the north, and I will follow him." Many a slave sister has formed the same plans.

## A PERILOUS PASSAGE IN THE SLAVE GIRL'S LIFE

After my lover went away, Dr. Flint contrived a new plan. He seemed to have an idea that my fear of my mistress was his greatest obstacle. In the blandest tones, he told me that he was going to build a small house for me, in a secluded place, four miles away from the town. I shuddered; but I was constrained to listen, while he talked of his intention to give me a home of my own, and to make a lady of me. Hitherto, I had escaped my dreaded fate, by being in the midst of people. My grandmother had already had high words with my master about me. She had told him pretty plainly what she thought of his character, and there was considerable gossip in the neighborhood about our affairs, to which the open-mouthed jealousy of Mrs. Flint contributed not a little. When my master said he was going to build a house for me, and that he could do it with little trouble and expense, I was in hopes something would happen to frustrate his scheme; but I soon heard that the house was actually begun. I vowed before my Maker that I would never enter it. I had rather toil on the plantation from dawn till dark; I had rather live and die in jail, than drag on, from day to day, through such a living death. I was determined that the master, whom I so hated and loathed, who had blighted the prospects of my youth, and made my life a desert, should not, after my long struggle with him, succeed at last in trampling his victim under his feet. I would do any thing, every thing, for the sake of defeating him. What *could* I do? I thought and thought, till I became desperate, and made a plunge into the abyss.

And now, reader, I come to a period in my unhappy life, which I would gladly forget if I could. The remembrance fills me with sorrow and shame. It pains me to tell you of it; but I have promised to tell you the truth, and I will do it honestly, let it cost me what it may. I will not try to screen myself behind the plea of compulsion from a master; for it was not so. Neither can I plead ignorance or thoughtlessness. For years, my master had done his utmost to pollute my mind with foul images, and to destroy the pure principles inculcated by my grandmother, and the good mistress of my childhood. The influences of slavery had had the same effect on me that they had on other young girls; they had made me prematurely knowing, concerning the evil ways of the world. I knew what I did, and I did it with deliberate calculation.

But, O, ye happy women, whose purity has been sheltered from childhood, who have been free to choose the objects of your affection, whose homes are protected by law, do not judge the poor desolate slave girl too severely! If slavery had been abolished, I, also, could have married the man of my choice; I could have had a home shielded by the laws; and I should have been spared the painful task of confessing what I am now about to relate; but all my prospects had been blighted by slavery. I wanted to keep myself pure; and, under the most adverse circumstances, I tried hard to preserve my self-respect; but I was struggling alone in the powerful grasp of the demon Slavery; and the monster proved too strong for me. I felt as if I was forsaken by God and man; as if all my efforts must be frustrated; and I became reckless in my despair.

I have told you that Dr. Flint's persecutions and his wife's jealousy had given rise to some gossip in the neighborhood. Among others, it chanced that a white unmarried gentleman had obtained some knowledge of the circumstances in which I was placed. He knew my grandmother, and often spoke to me in the street. He became interested for me, and asked questions about my master, which I answered in part. He expressed a great deal of sympathy, and a wish to aid me. He constantly sought opportunities to see me, and wrote to me frequently. I was a poor slave girl, only fifteen years old.

So much attention from a superior person was, of course, flattering; for human nature is the same in all. I also felt grateful for his sympathy, and encouraged by his kind words. It seemed to me a great thing to have such a friend. By degrees, a more tender feeling crept into my heart. He was an educated and eloquent gentleman; too eloquent, alas, for the poor slave girl who trusted in him. Of course I saw whither all this was tending. I knew the impassable gulf between us, but to be an object of interest to a man who is not married, and who is not her master, is agreeable to the pride and feelings of a slave, if her miserable situation has left her any pride or sentiment. It seems less degrading to give one's self, than to submit to compulsion. There is something akin to freedom in having a lover who has no control over you, except that which he gains by kindness and attachment. A master may treat you as rudely as he pleases, and you dare not speak; moreover, the wrong does not seem so great with an unmarried man, as with one who has a wife to be made unhappy. There may be sophistry in all this; but the condition of a slave confuses all principles of morality, and, in fact, renders the practice of them impossible.

When I found that my master had actually begun to build the lonely cottage, other feelings mixed with those I have described. Revenge, and calculations of interest, were added to flattered vanity and sincere gratitude for kindness. I knew nothing would enrage Dr. Flint, so much as to know that I favored another; and it was something to triumph over my tyrant even in that small way. I thought he would revenge himself by selling me, and I was sure my friend, Mr. Sands, would buy me. He was a man of more generosity and feeling than my master, and I thought my freedom could be easily obtained from him. The crisis of my fate now came so near that I was desperate. I shuddered to think of being the mother of children that should be owned by my old tyrant. I knew that as soon as a new fancy took him, his victims were sold far off to get rid of them; especially if they had children. I had seen several women sold, with his babies at the breast. He never allowed his offspring by slaves to remain long in sight of himself and his wife. Of a man who was not my master I could ask to have my children well supported; and in this case, I felt confident I should obtain the boon. I also felt quite sure that they would be made free. With all these thoughts revolving in my mind, and seeing no other way of escaping the doom I so much dreaded, I made a headlong plunge. Pity me, and pardon me, O virtuous reader! You never knew what it is to be a slave; to be entirely unprotected by law or custom; to have the laws reduce you to the condition of a chattel, entirely subject to the will of another. You never exhausted your ingenuity in avoiding the snares, and eluding the power of a hated tyrant; you never shuddered at the sound of his footsteps, and trembled within hearing of his voice. I know I did wrong. No one can feel it more sensibly than I do. The painful and humiliating memory will haunt me to my dying day. Still, in looking back, calmly, on the events of my life, I feel that the slave woman ought not to be judged by the same standard as others.

The months passed on. I had many unhappy hours. I secretly mourned over the sorrow I was bringing on my grandmother, who had so tried to shield me from harm. I knew that I was the greatest comfort of her old age, and that it was a source of pride to her that I had not degraded myself, like most of the slaves. I wanted to confess to her that I was no longer worthy of her love; but I could not utter the dreaded words.

As for Dr. Flint, I had a feeling of satisfaction and triumph in the thought of telling him. From time to time he told me of his intended arrangements, and I was silent. At last, he came and told me the cottage was completed, and ordered me to go to it. I told him I would never enter it. He said, "I have heard enough of such talk as that. You shall go, if you are carried by force; and you shall remain there."

I replied, "I will never go there. In a few months I shall be a mother."

He stood and looked at me in dumb amazement, and left the house without a word. I thought I should be happy in my triumph over him. But now that the truth was out, and my relatives would hear of it, I felt wretched. Humble as were their circumstances, they had pride in my good character. Now, how could I look them in the face? My self-respect was gone! I had resolved that I would be virtuous, though I was a slave. I had said, "Let the storm beat! I will brave it till I die." And now, how humiliated I felt!

I went to my grandmother. My lips moved to make confession, but the words stuck in my throat. I sat down in the shade of a tree at her door and began to sew. I think she saw something unusual was the matter with me. The mother of slaves is very watchful. She knows there is no security for her children. After they have entered their teens she lives in daily expectation of trouble. This leads to many questions. If the girl is of a sensitive nature, timidity keeps her from answering truthfully, and this well-meant course has a tendency to drive her from maternal counsels. Presently, in came my mistress, like a mad woman, and accused me concerning her husband.

My grandmother, whose suspicions had been previously awakened, believed what she said. She exclaimed, "O Linda! has it come to this? I had rather see you dead than to see you as you now are. You are a disgrace to your dead mother." She tore from my fingers my mother's wedding ring and her silver thimble. "Go away!" she exclaimed, "and never come to my house, again." Her reproaches fell so hot and heavy, that they left me no chance to answer. Bitter tears, such as the eyes never shed but once, were my only answer.

I rose from my seat, but fell back again, sobbing. She did not speak to me; but the tears were running down her furrowed cheeks, and they scorched me like fire. She had always been so kind to me! So kind! How I longed to throw myself at her feet, and tell her all the truth! But she had ordered me to go, and never to come there again. After a few minutes, I mustered strength, and started to obey her. With what feelings did I now close that little gate, which I used to open with such an eager hand in my childhood! It closed upon me with a sound I never heard before.

Where could I go? I was afraid to return to my master's. I walked on recklessly, not caring where I went, or what would become of me. When I had gone four or five miles, fatigue compelled me to stop. I sat down on the stump of an old tree. The stars were shining through the boughs above me. How they mocked me, with their bright, calm light! The hours passed by, and as I sat there alone a chilliness and deadly sickness came over me. I sank on the ground. My mind was full of horrid thoughts. I prayed to die; but the prayer was not answered.

At last, with great effort I roused myself, and walked some distance further, to the house of a woman who had been a friend of my mother. When I told her why I was there, she spoke soothingly to me; but I could not be comforted. I thought I could bear my shame if I could only be reconciled to my grandmother. I longed to open my heart to her. I thought if she could know the real state of the case, and all I had been bearing for years, she would perhaps judge me less harshly. My friend advised me to send for her. I did so; but days of agonizing suspense passed before she came.

Had she utterly forsaken me? No. She came at last. I knelt before her, and told her the things that had poisoned my life; how long I had been persecuted; that I saw no way of escape; and in an hour of extremity I had become desperate. She listened in silence. I told her I would bear any thing and do any thing, if in time I had hopes of obtaining her forgiveness. I begged of her to pity me, for my dead mother's sake.

And she did pity me. She did not say, "I forgive you;" but she looked at me lovingly, with her eyes full of tears. She laid her old hand gently on my head, and murmured, "Poor child! Poor child!"

THE NEW TIE TO LIFE

I returned to my good grandmother's house. She had an interview with Mr. Sands. When she asked him why he could not have left her one ewe lamb,—whether there were not plenty of slaves who did not care about character,—he made no answer; but he spoke kind and encouraging words. He promised to care for my child, and to buy me, be the conditions what they might.

I had not seen Dr. Flint for five days. I had never seen him since I made the avowal to him. He talked of the disgrace I had brought on myself; how I had sinned against my master, and mortified my old grandmother. He intimated that if I had accepted his proposals, he, as a physician, could have saved me from exposure. He even condescended to pity me. Could he have offered wormwood more bitter? He, whose persecutions had been the cause of my sin!

"Linda," said he, "though you have been criminal towards me, I feel for you, and I can pardon you if you obey my wishes. Tell me whether the fellow you wanted to marry is the father of your child. If you deceive me, you shall feel the fires of hell."

I did not feel as proud as I had done. My strongest weapon with him was gone. I was lowered in my own estimation, and had resolved to bear his abuse in silence. But when he spoke contemptuously of the lover who had always treated me honorably; when I remembered that but for him I might have been a virtuous, free, and happy wife, I lost my patience. "I have sinned against God and myself," I replied; "but not against you."

He clinched his teeth, and muttered, "Curse you!" He came towards me, with ill-suppressed rage, and exclaimed, "You obstinate girl! I could grind your bones to powder! You have thrown yourself away on some worthless rascal. You are weak-minded, and have been easily persuaded by those who don't care a straw for you. The future will settle accounts between us. You are blinded now; but hereafter you will be convinced that your master was your best friend. My lenity [mildness] towards you is a proof of it. I might have punished you in many ways. I might have had you whipped till you fell dead under the lash. But I wanted you to live; I would have bettered your condition. Others cannot do it. You are my slave. Your mistress, disgusted by your conduct, forbids you to return to the house; therefore I leave you here for the present; but I shall see you often. I will call tomorrow."

He came with frowning brows, that showed a dissatisfied state of mind. After asking about my health, he inquired whether my board was paid, and who visited me. He then went on to say that he had neglected his duty; that as a physician there were certain things that he ought to have explained to me. Then followed talk such as would have made the most shameless blush. He ordered me to stand up before him. I obeyed. "I command you," said he, "to tell me whether the father of your child is white or black." I hesitated. "Answer me this instant!" he exclaimed. I did answer. He sprang upon me like a wolf, and grabbed my arm as if he would have broken it. "Do you love him?" said he, in a hissing tone.

"I am thankful that I do not despise him," I replied.

He raised his hand to strike me; but it fell again. I don't know what arrested the blow. He sat down, with lips tightly compressed. At last he spoke. "I came here," said he, "to make you a friendly proposition; but your ingratitude chafes me beyond endurance. You turn aside all my good intentions towards you. I don't know what it is that keeps me from killing you." Again he rose, as if he had a mind to strike me.

But he resumed. "On one condition I will forgive your insolence and crime. You must henceforth have no communication of any kind with the father of your child. You must not ask any thing from him, or receive any thing from him. I will take care of you and your child. You had better promise this at once, and not wait till you are deserted by him. This is the last act of mercy I shall show towards you."

I said something about being unwilling to have my child supported by a man who had cursed it and me also. He rejoined, that a woman who had sunk to my level had no right to expect any thing else. He asked, for the last time, would I accept his kindness? I answered that I would not.

"Very well," said he; "then take the consequences of your wayward course. Never look to me for help. You are my slave, and shall always be my slave. I will never sell you, that you may depend upon."

Hope died away in my heart as he closed the door after him. I had calculated that in his rage he would sell me to a slave-trader; and I knew the father of my child was on the watch to buy me.

About this time my uncle Phillip was expected to return from a voyage. The day before his departure I had officiated as bridesmaid to a young friend. My heart was then ill at ease, but my smiling countenance did not betray it. Only a year had passed; but what fearful changes it had wrought! My heart had grown gray in misery. Lives that flash in sunshine, and lives that are born in tears, receive their hue from circumstances. None of us know what a year may bring forth.

I felt no joy when they told me my uncle had come. He wanted to see me, though he knew what had happened. I shrank from him at first; but at last consented that he should come to my room. He received me as he always had done. O, how my heart smote me when I felt his tears on my burning cheeks! The words of my grandmother came to my mind,—"Perhaps your mother and father are taken from the evil days to come." My disappointed heart could now praise God that it was so. But why, thought I, did my relatives ever cherish hopes for me? What was there to save me from the usual fate of slave girls? Many more beautiful and more intelligent than I had experienced a similar fate, or a far worse one. How could they hope that I should escape?

My uncle's stay was short, and I was not sorry for it. I was too ill in mind and body to enjoy my friends as I had done. For some weeks I was unable to leave my bed. I could not have any doctor but my master, and I would not have him sent for. At last, alarmed by my increasing illness, they sent for him. I was very weak and nervous; and as soon as he entered the room, I began to scream. They told him my state was very critical. He had no wish to hasten me out of the world, and he withdrew.

When my babe was born, they said it was premature. It weighed only four pounds; but God let it live. I heard the doctor say I could not survive till morning. I had often prayed for death; but now I did not want to die, unless my child could die too. Many weeks passed before

I was able to leave my bed. I was a mere wreck of my former self. For a year there was scarcely a day when I was free from chills and fever. My babe also was sickly. His little limbs were often racked with pain. Dr. Flint continued his visits, to look after my health; and he did not fail to remind me that my child was an addition to his stock of slaves.

I felt too feeble to dispute with him, and listened to his remarks in silence. His visits were less frequent; but his busy spirit could not remain quiet. He employed my brother in his office, and he was made the medium of frequent notes and messages to me. William was a bright lad, and of much use to the doctor. He had learned to put up medicines, to leech, cup, and bleed. He had taught himself to read and spell. I was proud of my brother; and the old doctor suspected as much.

One day, when I had not seen him for several weeks, I heard his steps approaching the door. I dreaded the encounter, and hid myself. He inquired for me, of course; but I was nowhere to be found. He went to his office, and despatched William with a note. The color mounted to my brother's face when he gave it to me; and he said, "Don't you hate me, Linda, for bringing you these things?" I told him I could not blame him; he was a slave, and obliged to obey his master's will.

The note ordered me to come to his office. I went. He demanded to know where I was when he called. I told him I was at home. He flew into a passion, and said he knew better. Then he launched out upon his usual themes,—my crimes against him, and my ingratitude for his forbearance. The laws were laid down to me anew, and I was dismissed. I felt humiliated that my brother should stand by, and listen to such language as would be addressed only to a slave. Poor boy! He was powerless to defend me; but I saw the tears, which he vainly strove to keep back.

This manifestation of feeling irritated the doctor. William could do nothing to please him. One morning he did not arrive at the office so early as usual; and that circumstance afforded his master an opportunity to vent his spleen. He was put in jail. The next day my brother sent a trader to the doctor, with a request to be sold. His master was greatly incensed at what he called his insolence. He said he had put him there to reflect upon his bad conduct, and he certainly was not giving any evidence of repentance. For two days he harassed himself to find somebody to do his office work; but every thing went wrong without William. He was released, and ordered to take his old stand, with many threats, if he was not careful about his future behavior.

As the months passed on, my boy improved in health. When he was a year old, they called him beautiful. The little vine was taking deep root in my existence, though its clinging fondness excited a mixture of love and pain. When I was most sorely oppressed I found a solace in his smiles. I loved to watch his infant slumbers; but always there was a dark cloud over my enjoyment. I could never forget that he was a slave. Sometimes I wished that he might die in infancy. God tried me. My darling became very ill. The bright eyes grew dull, and the little feet and hands were so icy cold that I thought death had already touched them. I had prayed for his death, but never so earnestly as I now prayed for his life; and my prayer was heard. Alas, what mockery it is for a slave mother to try to pray back her dying child to life! Death is better than slavery.

It was a sad thought that I had no name to give my child. His father caressed him and treated him kindly, whenever he had a chance to see him. He was not unwilling that he should bear his name; but he had no legal claim to it; and if I had bestowed it upon him, my master would have regarded it as a new crime, a new piece of insolence, and would, perhaps, revenge it on the boy. O, the serpent of Slavery has many and poisonous fangs!

Jacobs stayed with her grandmother, and soon found herself pregnant again. Dr. Norcom (called Dr. Flint in Jacobs's book), who had previously thrown her down the stairs, now cut off all her hair. At nineteen years old, Jacobs gave birth to a daughter. Once again the doctor threatened her life; at one point he even hurled her son across her room, and he repeatedly hurt her. When she persisted in refusing to submit to his demands, he sent her to work on his son's plantation.

One night at midnight—the night before Jacobs's children were to be brought to the plantation, there to become plantation slaves—Jacobs ran away and hid in a friend's house, thus making the doctor lose interest in her children. He offered a $300 reward for her ($6,000 in today's money), and searched assiduously. Jacobs, in the meantime, was bitten by a snake, and had to move from house to house.

The doctor, after looking for Jacobs in New York, became discouraged, and sold her children and brother to a slave trader, who in turn sold them to Samuel Sawyer (called Mr. Sands in Jacobs's book), the children's father. Jacobs's wishes had come true.

Meanwhile, Jacobs was put in a new hiding place: in a garret at the top of a shed in her grandmother's place. In this stifling, windowless room, which was nine feet long, seven feet wide, and three feet high in the middle, she spent, incredibly enough, the next seven years. Her sufferings were terrible: from the heat, from the cold, from inaction (she feared she'd be crippled for life). Her only blessings were the occasional nighttime company of her grandmother and her relatives, and the ability to watch her children (who had no idea where she was) play through a one-inch hole she had drilled.

Eventually, Jacobs escaped by boat to New York, where she was reunited with her children and her brother. She was still afraid of being found by Dr. Norcom, who made several trips to the city to look for her, so she and her family moved to Boston for a few years. Finally Dr. Norcom died, and Jacobs was now the property of his daughter, who also came up to New York to look for her. Against Jacobs's wishes, one of her friends bought her freedom from Dr. Norcom's son-in-law for $300.

In 1862, Jacobs, along with other black women, worked to help the black refugees following the Union Army through the South. Throughout the 1860s, she and her daughter worked in various Southern cities distributing clothing and supplies; organizing schools, nursing homes, and orphanages; and reporting on their own work in Northern newspapers. In the mid-1870s, Jacobs and her daughter relocated to Washington, D.C., where she spent the next twenty years.

# J. D. GREEN

**J**acob D. Green (1813–?) was the only slave writer to make full use of the *trickster* tradition. This African American tradition stretches from African folktales to contemporary rap music. In it, the trickster is a cunning character who always tricks his enemies, often with terrifying results—sometimes for those enemies, and sometimes for himself. Nothing in the trickster's world is right or wrong, everything always turns out the opposite of what you'd expect, and the trickster is faithful to no one and is never caught or punished.

In his book, *Narrative of the Life of J. D. Green, a Runaway Slave*, from Kentucky, Green paints a picture of himself as a human "Brer Rabbit," exposing both blacks and whites to his cruel and hilarious trickery. Instead of bragging about his heroism, Green revels in a gleeful wickedness. Everything always turns out exactly the opposite of what we expect—humor turns into horror and back again, and the positions of the characters are constantly reversed. As Green's master puts it at one point, "you black vagabond, stay on this plantation three months longer, and you will be the master and I the slave."

## "OH! HOW DREADFUL IT IS TO BE BLACK!"

One morning after my mother was sold [Green was twelve years old at the time], a white boy was stealing corn out of my master's barn, and I said for this act we black boys will be whipped until one of us confesses to have done what we are all innocent of, as such is the case in every instance; and I thought, Oh, that master was here, or the overseer, I would then let them see what becomes of the corn. But, I saw he was off with the corn to the extent of half a bushel, and I will say nothing about it until they miss it, and if I tell them they wont believe me if he denies it, because he is white and I am black. Oh! how dreadful it is to be black! Why was I born black? It would have been better had I not been born at all.

Only yesterday, my mother was sold to go to not one of us knows where, and I am left alone, and I have no hope of seeing her again. At this moment a raven alighted on a tree over my head, and I cried, "Oh, Raven! if I had wings like you, I would soon find my mother and be happy again." Before parting she advised me to be a good boy, and she would pray for me, and I must pray for her, and hoped we might meet again in heaven, and I at once commenced to pray, to the best of my knowledge, "Our Father art in Heaven, be Thy name, kingdom come.—Amen."

But, at this time, words of my master obtruded into my mind that God did not care for black folks, as he did not make them, but the devil did. Then I thought of the old saying amongst us, as stated by our master, that, when God was making man, He made white man out of the best clay, as potters make china, and the devil was watching, and he immediately took up some black mud and made a black man, and called him a nigger.

My master was continually impressing upon me the necessity of being a good boy, and used to say, that if I was good, and behaved as well to him as my mother had done, I should go to Heaven without a question being asked. My mother having often said the same, I determined from that day to be a good boy, and constantly frequented the Meeting-house attended by the blacks where I learned from the minister, Mr. Cobb, how much the Lord had done for the blacks and for their salvation; and he was in the habit of reminding us what advantages he had given us for our benefit, for when we were in our native country, Africa, we were destitute of Bible light, worshipping idols of sticks and stones, and barbarously murdering one another, God put it into the hearts of these good slaveholders to venture across the bosom of the hazardous Atlantic to Africa, and snatch us poor negroes as brands from the eternal burning, and bring us where we might sit under the droppings of his sanctuary, and learn the ways of industry and the way to God. "Oh, niggers! how happy are your eyes which see this heavenly light; many millions of niggers desired it long, but died without the sight. I frequently envy your situations, because God's special blessing seems to be ever over you, as though you were a select people, for how much happier is your position than that of a free man, who, if sick, must pay his doctor's bill; if hungry, must supply his wants by his own exertions; if thirsty, must refresh himself by his own aid. And yet you, oh, niggers! your master has all this care for you. He supplies your daily wants; your meat and your drink he provides; and when you are sick he finds the best skill to bring you to health as soon as possible, for your sickness is his loss, and your health his gain; and, above all when you die (if you are obedient to your masters, and good niggers), your black faces will shine like black jugs around the throne of God."

Such was the religious instruction I was in the habit of receiving until I was about seventeen years old; and told that when at any time I happened to be offended, or struck by a white boy I was not to offend or strike in return, unless it was another black, then I might fight as hard as I chose in my own defense.

## "A FEELING OF REVENGE IN MY BOSOM"

It happened about this time there was a white boy who was continually stealing my tops and marbles, and one morning when doing so I caught him, and we had a battle, and I had him down on the ground when Mr. Burmey came up. He kicked me away from the white boy, saying if I belonged to him he would cut off my hands for *daring* to strike a white boy; this without asking the cause of the quarrel, or of ascertaining who was to blame. The kick was so severe that I was sometime before I forgot it, and created such a feeling of revenge in my bosom that I was determined when I became a man I would pay him back in his own coin.

I went out one day, and measured myself by a tree in the wood, and cut a notch in the tree to ascertain how fast I grew. I went at different times for the space of two months and found I was no taller, and I began to fear he would die before I should have grown to man's estate, and I resolved if he did I would make his children suffer by punishing them instead of their father.

At this time my master's wife had two lovers, this same Burmey and one Rogers, and they despised each other from feelings of jealousy. Master's wife seemed to favour Burmey most, who was a great smoker, and she provided him with a large pipe with a German silver bowl, which screwed on the top; this pipe she usually kept on the mantel piece, ready filled with tobacco.

One morning I was dusting and sweeping out the dining-room, and saw the pipe on the mantel-piece. I took it down, and went to my young master William's powder closet and took out his powder horn, and after taking half of the tobacco out of the pipe filled it nearly full with powder, and covered it over with tobacco to make it appear as usual when filled with tobacco, replaced it, and left.

Rogers came in about eight o'clock in the morning, and remained until eleven, when Mr. Burmey came, and in about an hour I saw a great

number running about from all parts of the plantation. I left the barn where I was thrashing buck-wheat, and followed the rest to the house, where I saw Mr. Burmey lying back in the arm chair in a state of insensibility, his mouth bleeding profusely; and from particulars given it appeared he took the pipe as usual and lighted it, and had just got it to his mouth when the powder exploded, and the party suspected was Rogers, who had been there immediately preceding; and Burmey's son went to Rogers and they fought about the matter. Law ensued, which cost Rogers 800 dollars, Burmey 600 dollars and his face disfigured; and my master's wife came in for a deal of scandal, which caused further proceedings at law, costing the master 1400 dollars, and I was never once suspected or charged with the deed.

## "I WAS CERTAIN THERE WAS A FLOGGING IN IT"

I was in the habit of driving the master; and on one occasion I had to drive him to Baltimore where two of his sons were studying law; and while there, I stole some sweet potatoes to roast when I got home; and how master got to know I had them I never knew; but when I got home he gave me a note to Mr. Cobb, the overseer, and told me to tell Dick, (another slave on the plantation) to come to Baltimore to him on the following evening, and as soon as I took the note in my hand I was certain there was a flogging in it for me, though he said nothing to me. I held the note that night and following day, afraid to give it to Mr. Cobb, so confident was I what would be the result. Towards evening I began to reason thus—If I give Cobb the note I shall be whipped; if I withhold the note from him I shall be whipped, so a whipping appears plain in either case.

Now Dick having arranged to meet his sweetheart this night assumed sickness, so that he could have an excuse for not meeting master at Baltimore, and he wanted me to go instead of him. I agreed to go, providing he would take the note I had to Mr. Cobb, as I had forgot to give it him, to which he consented, and off I went; and I heard that when he delivered the note to Mr. Cobb, he ordered him to go to the whipping-post, and when he asked what he had done he was knocked down, and afterwards put to the post and thirty-nine lashes were administered, and failed seeing his sweetheart as well.

When I arrived at Baltimore my master and young master took their seats and I drove away without any question until we had gone three miles, when he asked what I was doing there that night. I very politely said Dick was not well, and I had come in his place. He than asked me if Mr. Cobb got his note, I answered, yes, sir. He then asked me how I felt, and I said first rate, sir. "The devil you do," said he. I said, yes sir. He said "nigger, did Mr. Cobb flog you?" No sir. I have done nothing wrong. "You never do," he answered; and said no more until he got home.

Being a man who could not bear to have any order of his disobeyed or unfulfilled, he immediately called for Mr. Cobb, and was told he was in bed; and when he appeared, the master asked if he got the note sent by the nigger. Mr. Cobb said "Yes." "Then why," said master, "did you not perform my orders in the note?" "I did, sir," replied Cobb; when the master said, "I told you to give that nigger thirty-nine lashes," Mr. Cobb says, "So I did, sir;" when master replied, "He says you never licked him at all." Upon which Cobb said, "He is a liar:" when my master called for me (who had been hearing the whole dialogue at the door), I turned on my toes and went a short distance, and I shouted with a loud voice that I was coming, (to prevent them knowing that I had been listening) and appeared before them and said "here I am master, do you want me." He said "Yes. Did you not tell me that Mr. Cobb had not flogged you," and I said "yes I did; he has not flogged me to-day, sir." Mr. Cobb answered, "I did not flog him. You did not tell me to flog him. You told me to flog that other nigger." "What other nigger," enquired Master. Cobb said, "Dick." Master then said, "I did not, I told you to flog this nigger here," Cobb then produced the letter, and read it as follows:

"Mr. Cobb will give the bearer 39 lashes on delivery."

R.T. Earle.

I then left the room and explanations took place. When I was again called in. "How came Dick to have had the letter," and I then said I had forgot to deliver it until Dick wanted me to go to Baltimore in his place, and I agreed providing he would take the letter. Master then said "you lie, you infernal villain," and laid hold of a pair of tongs and said he would dash my brains out if I did not tell him the truth. I then said I thought there was something in the note that boded no good to me, and I did not intend to give it to him. He said, "you black vagabond, stay on his plantation three months longer, and you will be master and I the slave; no wonder you said you felt first rate when I asked you, but I will sell you to go to Georgia the first chance I get."

Then laying the tongs down he opened the door and ordered me out. I knew he had on heavy cow-hide boots, and I knew he would try to assist me in my outward progress, and though expecting it, and went as quick as I could, I was materially assisted by a heavy kick from my master's foot. This did not end the matter, for when Dick found out I had caused his being flogged, we had continual fightings for several months.

### "A NEGRO SHINDY"

When I was sixteen I was very fond of dancing, and was invited privately to a negro shindy or dance, about twelve miles from home, and for this purpose I got Aunt Dinah to starch the collars for my two linen shirts, which were the first standing collars I had ever worn in my life; I had a good pair of trousers, and a jacket, but no necktie, nor no pocket handkerchief, so I stole aunt Dinah's checked apron, and tore it in two—one part for a necktie, the other for a pocket handkerchief. I had twenty-four cents, or pennies which I divided equally with fifty large brass buttons in my right and left pockets. Now, thought I to myself, when I get on the floor and begin to dance—oh! how the niggers will stare to hear the money jingle. I was combing my hair to get the knots out of it: I then went and looked in an old piece of broken looking-glass, and I thought, without joking, that I was the best looking negro that I had ever seen in my life.

About ten o'clock I stole out to the stable when all was still; and while I was getting on one of my master's horses I said to myself— Master was in here at six o'clock and saw all these horses clean, so I must look out and be back time enough to have you clean when he gets up in the morning. I thought what a dash I should cut among the pretty yellow and Sambo [in this context, Sambo simply means black] gals, and I felt quite confident, of course, that I should have my pick among the best looking ones, for my good clothes, and my abundance of money, and my own good looks—in fact, I thought no mean things of my self.

When I arrived at the place where the dance was, it was at an old house in the woods, which had many years before been a negro meeting-house; there was a large crowd there, and about one hundred horses tied round the fence—for some of them were far from home, and, like myself, they were all runaways, and their horses, like mine, had to be home and cleaned before their masters were up in the morning. In getting my horse close up to the fence a nail caught my trousers at the thigh, and split them clean up to the seat; of course my shirt tail fell out behind, like a woman's apron before. This dreadful misfortune almost unmanned me, and curtailed both my pride and pleasure for the night. I cried until I could cry no more.

However, I was determined I would not be done out of my sport after being at the expense of coming, so I went round and borrowed some pins, and pinned up my shirt tail as well as I could. I then went into the dance, and told the fiddler to play me a jig. Che, che, che, went the fiddle, when the banjo responded with a thrum, thrum, thrum, with the loud cracking of the bone player. I seized a little Sambo gal, and round and round the room we went, my money and my buttons going jingle, jingle, jingle, seemed to take a lively part with the music, and to my great satisfaction every eye seemed to be upon me, and I could not help thinking about what an impression I should leave behind upon those pretty yellow and Sambo gals, who were gazing at me, thinking I was the richest and handsomest nigger they had ever seen: but unfortunately the pins in my breeches gave way, and to my great confusion my shirt tail fell out; and what made my situation still more disgraceful was the mischievous conduct of my partner, the gal that I was dancing with, who instead of trying to conceal my shame caught my shirt tail behind and held it up.

The roar of laughter that came from both men and gals almost deafened me, and I would at this moment have sunk through the floor, so I endeavored to creep out as slily as I could; but even this I was not permitted to do until I had undergone a hauling around the room by my unfortunate shirt tail: and this part of the programme was performed by the gals, set on by the boys—every nigger who could not stand up and laugh, because laughing made them weak, fell down on the floor and rolled round and round. When the gals saw their own turn they let me go, and I hurried outside and stood behind the house, beneath a beautiful bright moon, which saw me that night the most wretched of all negroes in the land of Dixie: and what made me feel, in my own opinion, that my humiliation was just as complete as the triumph of the negroes inside was glorious, was that the gals had turned my pockets out, and found that the hundreds of dollars they had thought my pockets contained, consisted of 24 cents or pennies, and 50 brass buttons. Everything was alive and happy inside the room, but no one knew or cared how miserable I was—the joy and life of the dance that night seemed entirely at my expense, all through my unfortunate shirt tail.

The first thing I thought of now was revenge. Take your comfort, niggers now, said I to myself, for sorrow shall be yours in the morning, so I took out my knife and went round the fence and cut every horse loose, and they all ran away. I then got on my horse and set off home. As I rode on I thought to myself—I only wish I could be somewhere close enough to see how those negroes will act when they come out and find all their horses gone. And then I laughed right out when I thought of the sport they had had out of my misfortune, and that some were ten to twelve, and some fifteen miles away from home. Well, thought I, your masters will have to reckon with you to-morrow; you have had glad hearts to-night at my expense, but you will have sore backs to-morrow at your own.

Now, when I got home, the stable was in a very bad situation, and I was afraid to bring my horse in until I could strike a light. When this was done, I took the saddle and bridle off outside. No sooner had I done this than my horse reared over the bars and ran way into the meadow. I chased him till daylight, and for my life I could not catch him.

My feelings now may be better imagined than described. When the reader remembers that this horse, with all the rest, master had seen clean at six o'clock the night before, and all safe in the stable, and now to see him in the meadow, with all the marks of having been driven somewhere and by somebody, what excuse could I make, or what story could I invent in order to save my poor back from that awful flogging which I knew must be the result of the revelation of the truth. I studied and tried, but could think of no lie that would stand muster.

At last I went into the stable and turned all the rest out, and left the stable door open, and creeping into the house, took off my fine clothes and put on those which I had been wearing all the week, and laid myself down on my straw.

I had not lain long before I heard master shouting for me, for all those horses, eight in number, were under my care; and although he shouted for me at the top of his voice, I lay still and pretended not to hear him: but soon after I heard a light step coming up stairs, and a rap at my door—then I commenced to snore as loud as possible, still the knocking continued. At last I pretended to awake, and called out, who's there—that you, Lizzy? oh my! what's up, what time is it, and so on.

Lizzy said master wanted me immediately; yes, Lizzy, said I, tell master I'm coming. I bothered about the room long enough to give colour to the impression that I had just finished dressing myself; I then came and said, here I am, master, when he demanded of me, what were my horses doing in the meadow? Here I put on an expression of such wonder and surprise—looking first into the meadow and then at the stable door, and to master's satisfaction, I seemed so completely confounded that my deception took upon him the desired effect. Then I affected to roar right out, crying, now master, you saw my horses all clean last night before I went to bed, and now some of those negroes have turned them out so that I should have them to clean over again: well, I declare! it's too bad, and I roared and cried as I went towards the meadow to drive them up; but master believing what I said, called me back and told me to call Mr. Cobb, and when Mr. Cobb came master told him to blow the horn; when the horn was blown, the negroes were to be seen coming from all parts of the plantation, and forming around in front of the balcony.

Master then came out and said, now I saw this boy's horses clean last night and in the stable, so now tell me which of you turned them out? Of course they all denied it, then master ordered them all to go down into the meadow and drive up the horses and clean them, me excepted; so they went and drove them up and set to work and cleaned them.

On Monday morning we all turned out to work until breakfast, when the horn was blown, and we all repaired to the house. Here master again demanded to know who turned the horses loose, and when they all denied it, he tied them all up and gave them each 39 lashes. Not yet satisfied, but determined to have a confession, as was always his custom on such occasions, he came to me and asked me which one I had reason to suspect.

My poor guilty heart already bleeding for the suffering I had caused my fellow slaves, was now almost driven to confession. What must I do, select another victim for further punishment, or confess the truth and bear the consequence? My conscience now rebuked me, like an armed man; but I happened to be one of those boys who, among all even of my mother's children loved myself best, and therefore had no disposition to satisfy my conscience at the expense of a very sore back, so I very soon thought of Dick, a negro who, like Ishmael [in the Bible: see *Genesis* 16], had his hand out against every man, and all our hands were out against him; this negro was a lickspittle or tell-tale, as little boys call them—we could not steal a bit of tea or sugar, or any other kind of nourishment for our sick, or do anything else we did not want to be known, but if he got to know it he would run and tell master or mistress, or the overseer, so we all wanted him dead; and now I thought of him—he was just the proper sacrifice for me to lay upon the altar of confession, so I told master I believed that it was Dick: moreover, I told him that I had seen him in and out of the stable on Saturday night, so master tied Dick up and gave him 39 lashes more, and washed his back down with salt and water, and told him that at night if he did not confess, he would give him as much more; so at night, when master went out to Dick again, he asked if he had made up his mind to tell him the truth, Dick said, yes, master;—well, said master, let me hear it. Well master, said Dick, I did turn the horses out; but will never do so again. So master, satisfied with this confession, struck Dick no more, and ordered him to be untied; but Dick had a sore back for many weeks.

And now to return to the negroes I had left at the dance, when they discovered that their horses were gone there was the greatest consternation amongst them, the forebodings of the awful consequences if they dared to go home induced many that night to seek salvation in the direction and guidance of the north star. Several who started off on that memorable night I have since shook hands with in Canada. They told me there were sixteen of them went off together, four of them were shot or killed by the bloodhounds, and one was captured while asleep in a barn; the rest of those who were at the dance either went home and took their floggings, or strayed into the woods until starved out, and then surrendered. One of those I saw in Toronto, is Dan Patterson; he has a house of his own, with a fine horse and cart, and he has a beautiful Sambo woman for his wife, and four fine healthy-looking children. But, like myself, he had left a wife and six children in slavery.

## "DEEPLY SMITTEN IN LOVE"

When I was about seventeen, I was deeply smitten in love with a yellow girl belonging to Doctor Tillotson. This girl's name was Mary, of whose loveliness I dreamt every night. I certainly thought she was the prettiest girl I had ever seen in my life. Her colour was very fair, approaching almost to white; her countenance was frank and open, and very inviting; her voice was as sweet as the dulcimer, her smiles to me were like the May morning sunbeams in the spring, one glance of her large dark eyes broke my heart in pieces, with a stroke like that of an earthquake. O, I thought, this girl would make me a paradise, and to enjoy her love I thought would be heaven.

In spite of either patrols or dogs, who stood in my way, every night nearly I was in Mary's company. I learned from her that she had already had a child to her master in Mobile, and that her mistress had sold her down here for revenge; and she told me also of the sufferings that she had undergone from her mistress on account of jealousy—her baby, she said, her mistress sold out of her arms only eleven months old, to a lady in Marysville, Kentucky. Having never before felt a passion like this, or of the gentle power, so peculiar to women, that, hard as I worked all day, I could not sleep at night for thinking of this almost angel in human shape. We kept company about six weeks, during which time I was at some times as wretched as I was happy at others.

Much to my annoyance Mary was adored by every negro in the neighbourhood, and this excited my jealousy and made me miserable. I was almost crazy when I saw another negro talking to her. Again and again I tried my best to get her to give up speaking to them, but she refused to comply. There was one negro who was in the habit of calling on Mary whom I dreaded more than all the rest of them put together, this negro was Dan, he belonged to Rogers; and notwithstanding I believed myself to be the best looking negro to be found anywhere in the neighbourhood, still I was aware that I was not the best of talkers. Dan was a sweet and easy talker, and a good bone and banjo player. I was led to fear that he would displace me in Mary's affections, and in this I was not mistaken.

One night I went over to see Mary, and in looking through the window, saw Mary—my sweet and beloved Mary—sitting upon Dan's knee; and here it is impossible to describe the feeling that came over me at this unwelcome sight. My teeth clenched and bit my tongue— my head grew dizzy, and began to swim round and round, and at last I found myself getting up from the ground, having stumbled from the effects of what I had seen. I wandered towards home, and arriving there threw myself on the straw and cried all night. My first determination was to kill Dan; but then I thought they would hang me and the devil would have us both, and some other negro will get Mary, then the thought of killing Dan passed away.

Next morning, when the horn blew for breakfast, I continued my work, my appetite having left me; at dinner time it was the same. At sun-down I went to the barn and got a rope and put it under my jacket, and started off to see Mary, whom I found sitting in the kitchen, smoking her pipe, for smoking was as common among the girls as among the men. Mary, said I, I was over here last night and saw you through the window sitting on Dan's knee. Now, Mary, I want you to tell me at once whose you mean to be—mine or Dan's?

Dan's, she replied, with an important toss of her head, which went through my very soul, like the shock from a galvanic [electric] battery.

I rested for a minute or so on an old oak table that stood by. Mary's answer had unstrung every nerve in me, and left me so weak that I could scarcely keep from falling.

Now I was not at that time, and don't think I ever shall be one of those fools who would cut off his nose to spite his face, much less kill myself because a girl refused to love me. Life to me was always preferable, under any circumstances; but in this case I played the most dexterous card I had. Mary, said I sternly, if you don't give Dan up and swear to be mine, I will hang myself this night.

To this she replied, hang on if you are fool enough, and continued smoking her pipe as though not the least alarmed.

I took out the rope from under my jacket, and got upon a three-legged stool, and putting the rope first over the beam in the ceiling, then made a slip-knot, and brought it down round my neck, taking good care to have it short enough that it would not choke me, and in this way I stood upon the stool for some considerable time, groaning and struggling, and making every kind of noise that might make her believe that I was choking or strangling; but still Mary sat deliberately smoking her pipe with the utmost coolness, and seemed to take no notice of me or what I was doing.

I thought my situation worse now than if I had not commenced this job at all. My object in pretending to hang myself was to frighten Mary into compliance with my demand, and her conduct turned out to be everything but what I had expected. I had thought that the moment I ascended the stool she would have clung to me and tried to dissuade me from committing suicide, and in this case my plan was to persist in carrying it out, unless she would consent to give Dan up; but instead of this she sat smoking her pipe apparently at ease and unmoved. Now I found I had been mistaken—what was I to do, to hang or kill myself was the last thing I meant to do—in fact I had not the courage to do it for five hundred Marys. But now, after mounting the stool and adjusting the rope round my neck, I was positively ashamed to come down without hanging myself, and then I stood like a fool.

At this moment in came the dog Carlo, racing after the cat, right across the kitchen floor, and the dog coming in contact with the stool, knocked it right away from under my feet, and brought my neck suddenly to the full length of the rope, which barely allowed my toes to touch the floor. Here I seized the rope with both hands to keep the weight of my whole body off my neck, and in this situation I soon found I must hang, and that dead enough, unless I had some assistance, for the stool had rolled entirely out of the reach of my feet, and the knot I had tied behind the beam I could not reach for my life. My arms began to tremble with holding on to the rope, and still my mortification and pride for some time refused to let me call on Mary for assistance. Such a moment of terror and suspense! heaven forbid that I should ever see or experience again. Thoughts rushed into my mind of every bad deed that I had done in my life; and I thought that old cloven foot, as we called the devil, was waiting to nab me. The stretch upon my arms exhausted me, with holding on by the rope, nothing was left me but despair, my pride and courage gave up the ghost, and I roared out, Mary! for God's sake cut the rope! No, answered Mary, you went up there to hang yourself so now hang on. Oh! Mary, Mary! I did not mean to hang! I was only doing so to see what you would say. Well, then, said Mary; you hear what I have to say—hang on. Oh, Mary! for heaven's sake cut this rope, or I shall strangle to death!—oh, dear, good Mary, save me this time: and I roared out like a jackass, and must too have fainted, for when I came round Doctor Tillotson and his wife and Mary stood over me as I lay on the floor.

How I got upon the floor, or who cut the rope I never knew. Doctor Tillotson had hold of my wrist, feeling my pulse; while mistress held a camphor [the active ingredient in Vicks VapoRub] bottle in one hand and a bottle of hartshorn [smelling salts made of ammonia] in the other. The doctor helped me up from the floor and set me in a chair, when I discovered that I was bleeding very freely from the nose and mouth. He called for a basin and bled me [doctors used to let some blood flow out in the belief that it would help cure the patient] in my left arm, and then sent me over home by two of his men. Next day my neck was dreadfully swollen, and my throat was so sore that it was with difficulty that I could swallow meat for more than a week. At the end of a fortnight, master having learnt all the particulars respecting my sickness, called me to account, and gave me seventy-eight lashes, and this was the end of my crazy love and courtship with Mary.

* * *

In a typical reversal of fortune, Dan happened to come across Mary as she was being raped by her master's son, whom he stabbed through the back with a pitchfork. Mary drowned herself, and Green had to identify the body; Dan was burned at the stake. The ringleaders behind Dan's lynching, the sons of Dr. Burmey (whose pipe had exploded), got their desserts when they burned to death in a barn.

When Green was twenty, his master forced him to marry Jane, another slave, who, after five months, gave birth to the same master's child. Unperturbed, Green stayed with his wife for six years and had two more children with her, but then she was sold with the children. At this point, Green determined to run away.

He had a very adventurous journey, characterized by his usual trickery, and finally settled in a town called Derby, near

Philadelphia, where he remained three years. However, when he lost his job, he was arrested and sent back to Maryland, where he was sold back into slavery, and was transported to Tennessee. He worked there another three-and-a-half years, and then escaped aboard a boat to New York City. He was recaptured a few months later in Utica, New York, but on the way back South he escaped off a steamboat near Cleveland. A few months later he was recaptured once again, this time in Zanesville, Ohio, and was sold as a coachman to a Louisville, Kentucky, slaveowner, with whom he stayed for twelve months before running away once again. This time, having had enough of being recaptured, he went to Toronto, where he stayed for three years, and then shipped for England, where he published his narrative.

# ELIZABETH KECKLEY

When **Elizabeth Keckley** (c. 1818–1907) published her autobiography in 1868, she immediately became one of the most famous black women in America. Entitled *Behind the Scenes; or Thirty Years a Slave, and Four Years in the White House*, the book offered to a curious public an intimate view of Abraham and Mary Todd Lincoln's private lives—Keckley had been Mrs. Lincoln's seamstress during her years in the White House.

Unfortunately, the method by which the book was promoted and sold caused it to be thoroughly condemned by the press, who saw Keckley as, in Keckley's own words, "an angry negro servant." The *New York Citizen* called it "grossly and shamelessly indecent"; Mrs. Lincoln never spoke to Keckley again; Robert Lincoln demanded that the book be suppressed; and it was withdrawn from the shelves.

Keckley's book was not, however, the standard tell-all. It was a strong, truthful, eloquent, and stirring autobiography. Keckley's account of her youth in slavery is dignified and unflinching; her subsequent triumphs only serve to prove that her mistress, who repeatedly told her she would never be worth her salt, was very wrong.

Keckley's was the first important slave narrative written after the war, and, like other slave narratives of the period, it emphasized progress and achievement over suffering and injustice. The pre–Civil War narratives emphasized anti-slavery feeling, but since slavery had come to an end, the later ones shifted their focus to the ability of African Americans to rise above their lowly status. So while Keckley never shrank from describing the hell of slavery, she saw it as ultimately redeemed by the progress of the nation to a land of the truly free.

### "YOUTH'S IMPORTANT LESSON OF SELF-RELIANCE"

My life has been an eventful one. I was born a slave—was the child of slave parents—therefore I came upon the earth free in God-like thought, but fettered in action. My birthplace was Dinwiddie Court-House, in Virginia. My recollections of childhood are distinct, perhaps for the reason that many stirring incidents are associated with that period. I am now on the shady side of forty, and as I sit alone in my room the brain is busy, and a rapidly moving panorama brings scene after scene before me, some pleasant and others sad; and when I thus greet old familiar faces, I often find myself wondering if I am not living the past over again. The visions are so terribly distinct that I almost imagine them to be real.

I presume that I must have been four years old when I first began to remember; at least, I cannot now recall anything occurring previous to this period. My master, Col. A. Burwell, was somewhat unsettled in his business affairs, and while I was yet an infant he made several removals. While living at Hampton Sidney College, Prince Edward County, Va., Mrs. Burwell gave birth to a daughter, a sweet, black-eyed baby, my earliest and fondest pet. To take care of this baby was my first duty. True, I was but a child myself—only four years old—but then I had been raised in a hardy school—had been taught to rely upon myself, and to prepare myself to render assistance to others. The lesson was not a bitter one, for I was too young to indulge in philosophy, and the precepts that I then treasured and practised I believe developed those principles of character which have enabled me to triumph over so many difficulties. Notwithstanding all the wrongs that slavery heaped upon me, I can bless it for one thing—youth's important lesson of self-reliance.

The baby was named Elizabeth, and it was pleasant to me to be assigned a duty in connection with it, for the discharge of that duty transferred me from the rude cabin to the household of my master. My simple attire was a short dress and a little white apron. My old mistress encouraged me in rocking the cradle, by telling me that if I would watch over the baby well, keep the flies out of its face, and not let it cry, I should be its little maid. This was a golden promise, and I required no better inducement for the faithful performance of my task. I began to rock the cradle most industriously, when lo! out pitched little pet on the floor. I instantly cried out, "Oh! the baby is on the floor;" and, not knowing what to do, I seized the fire-shovel in my perplexity, and was trying to shovel up my tender charge, when my mistress called to me to let the child alone, and then ordered that I be taken out and lashed for my carelessness.

The blows were not administered with a light hand, I assure you, and doubtless the severity of the lashing has made me remember the incident so well. This was the first time I was punished in this cruel way, but not the last. The black-eyed baby that I called my pet grew into a self-willed girl, and in after years was the cause of much trouble to me.

## "THE SEPARATION OF MY PARENTS"

I grew strong and healthy, and, notwithstanding I knit socks and attended to various kinds of work, I was repeatedly told, when even fourteen years old, that I would never be worth my salt. When I was eight, Mr. Burwell's family consisted of six sons and four daughters, with a large family of servants. My mother was kind and forbearing;

Mrs. Burwell a hard task-master; and as mother had so much work to do in making clothes, etc., for the family, besides the slaves, I determined to render her all the assistance in my power, and in rendering her such assistance my young energies were taxed to the utmost.

I was my mother's only child, which made her love for me all the stronger. I did not know much of my father, for he was the slave of another man, and when Mr. Burwell moved from Dinwiddie he was separated from us, and only allowed to visit my mother twice a year—during the Easter holidays and Christmas. At last Mr. Burwell determined to reward my mother, by making an arrangement with the owner of my father, by which the separation of my parents could be brought to an end. It was a bright day, indeed, for my mother when it was announced that my father was coming to live with us. The old weary look faded from her face, and she worked as if her heart was in every task. But the golden days did not last long. The radiant dream faded all too soon.

In the morning my father called me to him and kissed me, then held me out at arms' length as if he were regarding his child with pride. "She is growing into a large fine girl," he remarked to my mother. "I dun no which I like best, you or Lizzie, as both are so dear to me." My mother's name was Agnes, and my father delighted to call me his "Little Lizzie." While yet my father and mother were speaking hopefully, joyfully of the future, Mr. Burwell came to the cabin, with a letter in his hand. He was a kind master in some things, and as gently as possible informed my parents that they must part; for in two hours my father must join his master at Dinwiddie, and go with him to the West, where he had determined to make his future home. The announcement fell upon the little circle in that rude-log cabin like a thunderbolt. I can remember the scene as if it were but yesterday;—how my father cried out against the cruel separation; his last kiss; his wild straining of my mother to his bosom; the solemn prayer to Heaven; the tears and sobs—the fearful anguish of broken hearts. The last kiss, the last good-by; and he, my father, was gone, gone forever.

Deep as was the distress of my mother in parting with my father, her sorrow did not screen her from insult. My old mistress said to her: "Stop your nonsense; there is no necessity for you putting on airs. Your husband is not the only slave that has been sold from his family, and you are not the only one that has had to part. There are plenty more men about here, and if you want a husband so badly, stop your crying and go and find another." To these unfeeling words my mother made no reply. She turned away in stoical silence, with a curl of that loathing scorn upon her lips which swelled in her heart.

My father and mother never met again in this world. They kept up a regular correspondence for years, and the most precious mementoes of my existence are the faded old letters that he wrote, full of love, and always hoping that the future would bring brighter days. In nearly every letter is a message for me. "Tell my darling little Lizzie," he writes, "to be a good girl, and to learn her book. Kiss her for me, and tell her that I will come to see her some day." Thus he wrote time and again, but he never came. He lived in hope, but died without ever seeing his wife and child.

The last letter that my mother received from my father was dated Shelbyville, Tennessee, March 20, 1839. He writes in a cheerful strain, and hopes to see her soon. Alas! he looked forward to a meeting in vain. Year after year the one great hope swelled in his heart, but the hope was only realized beyond the dark portals of the grave.

"THE SAVAGE EFFORTS TO SUBDUE MY PRIDE"

I must pass rapidly over the stirring events of my early life. When I was about fourteen years old I went to live with my master's eldest son, a Presbyterian minister. His salary was small, and he was burdened with a helpless wife, a girl that he had married in the humble walks of life.

She was morbidly sensitive, and imagined that I regarded her with contemptuous feelings because she was of poor parentage. I was their only servant, and a gracious loan at that. They were not able to buy me, so my old master sought to render them assistance by allowing them the benefit of my services. From the very first I did the work of three servants, and yet I was scolded and regarded with distrust.

The years passed slowly, and I continued to serve them, and at the same time grew into strong, healthy womanhood. I was nearly eighteen when we removed from Virginia to Hillsboro', North Carolina, where young Mr. Burwell took charge of a church. The salary was small, and we still had to practise the closest economy. Mr. Bingham, a hard, cruel man, the village schoolmaster, was a member of my young master's church, and he was a frequent visitor to the parsonage. She whom I called mistress seemed to be desirous to wreak vengeance on me for something, and Bingham became her ready tool. During this time my master was unusually kind to me; he was naturally a good-hearted man, but was influenced by his wife.

It was Saturday evening, and while I was bending over the bed, watching the baby that I had just hushed into slumber, Mr. Bingham came to the door and asked me to go with him to his study. Wondering what he meant by his strange request, I followed him, and when we had entered the study he closed the door, and in his blunt way remarked: "Lizzie, I am going to flog you."

I was thunderstruck, and tried to think if I had been remiss in anything. I could not recollect of doing anything to deserve punishment, and with surprise exclaimed: "Whip me, Mr. Bingham! what for?"

"No matter," he replied, "I am going to whip you, so take down your dress this instant."

Recollect, I was eighteen years of age, was a woman fully developed, and yet this man coolly bade me take down my dress. I drew myself up proudly, firmly, and said: "No, Mr. Bingham, I shall not take down my dress before you. Moreover, you shall not whip me unless you prove the stronger. Nobody has a right to whip me but my own master, and nobody shall do so if I can prevent it."

My words seemed to exasperate him. He seized a rope, caught me roughly, and tried to tie me. I resisted with all my strength, but he was the stronger of the two, and after a hard struggle succeeded in binding my hands and tearing my dress from my back. Then he picked up a rawhide, and began to ply it freely over my shoulders. With steady hand and practised eye he would raise the instrument of torture, nerve himself for a blow, and with fearful force the rawhide descended upon the quivering flesh. It cut the skin, raised great welts, and the warm blood trickled down my back. Oh God! I can feel the torture now—the terrible, excruciating agony of those moments. I did not scream; I was too proud to let my tormentor know what I was suffering. I closed my lips firmly, that not even a groan might escape from them, and I stood like a statue while the keen lash cut deep into my flesh. As soon as I was released, stunned with pain, bruised and bleeding, I went home and rushed into the presence of the pastor and his wife, wildly exclaiming: "Master Robert, why did you let Mr. Bingham flog me? What have I done that I should be so punished?"

"Go away," he gruffly answered, "do not bother me."

I would not be put off thus. "What *have* I done? I *will* know why I have been flogged."

I saw his cheeks flush with anger, but I did not move. He rose to his feet, and on my refusing to go without an explanation, seized a chair, struck me, and felled me to the floor. I rose, bewildered, almost dead with pain, crept to my room, dressed my bruised arms and back as best I could, and then lay down, but not to sleep. No, I could not sleep, for I was suffering mental as well as bodily torture. My spirit rebelled against the unjustness that had been inflicted upon me, and though I tried to smother my anger and to forgive those who had been so cruel to me, it was impossible. The next morning I was more calm, and I believe that I could then have forgiven everything for the sake of one kind word. But the kind word was not proffered, and it may be possible that I grew somewhat wayward and sullen. Though I had faults, I know now, as I felt then, harshness was the poorest inducement for the correction of them. It seems that Mr. Bingham had pledged himself to Mrs. Burwell to subdue what he called my "stubborn pride."

On Friday following the Saturday on which I was so savagely beaten, Mr. Bingham again directed me come to his study. I went, but with the determination to offer resistance should he attempt to flog me again. On entering the room I found him prepared with a new rope and a new cowhide. I told him that I was ready to die, but that he could not conquer me. In struggling with him I bit his finger severely, when he seized a heavy stick and beat me with it in a shameful manner. Again I went home sore and bleeding, but with pride as strong and defiant as ever.

The following Thursday Mr. Bingham again tried to conquer me, but in vain. We struggled, and he struck me many savage blows. As I stood bleeding before him, nearly exhausted with his efforts, he burst into tears, and declared that it would be a sin to beat me any more. My suffering at last subdued his hard heart; he asked my forgiveness, and afterwards was an altered man. He was never known to strike one of his servants from that day forward.

Mr. Burwell, he who preached the love of Heaven, who glorified the precepts and examples of Christ, who expounded the Holy Scriptures Sabbath after Sabbath from the pulpit, when Mr. Bingham refused to whip me any more, was urged by his wife to punish me himself. One morning he went to the wood-pile, took an oak broom, cut the handle off, and with this heavy handle attempted to conquer me.

I fought him, but he proved the strongest. At the sight of my bleeding form, his wife fell upon her knees and begged him to desist. My distress even touched her cold, jealous heart. I was so badly bruised that I was unable to leave my bed for five days. I will not dwell upon the bitter anguish of these hours, for even the thought of them now makes me shudder.

The Rev. Mr. Burwell was not yet satisfied. He resolved to make another attempt to subdue my proud, rebellious spirit—made the attempt and again failed, when he told me, with an air of penitence, that he should never strike me another blow; and faithfully he kept his word. These revolting scenes created a great sensation at the time, were the talk of the town and neighborhood, and I flatter myself that the actions of those who had conspired against me were not viewed in a light to reflect much credit upon them.

The savage efforts to subdue my pride were not the only things that brought me suffering and deep mortification during my residence at Hillsboro'. I was regarded as fair-looking for one of my race, and for four years a white man—I spare the world his name—had base designs upon me. I do not care to dwell upon this subject, for it is one that is fraught with pain. Suffice it to say, that he persecuted me for four years, and I—I—became a mother. The child of which he was the father was the only child that I ever brought into the world. If my poor boy ever suffered any humiliating pangs on account of birth, he could not blame his mother, for God knows that she did not wish to give him life; he must blame the edicts of that society which deemed it no crime to undermine the virtue of girls in my then position.

* * *

Shortly afterward, Keckley and her mother accompanied her new master, Mr. Garland, who had married one of Mr. Burwell's daughters, to St. Louis. There they faced such dire poverty that the family proposed to send Keckley's mother out to work. Keckley convinced Garland to send herself out to work instead, and by application and industry, Keckley soon became a skilled seamstress—so skilled that, as she wrote,

> The best ladies in St. Louis were my patrons, and when my reputation was once established I never lacked for orders. With my needle I kept bread in the mouths of seventeen persons for two years and five months. While I was working so hard that others might live in comparative comfort, and move in those circles of society to which their birth gave them entrance, the thought often occurred to me whether I was really worth my salt or not; and then perhaps the lips curled with a bitter sneer.

Keckley soon managed to persuade her master to allow her to buy her freedom; her master gave her a price of $1,200 (over $25,000 in today's currency). (She could have easily escaped, but wanted to be legally free.) She soon married, but her husband had deceived her: he had pretended to be a free man, but he was really a slave, and Keckley left him after eight hard years. She made many friends in St. Louis, however, and they loaned her enough money to buy her freedom.

In 1860, at the age of forty-two, Keckley moved to Baltimore, and six months later to Washington, D.C. There, she rented an apartment and set up her own business. Among her customers was Varina Davis, wife of Jefferson Davis, future president of the Confederate States of America. Mary Todd Lincoln was another frequent customer, and Keckley was soon making all of the first lady's clothes, traveling with her, and being her constant companion.

Keckley's son, George, was killed fighting for the Union, and shortly thereafter she helped to found the Contraband Relief Association, an organization of African American women who aided former slaves in the Washington area. Prominent abolitionists, including Frederick Douglass, donated to her cause, as did Mrs. Lincoln.

Keckley was a sharp observer and spent considerable time at the White House and traveling with Mrs. Lincoln, and her book is full of intimate details about the Lincoln family. After President Lincoln's assassination, Mrs. Lincoln turned to Keckley as her close friend and comforter. When Mrs. Lincoln came to financial trouble, Keckley helped find her support.

But when she published *Behind the Scenes*, all of that came to an abrupt end. Newspapers, friends, Mrs. Lincoln, and prominent African Americans condemned Keckley for her perceived betrayal of President Lincoln. In fact, *Behind the Scenes* presents the Lincolns in a largely favorable light, but the publicity surrounding its publication prevented anyone from seeing this. From the height of success, Keckley plunged into a life of poverty. She lost all her clients and lived solely on the pension she received as the mother of a fallen Union soldier. She ended up dying in the Home for Destitute Women and Children in Washington, a home she had helped found some forty years earlier.

# WILLIAM H. ROBINSON

**W**illiam H. Robinson (1848–?) published his autobiography, *From Log Cabin to Pulpit, or, Fifteen Years in Slavery* in 1904; it went through three editions, the last in 1913. Robinson is a now forgotten figure: his book has never been republished, and few people are aware of its existence. Yet it offers one of the most concise and memorable depictions of a childhood spent in slavery.

Robinson was born in Wilmington, North Carolina. His parents belonged to an exceptionally wealthy man named Thomas Cowens, who owned two farms and over five hundred slaves. Robinson's father was an engineer who towed vessels into and out of Wilmington harbor, and he made an elaborate arrangement with Cowens to buy his own freedom, paying $800 down. But Cowens then broke his word and sold him. As Robinson's father was being led away to Richmond, Virginia to be auctioned off, he told his son, "William, never pull off your shirt to be whipped. I want you to die in defense of your mother; for once I lay in the woods eleven months for trying to prevent your mother from being whipped."

His words resonated for the rest of his son's life. Unlike some other post–Civil War slave narratives, William Robinson's never dwells on the "benevolent" aspects of slavery. As he wrote in his preface, "My book reveals in every chapter either the pathetic moan of slaves in almost utter despair, yet panting, groaning, bitterly wailing and still hoping for freedom, or of slaves with their hearts lifted to God, praying for deliverance from the cruel bonds, the auction block, and years of unrequited grinding toil for those who had no right to their labor."

## "MY MASTER ... HAD DIED"

About a month after I entered upon my new occupation [and about seven weeks after my father was sold] my master told me one day, while sitting on the porch, to light his pipe. He smoked a pipe with a long reed stem and would rest the bowl of it on a shelf. After I lit the pipe he ordered me to bring him a glass of water. I went for it, but on returning I found he had turned a sallow complexion. I spoke to him but he did not answer. I called old mistress, (this is the way we distinguished her from the children, as we called all, from the least to the biggest, mistress and master.) She came and spoke to him, but there was no reply. He had died sitting there in his chair.

It was the custom among the slave holders to have the older slaves come and view the remains of their masters or mistresses while they lay in state, and if the master was a man of any humanity, or what we termed a good master, they would actually shed tears over his body. So as usual, they called the slaves in, but old mistress did not know that Master Tom had incurred the ill-will of every slave on the place by selling [my] father.

Father was almost a prophet among my people, because he secured all the news through his Quaker friends, and other white men that were friendly to him, with whom he came in contact. Then he would tell it to our people. Of course the slaves held him in high esteem, and when Master Tom sold him they never again had any good feeling for him. They came as usual, but just outside the door they wet their fingers with saliva and made "crocodile tears" and passed on pretending to be crying, and saying, "Poor Massa Tom is gone." Of course they didn't say where he had gone.

This may appear very deceptive, but had we not made some demonstration of grief our very lives would have been in danger.

## "THE MEANEST OF ALL THE COWENS FAMILY"

About three weeks later they began to look up the will, for boys then were like a good many are today, just waiting for the old man to die, so they could run through with what he had accumulated. We have many young men of that class today. They are not worthy to bear their father's name. It was found in the will that mother and three of the children had fallen to Scott Cowens—the meanest of all the Cowens family. He was a drunkard and a gambler, for he had taken three different women's sons, between the ages of twelve and fourteen years, and gambled them off and came back home without them, leaving the parents in anguish. We went to his home, mother as cook, the rest as servants in general.

We had been there but a few months when he called my mother one day and asked her why she said "that God had sent swift judgment upon his father." Of course mother denied it, but in her grief she had thoughtlessly said it, and somehow it had reached his ears. He threatened mother very strongly, but didn't strike her.

He left home one evening, telling me to be ready to accompany him when he returned. He did not come back until the next morning. I saw at once that he had been drinking heavily. He sat down to the breakfast table and ordered me to bring him a glass of cool water right from the spring. I put the glass of water in front of him. He immediately picked it up and threw the water in my face, saying "I will show you how to bring me dirty water to drink."

One morning a few days later, he found fault with the biscuits and asked me what was the matter with them. I told him I didn't know. He then jumped up from the table and called mother. We, from the least to the largest, were taught when called by our mistress or master to answer and go toward that voice. So mother was coming to him and he met her on the porch, between the kitchen and the dining room. He asked mother why she was crying—I had told her about his throwing the water in my face—and before she could answer him he knocked her from the porch to the ground. This was more than I could endure. An ax handle was on the opposite side from which mother fell. He stood over her, cursing and kicking her, and I knocked him down with the ax handle.

## "MY ONLY HOPE OF ESCAPE"

I knew my only hope of escape was to run away, so I started at once. I had often heard ex-runaway slaves, men and women, tell the adventures of when they were in the woods and about their hiding places or rendezvous. I had heard it told so often at my father's fireside that I knew almost directly where they were, for I had passed close by them many times, so I started to look for them. I went to the three mile farm, arriving there about the time they were going to dinner. I went to an old mother—we were taught to call each old woman mother, and they called us son or daughter. It seemed there was a natural bond of sympathy existing in the heart of every woman for the children of others. I told her what I had done. She gave me a chunk of fat meat and half of a corn dodger and directed me the way to a hiding place. Then with her hand upon my head she prayed one of those fervent prayers for God to hasten the day when the cruel chains of slavery would fall, and women's children would not be forced to leave home and take refuge among the beasts of the forest for trying to protect their mothers.

Quite late that night I got opposite the hiding place. It was a low swampy place back of a thick cane brake. It was so dark and the cane so thick when I got to the place where I had been directed to turn in I was afraid to venture. But as I stood there I imagined I could hear the baying of blood hounds, and so strong was the imagination that it drove me in. I had several things to fear, for that country was infested with bears. More than once I had seen a bear come out of a corn field with his arms full of corn, go up to the fence and throw it over, get over, pick it up like a man, and walk off. Then we had reptiles, such as water moccasins and rattle snakes. Sometimes I could walk upright, sometimes I was compelled to crawl through the cane. About three o'clock the next morning I came out of the cane brake on the banks of a large pond of almost stagnant water. I could see the rocky mound or cave that I had heard so much talk of.

There was no boat around and I was afraid to go into the water, but the same impulse that drove me into the cane brake caused me to go into the water. With a long reed for a staff I waded into the water until I heard the voice of a man, in the real coarse negro dialect, "who is dat?"

My hair was not extremely long, yet it seemed so to me, as I imagined I felt my hat going up, and I answered "dis is me." (Of course he knew who "me" was.)

He then began to question me as to my name and my parents' name. It was necessary for him to be very cautious whom he admitted, because white men often disguised themselves and played the role of a runaway, and in this way many runaways had been captured.

I finally succeeded in convincing him that I was not a spy but an actual runaway. Then he allowed me to advance, and as I sat on the top of the rocky mound with him he prayed long and earnestly for the time to come when God would raise up a deliverer to lead us in some way out of bondage. And while he was thus praying I heard this peculiar sound, "gaw goo." The old man saw I was in a terrible dilemma, and he said, "son, you need not be uneasy, that is only some men below snoring." In a few minutes I looked across the field and saw two men coming with poles on their backs, and I got excited again, and called his attention to the fact. He assured me that they were men who had been off seeking food. They were stealing.

Our people in those days were naturally good hunters, but never shot anything larger than a coon nor smaller than a chicken, always good on the wing with the latter. They threw their game down. It consisted of some fat hens and meat they had returned to their homes and secured.

There was always an understanding between the slaves, that if one ran away they would put something to eat at a certain place; also a mowing scythe, with the crooked handle replaced with a straight stick with which to fight the bloodhounds.

The cook came out, made a hot fire of hickory bark, thoroughly wet the chickens and wrapped them in cabbage leaves and put them in the bed of ashes; then he proceeded to make his bread by mixing the corn meal in an old wooden tray and forming it into dodgers [cakes], rolling them in cabbage leaves and baking in the ashes. These are known as ash cakes, the most nutritious bread ever eaten. Of course the chickens retained all their nutriment because the intestines had not been taken out of them. But now he returned to them and catching them by both feet he stripped the skin and feathers off, then took the intestines out and put red pepper and salt in them and then returned them to the oven to brown. Parched some corn meal for coffee. Breakfast being ready, the guests came from the sleeping place, fifteen in number, the two huntsmen made seventeen, the old man and myself making nineteen in all, all runaways.

Among them was a man named Frank Anderson. His father, James Anderson, a white man of Wilmington, was his master. Yet he was a runaway slave, with a standing reward of one hundred dollars for his head.

He had been a fugitive eleven months, and had stripes on his back like the ridges of a wash board, put there by his father's overseer and by the command of that father, simply because he had so much of his father's blood in him that he would not allow them to lacerate his back only when they overpowered him.

Uncle Amos, as the watchman was called, was a prophet among us. He would watch every night, and took me as his companion, as I was the only boy. So I slept in the day and watched with him at night. He was a great astrologer, although he could not read a word; but strange to say, he would go out and lie flat on his back and watch the moon and stars, go through some peculiar movement with his hands, then the next morning he could tell almost anything you wanted to know. Many times it came just as he prophesied.

One morning, after I had been to the hiding place about three weeks, the runaways inquired, as was the custom, "if everything was all right, or what would happen." If he answered them in the affirmative, they were perfectly satisfied with his decision. But on this memorable morning he told them that we would have to get away at once, for if we did not we would be attacked within three days by negro hunters, for said he, "God has shown me the hounds and the men, and that some one will lose his life if the attack is made here."

So they decided to go to another rendezvous fourteen miles away. Uncle Amos advised each one to get his weapon in shape, and get provisions enough that night to last a few days, or until they learned something about the country surrounding the other hiding place.

When men ran away, if in the day, they returned at night and secured a mowing scythe and took the crooked handle off and put a straight handle on it. Then they made a scabbard of bark, and would swing their saber to their side. This was to fight blood hounds with, and if the negro hunters got too close, many times they were hewn down.

On that night three different parties were out foraging, and returned with considerable provisions. But the next morning, while we were eating breakfast, negro hunters suddenly appeared with shot guns and drawn revolvers, and demanded every one of us to wade over to them. They had negro men to hold the hounds and cut the cane so they could pass through. These men had worked noiselessly all night, cutting the way through the cane.

I told Uncle Amos several times that I thought I heard something, but he seemed to think it more fear in me than reality, and he failed to give the proper attention.

We all jumped to our feet, with instructions from the old man to march over in a body, and each choose his man and dog to cut down when they reached the other shore, but the hunters were on the alert and demanded all to stand in a row, then march over one at a time. One of the hunters said to Frank Anderson, "if you run I'll blow your brains out." We formed a line and in a moment Frank Anderson bounded off like a deer. We heard the crack of a gun, saw Frank throw up both his hands and fall, and in a minute he lay cold in death. Murdered because he wouldn't consent to be tied up and whipped when he was late returning home from a Saturday night dance.

One by one we all marched over and were handcuffed to each other and marched off to the road, and the colored men who were with the hunters carried Frank over and put him in the mule cart which they had with them, and he could be tracked for thirteen miles by the blood which dropped through the cracks in the cart. His father rode over the sand stained by the blood of his son, whom he had commanded to be murdered.

This is but a small portion of the horrors through which my people passed. No tongue has ever been able to utter, nor has the pen been forged that can pen the horrors through which my people have passed. But they kept a constant knocking by faith at mercy's door, until God moved in his mighty power and touched the heart of Lincoln, who was a type of a second Moses, through whom he delivered us.

They surrendered us to the jailor or keeper of the negro pen. There was no jail after all, only negro pens for slaves. If a poor white man transgressed the law, they simply took what he had and gave him time to get out of the country. The Lords, who were our masters, hood-winked the law. If the negro transgressed, he paid the penalty with a lacerated back, from fifty to three hundred lashes. So you see there was no need for jails, only negro pens where slaves were bought and sold as goods and chattels.

These men received for capturing us the paltry sum of three dollars per head as the reward for the capture of runaway negroes, and the additional two hundred offered for the head of Frank Anderson, which had been a standing reward from his master, as he couldn't be captured in the first six months after he ran away. This was equivalent to his father's saying that it was better his own son should die than have all the other negroes spoiled. Nearly all of us were struck thirty-nine lashes according to the law, then returned to our several masters.

For some cause I was among the few exempted from the thirty-nine lashes. My master paid the stipulated amount of three dollars and ordered me home. I walked off in front of him under a storm of oaths and threats, and expecting him to kick me or knock me down at every step. But I was agreeably disappointed.

## "WHEN I ARRIVED HOME"

When I arrived home I found that my mother, one brother and one sister that were with her when I left, had been sold to negro traders, and three brothers who fell to Hezekiah Cowens were also sold away, and no one could tell me anything about their whereabouts. Of course my master wouldn't tell me. This was the hour of great sorrow and distress with me. My master gave me the task of piling up stove wood, and for three weeks nearly every stick of wood I picked up was wet with tears of grief and sorrow, weeping for that mother who was the best friend on earth to me, and for my brothers and sisters, and expecting every day to be whipped. And this suspense was one of the most severe punishments or whippings I could have undergone.

There was another old woman whom I called mother, doing the cooking. One day at the expiration of the third week, master sent me to the store to get some goods, and in the packages there was a cow-hide in its crude state, but I didn't see it wrapped up. After unwrapping the cow-hide my master asked me how I liked the looks of it. I told him that I didn't like it at all. We were in his bed room. He stood between me and the door. His wife came in with his decanter of whiskey, glass and water and he locked the door, then demanded me to pull off my shirt. I had not forgotten the promise I made my father, so I fully made up my mind to fight him until I got a chance to jump out of the window. But I looked toward the bureau and saw an old fashioned pistol which you load from the muzzle and fired with a cap. My master was standing very close to this and the sight of it knocked all the manhood out of me, so I reluctantly pulled off my shirt with their assistance, and he tied my hands behind me, my feet together, and ran a stick between them. This left me in a doubled up position on the floor.

He whipped and cursed me until he had cut my back to pieces. My mistress tried to take the whip from him, but he pushed her away so violently that once she fell on the floor. The second time she fell on the bed, but had secured the whip. He gave me a kick in my side, from which I have never recovered, and staggered from the room, being too drunk to whip me any more.

His wife untied me and at the same time the old mother came to the door and said, "Master Scott, I came here to break this door open, for it's a shame for any woman's son to be cut up as you have done that child." He knocked the old lady down.

I went up stairs and lay down on my stomach with my face across my arms. The next morning when I awoke the blood had dried the shirt in the wounds on my back. The cook had to grease the shirt so as to get it out of the wounds. Then he gave her medicine to heal my back. Every day after this when I would go to pile up wood I had to stoop my whole body, for my back was so sore that I couldn't bend it, and if I had not been so young (I was only eleven years,) the marks would have been visible until now, and like many other slaves, I would have carried them to judgment as a testimony against him.

After four or five weeks, when my back had become somewhat healed up, he told me one day if any one asked me if I had ever been whipped to tell them no. Is it not a wonder that negroes are not inveterate thieves and liars? They worked all the week for their masters, with only a peck of meal and three pounds of fat bacon, and after each day's labor they were compelled to go to their master's smoke house or chicken roost and steal enough to subsist upon the next day, to do that master's work, then, after this master had cut his back all to pieces he would compel him to tell a lie in order to sell him. But, thank God, we, like other nations, are born with the same natural instinct that others are, and although manhood was crushed for two hundred and forty odd years, yet, with the same surroundings and opportunities to develop them, we have risen above our environments.

One afternoon five negro traders came; my master called me, met me at the door, and repeated his former command "if any one asked me had I been whipped, to tell them no." I walked into the parlor; there sat five men wearing broad brimmed straw hats, their pants in their boots and a black snake whip across their shoulders. The first question they addressed to me was, had I ever been whipped. I suspect I was too slow in speaking, for the punishment had been too severe, and was too fresh in my memory for me to tell a lie on the spur of the moment. I had on a long straight gown which reached to my feet. The trader raised that and looked at my back and that told the story. They offered my master a small price for me, he refused it, and they left. I remained with him about three or four weeks longer, when one day he wrote a note and sent me to the trader's pen. The keeper, Mr. Howard, read it and told me to take it back to James, the negro turnkey, who also did all the whipping in the jail. He ordered me put in a cell and closed the big iron door, which told me that I was bound for Richmond, or some other slave market, and I was truly glad, for I now hated the soil upon which I was born.

## "FOOTSORE, HUNGRY AND BROKEN-HEARTED"

I was in the trader's pen about three weeks. There were from one to ten slaves brought in every day. All of my brothers and sisters save two had been sold from Wilmington. Other slaveholders passing through had bought them, and it was said they were taken to Georgia. At the end of three weeks the gang of three hundred and fifty was made up and we were chained and started for Richmond, Virginia. In this gang was a woman named Fannie Woods. She had two children, the oldest about eight years, the other a nursing baby. She was not handcuffed as the others were, but tied above the elbow so she could shift the nursing baby in her arms. She led the older one by the hand. The first half of the day the little boy kept up pretty well; after that he became a hindrance in the march. The trader came back several times and ordered her to keep up. She told him she was doing the best she could. He threatened each time to whip her if she did not keep up, and finally he ordered a negro, a strong muscular man six feet in height, who went along to give us water and help drive, to untie her, made her give the baby to another woman, then ordered her to take off her waist [blouse]. They buckled a strap around each wrist and strapped her to a large pine tree less than ten feet from the rest of us, and with a blacksnake whip the colored man was made to hit her fifty lashes on her bare back. The blood ran down as water but she never uttered a sound. She was ordered to put on her waist. They retied her and told her to see if they could keep up.

After going a few miles farther they sold the little boy she was leading to a man along the way. I heard the wails of the mother and the mourning of the other slaves on account of her sorrow, and heard the gruff voice of the trader as he ordered them to shut up. We marched until nine or ten o'clock, when we came to a boarding house that was kept especially for the accommodation of negro traders. This was a large log house of one room, about eighteen by twenty feet, with staples driven in all around the room and handcuffs attached to chains about four feet long. They would handcuff two or three slaves to each chain. In the summer they had nothing but the bare floor to lie upon; in the winter straw was put upon the floor. There was a very large fire place in this room.

We stopped at this boarding house. This was our first night's stop after leaving Wilmington. The keeper of the boarding house tried to buy Fannie Wood's baby, but there was a disagreement regarding the price. About five the next morning we started on. When we had gone about half a mile a colored boy came running down the road with a message from his master, and we were halted until his master came bringing a colored woman with him, and he bought the baby out of Fannie Woods' arms. As the colored woman was ordered to take it away I heard Fannie Woods cry, "Oh God, I would rather hear the clods fall on the coffin lid of my child than to hear its cries because it is taken from me." She said, "good bye, child." We were ordered to move on, and could hear the crying of the child in the distance as it was borne away by the other woman, and I could hear the deep sobs of a broken hearted mother. We could hear the groans of many as they prayed for God to have mercy upon us, and give us grace to endure the hard trials through which we must pass.

We marched all that day, and the second and third nights we stopped in the same kind of a place as the first night. They were buying and selling all along the way, so when we reached Richmond about ten o'clock the fourth night, there were about four hundred and fifty of us, footsore, hungry and broken-hearted.

## "THE AUCTIONEERING"

We were taken to Lee's negro traders' auction pen, which was a very large brick structure with a high brick wall all around it. A very large hall ran through the center. There was no furniture in it, not even a chair to sit upon. In this pen the handcuffs were taken off for the first time since we left home. There were possibly three or four hundred in there when we arrived. Many found relatives. One woman found her husband who had been sold from her three or four years before. But I was not so fortunate as to find any of my people.

The next morning the back door was open and we went down to wash. There were three or four pumps in the yard and long troughs near each. Some one would pump these troughs full of water and we would wash our faces and hands. There were no towels to wipe on, so some woman would give us her apron or dress skirt to dry our faces with. We then waited for our breakfast. The cooks handed out our tin pans with cabbage, or beans and corn bread, without knife, fork or spoon. Many having been sold before, and knowing how they would fare, carried such things with them. We sat around on the floor and ate our breakfast, after which we were ordered into a long hall, where we found wire cards [bent wire teeth set in rows in a thick piece of leather], such as are used for wool, flax or hemp. We were ordered to comb our hair with them. Of course when we started we had on our best clothes, which consisted of a pair of hemp pants and cotton shirt; most of us were barefoot. The women, and sometimes the men, wore red cotton bandanas on their heads. After our toilets were completed we were ordered into a little ten by twelve room; we went in, ten or twelve at once. There were five or six young ladies in the gang I went in with. The traders, forgetting the sacredness of their own mothers and sisters, paid no respect to us, but compelled each one of us to undress, so as to see if we were sound and healthy. I heard Fannie Woods as she pleaded to be exempt from this exposure. They gave her to understand that they would have her hit one hundred lashes if she did not get her clothes off at once. She still refused, and when they tried to take them off by force, fought them until they finally let her alone.

After this humiliating ordeal of examination was over we went into the auction room. This was a large room about forty by sixty feet, with benches around the sides, where we were permitted to sit until our turn came to get on the auction block. The auctioneering began about nine o'clock each day and lasted until noon, began again at one o'clock and continued until five p.m. This was a perpetual business every day in the year, and the prices were quoted on the bulletin and in the papers the same as our stock and wheat are quoted today. At these sales we could find the best people of the South buying and selling.

I remember when I got on the block, the first bid was one hundred and fifty dollars. It went up to seven hundred, when the bidding ceased. The negro trader went to the auctioneer and told him that I came from the Madagascar tribe and that my father was an engineer and a skilled mechanic. Then the bidding became brief. I recall that the auctioneer said, "right and title guaranteed," as he slapped me on the head, then continued by saying "he's sound as a silver dollar." I was knocked off at eleven hundred and fifty dollars.

A poor man in East Virginia, named William Scott, bought me, paying four hundred and fifty dollars cash and giving a mortgage on his sixty acres of land, his stock and everything he owned, including one colored girl, whom he had bought four years before.

The next morning after I was sold they brought a man to the traders' pen to be whipped. This man would not allow his overseer to whip him. He had chains on him that looked as though they were welded on. They took him upstairs in the big building where there were about seven or eight hundred men, women and children. It was about noon and they left him handcuffed while they went to dinner. He explained to us why they were about to whip him. He had gone to church without a pass on two occasions and refused to allow his master to whip him for so doing. His master declared he would whip him or kill him. They took the irons off, and ordered him to strip himself of all of his clothing. He promptly did so. His master said, "you might just as well have done this at home and you might have gotten off with a few hundred lashes." But to their surprise, when they told him to lie down, he began to knock men down right and left, with his feet and hands. Many went down before him. Then they picked out ten or twelve strong colored men, made them run in upon him, and though he knocked many of them down they were too many for him, so they overpowered him, and with straps fastened him taut upon the floor to six strong rings. These rings were arranged in two rows of three rings each, opposite each other and covering a space something over six feet in length.

Then his master, with four or five other men, came up to see him whipped, one man with his tally book, and a negro with his black snake whip and paddle; they brought their demijohn [large narrow-necked bottle] of whiskey, each one taking a drink before they began their bloody work. They even gave the negro who was compelled to do the whipping, a drink. After they were well drunk the whipping began. One man would count out until he counted nine, then with the tenth he would cry tally. When the whipping first began the slave would not say a word, but after awhile as they cut his back all to pieces, he would cry out, "pray, master," and in this way he pleaded for mercy until he grew so weak he could not utter a word. They gave him three hundred lashes, then washed his back with salt water and paddled it with a leather paddle about the size of a man's hand, with six holes in it. As they paddled him it sounded as a dead thud; you could hardly hear him grunt as each lick fell upon him. He was whipped from head to foot, and the floor where he was lying was a pool of blood when the brutal work was ended. His master congratulated the negro whipping master for the way he accomplished his part of the work, gave him another big drink of whiskey and ordered him to untie the man.

They all went down stairs and the other colored people who were in the room put the man's clothing on him. This was late in the afternoon. The next morning when I awoke I saw the men and women kneeling around in a circle, praying, groaning and crying. I walked up and looked to see what the trouble was, and I found the man they had whipped the day before cold in death. He was swollen so that his clothing had bursted off. A jury of white men came up and held a mock inquest. I never heard what the verdict was. The colored men came with a mule cart, rolled him up in a sheet and took him to his last resting place.

I stayed in this trader's pen three days after my new master bought me, and during this time I saw hundreds of mothers separated from their children. I heard the wail of many a child for its mother, and of the mother for her child. While one buyer had the mother, going in one direction, another with the child would be going the opposite way. I saw husband and wife bidding each other farewell and sisters and brothers being separated. There could not have been any darker days to them than these; it was with them as it was with Job, when he spake in the Third Chapter of Job, and said:

"Let the day perish wherein I was born, and the night in which it is said there is a man child conceived, let that day be darkness; let not God regard it from above, neither let the light shine upon it."

"Let darkness and the shadow of death stain it; let a cloud dwell upon it, let the blackness of the day terrify it. As for that night, let darkness seize upon it; let it not be joined unto the days of the year, let it not come into the number of the months. Lo, let that night be solitary, let no joyful voice come therein. Let them curse it that curse the day, who are ready to raise up their mourning. Let the stars of the twilight thereof be dark; let it look for light, but have none, neither let it see the dawning of the day; because it shut not up the doors of my mother's womb, nor hid sorrow from mine eyes."

These were the lamentations of the poor slaves, but still they prayed for the dawn and light of a better day. Like [the children of] Israel [in the Bible], many looked long and eagerly for freedom but died without the sight. Thank God, over three million lived to see the sunlight in all its brilliancy, and we can now look back and say: "The Lord has done great things for us, whereof we are glad" [*Psalm* 126:3].

"MY NEW MASTER"

On the fourth morning after I was sold, I got on the horse behind my new master. I had a handcuff on my right wrist, with a chain extending down to my right foot and locked around my ankle. We rode until late in the afternoon, when we stopped at a hotel. He chained me to the porch and left me until after supper time; then gave me a piece of bread and meat, and left me until about ten o'clock at night, while he talked. Then he came after me and we went up stairs to his room. He chained me to his bed post, and gave me a quilt to lie on by the side of his bed, on the floor.

The next morning we had breakfast by daylight and started again on our journey; to my surprise he didn't handcuff me this time. He talked very freely with me, told me he had a nice girl and if I acted all right we would have a good time, and he would soon buy my mother and father, when the poor fellow was not able to buy me; he had just finished paying the mortgage which he gave when he bought the girl, and remortgaged to buy me. About nine o'clock the succeeding night we arrived home; when quite a distance from the house he called out in a loud voice for Fanny to open the gate. As we neared the gate, she threw it open. I had ridden until my limbs would not hold me up when I slid off the horse, so I fell prostrate upon the ground, but with the assistance of the girl and my master, I was able to get on my feet.

His residence was a large log building of one room. He left me at the door and told me to stay there until he called me. Now, it was a custom with my people, when a white man went on the inside and closed the door and left a black man, woman or child outside, just so sure a black ear went to the key hole. I didn't want to make an exception to this rule, so when he went in, my ear went to the key hole. After the usual mode of family greeting of a man that had been away from home a week or ten days, he said: "The one who guesses what I have brought, may have it." The oldest boy said, "A pair of boots, for you promised me a pair;" the nine-year-old girl said, "A large china doll," but when the guessing came to the smallest one, a little girl between the age of three and four years, to my surprise she said, "A nigger." "Correct," said my master, "the nigger's yours; come in here, Bill." I went in and the formal introduction was made. He said, beginning with the boy, "This is your master Charles, this is your Miss Mary," but when it came to the youngest girl, he said, "this is your Miss Alice and you belong to her. Now, if you are a good and obedient nigger, when she is grown and at her death she will set you free." If I had believed this story I would have prayed to God to kill her then, wicked as it was. Then he gave me an introduction to his wife.

As long as I had been with him he had not introduced himself until now. He really grew enthusiastic in introducing himself; his face grew red, and his voice trembled as he said: "I want you to understand that I'm a nigger breaker. I hear you came from a family of niggers that won't be whipped, but I'll break you or kill you." I knew he could not afford to do the latter, for I had overheard Robert E. Lee [the Negro trader, not the future Confederate general], from whom he had bought me, say to him, "I understand you have abused the girl you bought from me, shamefully. If you abuse this boy it will cost you all you are worth."

He then called the girl, who was once a pretty octoroon, but now her face was much disfigured where the mistress had stuck the hot tongs to it because she was so overworked she would fall asleep while she would be carding wool at night. You could hardly see the traces of a once beautiful girl, now about fourteen years old.

He said, "you two have got a good home and can be happy here together." Jokingly, he said, "I'll have the preacher come over and marry you." He thought through this union—he had formed in his mind—that he would raise his own slaves.

After supper the mistress ordered her to bring in her tin pan and quart cup, at the same time wondering what dishes to give me to use. My master said. "Oh yes, I forgot to tell you I bought Bill a new pan and cup." The children scampered away for the old saddle bags. They brought my cup and pan, and after using the latter for a looking glass for a time, handed it to me. In the tin pans she put a little gravy and a corn dodger on each, and filled the cups with skimmed milk—the milk had been skimmed and skimmed until there was not an eye of cream to be seen on it. We called it blue John.

Fannie and I went into the kitchen. She said to me, "don't eat yet, we'll milk first." I was very hungry, but did as she asked me. We took our milk buckets and went to the cow pen; there were two cows, so we got them close together. Fannie milked both, for I had never before tried to milk. We poured our cup of blue John into the milk pail. She milked both our cups full, and with our hoe cakes of corn bread, we ate our supper, drinking the warm, unstrained milk. The mistress often complained, and spoke of selling the cows because they gave such poor milk. We would then milk the cows into the pail where we had poured our skimmed milk and return it to our mistress. We continued this as long as I was there, which was three or four months.

My master was overseer for a man on an adjoining farm, named Howard, for which he was paid thirty dollars per month. He would leave home at three o'clock in the morning, giving the girl and me our task the night before. He would eat his dinner each day in the field with the slaves, and return home at about nine or ten o'clock at night. He hired the slaves at night, and sometimes in the day he would slip them over to work in his crop. I have known the slaves many times to work in his field from ten o'clock at night until near day-break the next morning; yet he never allowed the girl or me to visit the slaves on any other farm, or them to visit us. He was the meanest overseer in that section of the country, for he would have a whipping bee every Monday morning.

He had whipping posts on the farm and the slaves were tied to this and whipped; you could hear the cries of slaves all around from that place. I have heard him laugh many times and tell how the slaves would squirm under the lash.

The farm on the other side of us belonged to a man named Wilkerson; he had seventy five or a hundred slaves, and he, also, was a cruel man. Every day, in going for the cows I would have to pass his farm. I heard him say to one of the rail splitters, "if you don't have your task of rails split tomorrow I will hit you one hundred lashes." The man told him he was doing all he could do and would die before he would take a single lick. I made it my business the next day to go after the cows about the time for him to go out; I saw him and four or five other men; he asked the rail splitter if he had his task completed. The man answered in the negative; he then ordered him to pull off his shirt, which the man did, then tied his pants around his waist with his suspenders. The reason the slaves would so readily pull off their shirts was so they could not have anything to hold them by, their flesh being moist they could not easily hold them. When his master told him to cross his hands he began to fight, knocking white men down as fast as they could come to him. Finally they made five or six other rail splitters, working near by, help take him. There were saw logs from five to six feet through, all round; some of the colored men caught him by the head and hands, while others had hold of his feet, and they bent him back over one of the saw-logs while he was fighting and cursing. His master seized the maul [a sledgehammer with a wedged end], which the man had been using to split rails with, and struck him across the abdomen; bent over in the position he was the lick sounded like a pop-gun, and the man's intestines ran out, and he died across the log; murdered because he could not perform the task imposed upon him. These are some of the horrible deeds which have stained the pages of American history, and which it will take centuries to mitigate.

### "RUNNING AWAY"

I would often talk to Fannie about running away; she would plead with me and beg me not to, because it would be so lonesome for her, but there was a constant yearning in my soul for that freedom which God intended for all human beings. Ultimately, after a careful planning of the route to be taken and a survey of the country, as far as I had been over, I made up my mind to leave. One morning my master sent me to the field to gather corn. I carried a basket and two sacks, and at noon I was to fill them and hitch up the mule cart and bring them home. I got the corn ready and sat down in the corn row. I realized then for the first time that there must be some efficacy in prayer. My mother had taught me to get on my knees and say my prayers, as far back as I could remember, yet I never knew the power there was in prayer, until on this memorable morning, I knelt down in a corn row and prayed with that fervent, childlike simplicity for God in some way to get me back to my mother or into Canada, or else let me die and go to heaven. The Queen of England had said that if the slaves could reach the shores of Canada she would protect them, if it took the whole navy of England to do so. While I was thus in prayer it seemed that all nature was in sympathy with me, for not even the rustling of the leaves could be heard. The only thing to break the monotony was the wooing of a turtle dove that sat in the branches of a distant tree, and seemed to be saying to me, "I am in deep sympathy with you." Reasoning came to me as audibly as though some one was speaking to me, saying "you shall see your mother again."

I became so much elated over this message, though received from an unseen power, that I jumped up and at once fully decided what course to take. Immediately I proceeded to put my decision into action, so I emptied the corn out of the two sacks and the basket; put the sacks in the basket on my arm and left that corn field with the full intention of going back to Richmond, Virginia.

It may seem strange to the reader that I would go back to this place of human misery; but I had learned from older men and women who had been sold to some poor man, that if they would run away and go back to their former master, and tell him "that your master was so mean that you could not live with him, and for this reason you had run away and come back to him," nine times out of ten he would accept this piece of deception practiced by the slave, and compel the poor man to take his money back, believing that the negro thought more of him than of the man he had sold him to, and for this reason I was going back to Richmond, Virginia.

I went about seven or eight miles that day through the woods, and about dusk I came in sight of a cabin in the distance. I was satisfied this was the home of some old mother or father who had outlived the days of their usefulness, and was given a peck of meal each week and cast off to fish or hunt for the rest of their living. I was not disappointed, for I found an old woman eighty years old; it was hard to discover until she spoke whether she was white or slave. The first words the old lady said were, "Son, you is a runaway, ain't you?" I told her that I was, and she told me "the overseer haven't been around yet cause dey aint done milking yit, but you take this path (as she pointed to a path) and follow it till you come to a log across de creek, with a fish box upon it; you sit there until you hear me singing this song, God has delivered Daniel, and why not deliver me?" She went into the house, while I went to the log mentioned. I sat there for three-quarters of an hour. I heard the milk maids while milking singing different melodies, then I heard the command of the overseer for them to take the cows to pasture, and in a short while I heard the feeble voice of the old mother as it rang out on the still, balmy air, singing:

He delivered Daniel from the lion's den,
Jonah from the body of the whale,
The Hebrew children from the fiery furnace,
And why not deliver poor me?

Hold up your head with courage bold,
And do not be afraid;
For my God delivered Daniel,
And He will deliver poor you.

I started for the house and met her coming. We went into the cabin where she had prepared supper, and I assure you I enjoyed it. The supper consisted of boiled fresh fish and "ash cake." As I ate she sat with her hands on my head, telling me how to get along in the world, and pointing me to that friend that sticketh closer than a brother. She repeatedly said, "if God be for you it is more than all the world against you." She made me a pallet [a makeshift bed] upon the floor, and I slept there until about three-thirty o'clock the next morning, when she awoke me and gave me breakfast of the same diet I had had the night previous for supper. She also gave me four or five onions, and told me upon the peril of my life, not to eat a single one of these onions, because they would make me sleepy and I would be liable to be caught. But she said negro hunters came along there every two or three hours in the day; and I learned for the first time how to decoy the blood hounds, for she told me whenever I heard the baying of hounds on my trail, to rub the onions on the bottoms of my feet and run, and after running a certain distance to stop and apply the onions again, then when I came to a large bushy tree, to rub the trunk as high up as I could reach, then climb the tree.

## "MY SAFE RETURN TO RICHMOND"

About four o'clock in the morning, at the old woman's command, I knelt by her side, she placed her hand upon my head and prayed fervently for my safe return to Richmond, and that God would touch Massa Lee's heart, that he might buy me back from my present owner. When she quit praying she told me that I would reach Richmond safely. She kissed me good bye, with tender, parting words, as a mother would her own son, and I left, with directions from her how to reach my intended destination. I had not gone far when an opportunity presented itself to test the efficacy of the onions, for about nine o'clock that day I heard the baying of the blood hounds in the distance behind me. I rubbed the onions on my feet as directed, and ran as fast as I could the distance of half a mile, when I repeated the application. I continued this process for about one mile and a half, going across the fields and through the woods, dodging the roads and farms where people were at work. I came to a thickly branched out tree in the woods. I rubbed onions on the trunk and climbed the tree. I could tell when the hounds came to the place where I first put the onions on my feet, because they would retrace their steps, until finally their voices died away, and I heard them no more that day. I traveled all of that day, and that night I slept in a low, swampy place between two huge logs, on some brush, with the two sacks over me which I took when I left the corn field. By daylight the next morning I started on my journey, but had not gone many miles when I came in sight of a river. I saw that I was not far from a house, and went close enough to see that a ford was near the house where they crossed the river. The white man who had charge of the ford lived in the house. So I knew I couldn't get across the river without taking a boat, and that he wouldn't hire me one without word from my master, therefore that necessitated my waiting until night, so I went back in the woods to wait.

I saw some colored men coming across the field and went to meet them, and learned through them their master's name and three or four slaves that he owned, and the name of a farmer on the other side of the river. They told me to go to the ferryman and tell him that Mr. Howard, my master, had sent me to take the basket and two sacks to Mr. Owens, who lived on the other side of the river. They told me that the ferryman would question me very minutely, but if he asked how long Mr. Howard had owned me to tell him he bought me from negro traders two weeks before—for traders had crossed there just two weeks ago with three or four hundred slaves. They then left me and told me to wait until they returned. I did so, but under great suspense, because one of the men belonged to a tribe of negroes known as the Guineas, who would divulge any secret for a little whiskey or wheat bread; therefore I was afraid I would be betrayed. But in a short time they returned, relieving me of the great suspense, and bringing me something to eat. They told me I was in an easy day's walk of Richmond after I crossed the river; told me what to say to Massa Lee when I got back, but not to go into Richmond until after dark. They prayed an ardent prayer for God's protection and guiding hand to go with me, and bade me good bye and God speed. I went to the ford, called out hello; the harsh voice of the ferryman cried out, "whose thar." At the same time he was coming towards the river, I was fast rehearsing in my mind the story I was to tell him. When he got near me his first words were, "where in hell are you going this time of night?" I started to tell him that Mr. Howard had sent me to Mr. Owen's to take the basket and sacks, but before I could finish telling him, he ordered me to pull off my hat: that he would teach me some manners if I came there talking to him with my hat on. He then asked how long Mr. Howard had owned me, at the same time flashing his lantern in my face. But when I told him he said, "yes, I remember seeing you in that gang; untie the boat." He sat down and lit his pipe while I pulled the boat over. When we reached the other side he said "tie her up thar." He looked at his watch and said "its a quarter up thar and a quarter back. I'll give you fifteen minutes each way, if you ain't back in that time I'll skin you alive." If he's waiting he is having a good long wait. I went on my way rejoicing.

After crossing the river that night I went but a short distance, when I made me a bed in a shock [pile] of fodder [food for the livestock]. The next morning before daylight as I came out of the shock two more runaways came out of the shock ahead of me. When they saw me they ran as fast as they could go and I after them. They did not wait to see whether I was white or black. They ran across a large field, and came to a fence. One, a very tall man, put his hand on the top and vaulted over. The other one attempted to follow but fell back. By that time I had caught up with him. He asked me why I did not tell him I was colored. I replied, "I couldn't catch you."

They were men who had been sold from Richmond and were now running away from their masters as I was, and trying to get back to Lee. They had with them plenty to eat, so we had about as good a time that day as runaways could have in the woods. Long before dusk we could see the statue of George Washington, which stood at Richmond, Virginia, with a negro boy chained at its base, and Washington pointing with his right hand, saying, "take the negro south." This very great man, who, with Hancock, in 1776, signed the Declaration of Independence, and said the colonies were and ought to be free, loosed them from the iron hand of Great Britain; and yet that was the inscription written on his statue, which adorned the public square of the once Capitol of the Southern Confederacy.

We hid around until dusk, when we went down to a spring and ate our lunch slaking our thirst from the clear cool water as it bubbled out from the spring, by lying flat down and lapping the water. I happened to be the first of the three to get up, and to my surprise there stood five negro hunters with their guns and revolvers pointing toward us. I said to my companions "here is some white men." They said "whar." Their eyes looked like great balls of cotton. The men commanded us to come to them. We dropped, each one of us in handcuffs, and we were marched into Richmond.

## "AT THE NEGRO TRADER'S"

When we arrived at the negro trader's pen, Mr Lee happened to be there. He wanted to know of the negro hunters where they found us; they told him. Then he began to interrogate each of us; I told him that "Massa Scott was so mean to me that I could not live with him, so I ran off and came back to you." The other two men told the same kind of story; so Mr. Lee ordered the negro hunters to take the handcuffs off, and if they wanted to make money to go and find negroes that were not coming back to him. They, with their hats in their hands, the same as the slaves, began to form excuses, when Lee ordered them off the premises without any reward. Had we not been returning to Mr. Lee they would have been entitled to three dollars per head. According to the law they were entitled to it at any rate, for we were runaways, but they were poor men with low occupations and their word didn't go as far as that of the slaves they were driving. One of the men he ordered locked up stairs, telling him that he had a good master, and if he behaved himself he would he treated all right. The man begged very hard not to be sent back, but his begging was all in vain. This man's master was wealthy, while mine and the other man's master were poor men, so he kept us and sent the other man back.

Mr. Lee told me that the man who had my mother had been there twice and wanted to buy me, and Scott, he said "was behind anyhow." I think he meant that his second payment was overdue—and he assured me that he shouldn't have me back. Mr. Lee wrote a note and sent me to his own house. I met an old colored mammy at the gate. She asked me, "where is you gwine?" I said, "to see Miss Lee." She said, "You look like gwine to see Miss Lee. Wha dat you got in your han?" I said, "a letter for her." She said, "gin it to me." She took the note, telling me to wait. Mrs. Lee raised the window and called me to come up. She asked about my parents, and said Mr. Scott should not take me back again. She told the colored mammy to take me and clean me up. When I got in the cabin I discovered it was wash day, for she had a kettle of hot water on the fire place. She took a couple of handfuls of soft soap out of the gourd and stirred it in the water. When she found I was not undressing she looked very much surprised and said, "gwine out of dem rags." She scrubbed my back till my flesh burned. About the time she was through the sixteen-year old maid came in with clothing for me. I tried to hide behind the old mother. The girl threw the clothes down and ran out. I put the clothes on and stayed at the trader's pen that evening. After that I was privileged to stay at the house, or pen, as I chose. I thought I was almost a free man, for I had on a pair of shoes, a nice suit of clothes and a large brass watch and chain.

Master Lee told me that a man named Jake Hadley, who lived in Greenville, Tennessee, had my mother, two brothers and a sister. He also said Mr. Hadley drove a big black horse so it seems that I thought there was only one black horse in all Virginia and that the Jew [Mr. Hadley] owned him; therefore I met with many disappointments. I waited and watched for more than a month for my new master to come, during which time I assisted Peter around the pen. Peter looked after the slaves, and did all the whipping. I cleaned the office and was errand boy. Most of my work was about the office. During the time I was there I saw thousands of slaves bought and sold. I saw one woman who had five children; she and two children, one a nursing baby, and a girl about eleven years old, were sold to negro traders, while the husband and the other three children were bought by a farmer who lived somewhere in east Virginia. The farmer went with the father and three children to see the mother and the other two children leave for Mississippi. As the boat pulled out from the shore and the husband and wife bade each other good bye, the woman, with one loud scream, made a sudden leap and landed in the deep water, with her baby clasped in her arms and the little girl handcuffed to her. She had preferred death to life separated from her husband and children. They were not picked up until the next day.

I saw another woman whipped seventy-five lashes on her bare back because she wouldn't strip her clothing any further down than her waist, to be examined. They took her back the second time, but she fought them until they were compelled to leave her alone.

### "MOTHER AND SIX CHILDREN TOGETHER AGAIN"

This is now the year of 1860. I was twelve years of age and had been a runaway twice in that time. I had now been at Lee's trader's pen four or five weeks, when one day I saw a man coming with a black horse and buggy; something from within seemed to whisper to me, "this is the man who owns your mother." My aspirations ran so high that I went out the back way and prayed that this might be he. He came into the office of the pen, and after a general conversation with Mr. Lee, he asked "if he had heard anything of that boy yet." I was watching every move and listening to every word passed. With a wink of the eye, Mr. Lee said, "no." Then he sent me to do something in the rear end of the building. I did it very quickly and returned to the office again; was very busily engaged with my dust brush. Never since I had been there had I found so much to be done in the office, and whenever I was sent away I would do my errand as quickly as possible and return to the office again.

Finally Mr. Hadley, for it was he, said: "boy, how would you like to belong to me and go down to Tennessee to live?" While I was satisfied that he was the man who owned my mother, I said, "I wouldn't like to go with you at all, 'cause Massa Lee said the man that had my mother was coming after me." As I spoke I couldn't keep from crying, and Mr. Lee could refrain no longer, so he said "William, this is Mr. Hadley, the man who has your mother, and brothers and sisters." And for once I saw that seemingly heartless man, who separated thousands of husbands and wives, mothers and children, sisters and brothers, touched to the very core, for he drew his handkerchief and wiped his eyes, instead of his nose, as he pretended to be doing.

Mr. Hadley was a very kind, fatherly acting man. He bought me a nice suit of clothes, and gave me money, telling me to buy my mother, brothers and sisters some presents. As a general thing all Jew slave owners were more lenient to their slaves than any other nationality, perhaps because they had been in bondage themselves. In a few days we started for home; we had to stop along the way in many little towns to attend to business, so that we were nearly four days in making the trip. These were four of the longest days I had ever experienced in my life, for I was anxious to meet my mother again. I was constantly inquiring "how much farther is it." On the fourth day in the afternoon I asked, "how long yet before we will reach home?" He said, "in a few days now." The words had scarcely left his lips, when I saw coming down the road my mother and new mistress. Mother came upon the side of the buggy my master was on, and almost dragged me out of the buggy across my master. She was rejoicing and blessing master for his deeds of kindness. In a few minutes my new mistress came up on the other side of the buggy; she pulled me over, and to my surprise, and for the first time in my life, a white woman kissed me. This was a very new feature to me, and naturally embarrassed me very much, so much so that I mentioned it many times afterwards. I couldn't understand how it was, I, a slave, and she my mistress, as others had been, and they were so heartless and cruel, and she so kind. But I afterwards learned that all the white people were not mean and cruel, for when I arrived home I found my mistress had prepared a grand dinner for us and invited in all the slaves. My mistress had two children, Samuel and Laura. I didn't call them master and mistress as I had heretofore called the white children, but called them each by their given name.

I had a glorious time in that home and felt almost as if I were free. My master owned a large farm three miles from Greenville, where we lived. But during the month of February he concluded to go to the old country—I think it was on account of the agitation of the slave question—he saw the war was coming on, so he decided to take us back to Wilmington and leave us there, with his wife and children, on his brother's farm, until he returned. Accordingly we all packed up and went back to Wilmington, N.C., my old birthplace. On arriving there we found another brother and sister, making mother and six children together again; father and the other six children we knew nothing of. Mr. Hadley went away but was gone only three weeks, when he returned, saying he had not gone any farther than Richmond, Virginia.

He stayed in Wilmington a month, and when he was ready to go back home he asked me and my sister "if we didn't want to stay with his brother awhile longer and come home later on." We, not having the least suspicion that he had sold us, told him that we would. So they went home, leaving us. After a couple of weeks, Mr. Dave Hadley—that was his brother's name—told us that he had bought us, but we could go every two or three months to Greenville to see mother.

It was not more than two weeks from the time I found that Massa Dave Hadley had bought me, when Joseph Cowens, the son of my original old master, came to Mr. Hadley's; he met me out in the yard and stopped me for a talk. He said, "it was a shame that his father had allowed my father to be sold away, that he was going to buy us all back and get us together again."

With this conversation he naturally won me, so when he asked me if I wouldn't like to belong to him, of course I said "yes." He went into the house and in a short time he and Massa Dave came out together, and Massa Dave told me that I now belonged to Joseph Cowens, and that he had bought my two brothers also, and in the next two months he was going to buy mother and the other two children. But when I got to his house and asked for my brothers, he said that he had hired them out for a year. I soon found out different; he had never bought my brothers, nor had any intention of buying them; or my mother, either.

## "BACK IN THE COWENS FAMILY"

I am now back in the Cowens family, my original master's son, and brother to Scott Cowens—the man I knocked off the porch for hitting my mother, and who was afterwards drowned. I went to Joseph Cowen's as general servant boy in the house, and was treated as well as could be expected from a Cowen. I stayed there quite satisfied, thinking that mother and the other children would come in a few months, as he had promised they would. The last of March we moved out on the Summer farm, three miles from town, and I had to drive him to town every morning and go for him every evening. He was a merchant and owned several ships. Now I had a great deal of freedom out on the farm, for I did nothing but drive Massa Joseph back and forth, to and from town, and wait table. I was in the cabins and among the slaves the most of my time in the day, but I slept at the "great house" in Massa Joseph's room. I had become almost a prophet among my people, because I would get the news from the white people, and in the day would tell it to the slaves in the fields and cabins.

He owned another farm five miles from town, and had a colored overseer on this farm. Uncle Tom was the meanest man you ever saw, in the presence of the white folks. He would draw back his whip as though he was going to knock down all around him, but I never knew him to strike an old person in my life.

The leading white men from town would come out two or three nights in a week and stay half of the night and gamble. I would take the whiskey, glasses and water in to them, then Massa Joe would send me off to bed, but I stood many an hour listening to them talk and discuss the question of the war, and whether it would be advisable to arm the negroes. They finally decided, as did the Egyptians, that if they did arm the negroes when the enemy came the slaves would join with the enemy and fight against them, so they thought it would not be expedient to do so.

Early Friday morning, April 12, 1861, I took my master to Wilmington. On the way we stopped and took in another man. As we neared Wilmington we could hear the booming of cannons, for the rebels had fired upon Ft. Sumter, and we could hear the echo of the guns as it came down the Cape Fear river and was borne out on the broad bosom of the Atlantic. My master, in great excitement, slapped his hands together, and with an oath, said, "it's come." Both of them grew deathly pale, and looked at each other as though they were surprised. My master hastily wrote a short note, sealed it and gave it to me, with directions to hurry home, cautioning me very particularly not to stop until I reached home and delivered the note to his wife.

I saw that every white man in Wilmington was greatly agitated and wore a look of anxiety. In a moment everything that had been told me by the Yankee soldiers, and by the underground railroad men, flashed in my mind; for many of them had told me that I would some day be free, and we looked forward to that day with great expectations.

I drove as fast as I could to the five mile farm, which was in charge of the colored overseer. Uncle Tom could read and write, and I wanted to know what was in the note. I had many times slipped him the newspapers from the house, and carried them back early the next morning before master called for them, and he taught me to listen carefully to every conversation held between the white people. I drove up to the fence, where fifty or sixty men and women worked in the field. I could hear them singing and shouting, for they too, had heard the booming of the cannon, and Uncle Tom had told them that that was a token of liberty. But when they saw the old "carry-all" drive up, each one ran to his or her work; the overseer came to the carriage, supposing master wanted to see him, but to his surprise master was not there. He called the slaves around and had me explain how master acted at the sound of the guns, then he made a speech to them, telling them to pray as they had never prayed before. I gave him the note I had for mistress; he looked at the envelope, studied for a moment, rubbed his head, and then thoroughly wet the seal; he opened the letter and read it. The letter read as follows:

"We have fired on Fort Sumter. I may possibly be called away to help whip the Yankees; may be gone three days, but not longer than that. You write a note and send William to Sawyer, [that is the overseer on the farm where we live] and tell him to keep a very close watch on the negroes, and see that there's no private talk among them. Have Martin, the overseer's son, aid you, and if Elliott or Fuller come on the place, give them no opportunity to talk with the negroes.

Your husband,
JOE COWENS."

After reading the note Uncle Tom told me to drive back and go around by the Salisbury road. This took me nearly two miles out of the way, but in the middle of this road was a large mud puddle. He told me to drive in there, very fast, then get out and wade in the water, and get the envelope wet and muddy. He showed me how to smear it over with my hands so mistress would not detect that it had been opened. He also showed me how to make saliva or crocodile tears. He said mistress would be on the porch watching for me, and that I should pretend to cry, at the same time get the envelope from my pocket, handing it to her with the left hand. She would take it with her right hand, tear it open and drop the envelope on the ground. As soon as she was gone I was to pick it up and destroy it. Mr. Fuller was in the house, having come to see master on business, so when mistress heard the carriage coming she came to the big gate to meet it, thinking master was returning, and left Mr. Fuller in the house. When I saw her coming I made some crocodile tears by wetting my fingers with saliva. As soon as she saw that master was not with me, she came rushing to the buggy and found me shedding tears as fast as I could. In a very tender tone, with her hand upon my head, she asked me what was the matter.

At this I broke down completely and cried aloud, at the same time feeling in my pocket for the envelope, and telling my sad story, between sobs, of how I had dropped it in the mud hole. She eagerly grasped it and tore it open, not noticing that it had ever been opened before, and patting me on the head, she said, "hush, mistress can read it." That instantly healed my pretended broken heart and dried up my manufactured tears.

She started for the house, forgetting she had not cautioned me, so she came back and told me "that Mr. Fuller was in the house, and for me not to mention anything to him or any one on the place, concerning the cannon firing." She then wrote a note and gave it to me to take to Mr. Sawyer. She had dropped the envelope and I was glad when she was out of sight. Picking up the envelope I put it in my mouth, chewed it up, removed a harness peg, put the pulp in the hole, and replaced the peg. If the old barn is still standing the envelope is there yet. I took the note to Mr. Sawyer and in a short time he was at the house in close consultation with her. Then he went after his son Martin, and they both went over to five mile farm, where Uncle Tom was overseer. She wrote another note to Mr. Bailey, a poor white man living about a mile away, and he came at once and took charge of our farm. He was once overseer on our place, but was so cruel that massa discharged him. So now he served as an extra two or three days at a time for the different overseers in the community, for which he received seventy-five cents per day, and what he could get the slaves to steal for him, for notwith-standing their inhumanity to the slaves, they kept up a constant trade with them. They stole their master's corn, wheat, chickens, hogs, etc., and carried them to the overseer, for which he would give them a little flour, and occasionally a dime or two, and very often when he was about to whip them he would let them off by their promising to bring him some meat or chickens. Master came home that night, and after supper five or six of the leading men from Wilmington came. After I brought in the demijohn, glasses and water, master told me that I could go to bed, because he would want me to go away with him early the next day. But instead of going to bed I pulled off my shoes, tip-toed down stairs and peeped through the keyhole, and not making an exception to the rule, my ear did its share of listening. They got into a hot discussion, and I heard one of them say, "if the Yankees whipped, every negro would be free." I became satisfied that the negro was the bone of contention, and that the light of liberty was probably about to dawn, so I went to bed.

On the morning of April 15th, 1861, I left home with my master to go to the war and whip the Yankees in three days; I carried a club for the first three days to knock off Yankees' horns with, for my master told me that they had horns. We were gone more than three months; we didn't whip them, but were gaining a victory in every battle that was fought, and this was encouraging to the rebels. You could hear the southern ladies singing "Old Lincoln and his hireling troops would never whip the South." We came home on a week's furlough, then returned to be gone six months, but before the expiration of the six months, my master was killed by a shell bursting at Greenville, Tennessee, near the place where John Morgan was killed.

## "THE RICHEST, FREEST MAN IN AMERICA"

After the death of my master I remained as cook for the company until November, 1863, when at Blue Springs, Tennessee, Generals Thomas and Burnside routed Hood and Forrest, after a short contest; and in the retreat, I, with many others, was captured. I was with the cooks' brigade. There were about fifty of us, and each one was riding one of those long eared fellows, that lean against the fence and say, "I have no one to love me" [a mule—mules cannot mate].

In the retreat we had quite a deep ditch, or gully, to cross. My animal was heavily loaded with camp kettles, tin pans and kitchen utensils in general. When the cavalry got to this ditch they commanded their horses to mount, and the horses leaped over, but I suspect in the excitement I forgot to give the necessary commands, for my long eared friend's fore feet reached the other shore safely, but his hind feet fell short of the mark, and down in the ditch we went; such a scramble you never saw. But I found that there were many rebel soldiers in there, who were tired of the Yankee lead and wanted to be captured. I was scrambling to get out, but they told me to lie still, and in a few moments Yankee soldiers—both cavalry and infantry, seemed to have popped up out of the earth; while some pursued the fleeing rebels, others took us to the general's headquarters. The rebels were sent to the northern prisons, and the cooks and colored servants that had been captured, were next brought before General Thomas and disposed of. I was the last man in the line, and when I came before the general, his first words to me were, "you're a fine looking fellow. Here we are fighting to free you and you are here dressed up in a suit of rebel uniform."

He then called his cook—a quaint looking, cross-eyed old man, who like myself, was "hewn out of a slab of ebony." He said, "Nathan, what shall we do with this boy?"

"Hang him to the highest tree we can find," said Nathan.

"Well, bring me the best rope you can find."

Nathan obeyed. He came with a rope as large around as his wrist, and about twenty feet long. The general asked him if he thought that would hold me; he answered in the affirmative, and General Thomas told him to throw it over the limb of a tall oak which stood near by.

But an officer by the name of Lane rode up and said: "General, maybe this boy will take the oath of allegiance." I would have taken most anything about this time.

Then the general inquired of me if I would take the oath. I told him I would.

By this time some one said, "hold up your right hand." Another said, "hold up your left hand," another said, "your right foot," and another said, "your left foot." I obeyed orders as fast as they were given until it came to the left foot. I had up all I could possibly get up.

After having all the fun they wanted with me, the general told Nathan to take me back and wash and clean me up. Uncle Nathan took me to his tent, where he had a kettle of boiling water. It looked as if he were going to scald a hog; then began the washing process. After the old man had rubbed and washed me until my flesh burned, and I had put on a castaway suit of General Thomas', I went to headquarters. After standing before the large mirror in the general's tent, I thought I was the richest, freest man in America.

They had carried the joke to such an extent—for I really thought they were going to hang me—that I was sick. They administered some medicine to me and I lay down across the general's bed, General Thomas himself having told me to. When I awoke about 3 p.m. I was between the two generals, Burnside and Thomas. When I moved towards one he would crowd against me, and if I moved towards the other he would crowd in, until I was squeezed as tightly as possible between the two. They were both awake, and I could feel their sides heaving until they could not restrain their laughter any longer, then General Thomas said, "lie still boy, this white won't rub off." This was my first day of freedom.

General Thomas questioned me concerning my parents, and on learning that my mother was in Greenville, Tennessee, he said; "you will see her within three days if the rebels don't whip us." Accordingly we left Blue Springs that day enroute to Madison Court House, Virginia, which brought us through Greenville where mother was. It was hard to prevent me from being the advance guard. For two days they were trying to hold me back, until we finally reached Greenville, and I saw the house in which mother lived. Seeing that no rebels were near, the officers allowed me to advance. Before I reached the house I saw mother and my Jewish mistress, Mrs. Hadley, standing on the porch. Everybody seemed very much excited, and the rebel army was retreating.

Having changed my uniform from the rebel gray to the Yankee blue, my mother did not recognize me until I was at the gate; then she came running and shouting "this is William."

I was saying in one breath—not waiting for one question to be answered before I asked another, "how are you? I am free, are you? Get ready to go to the Yankees; has master the same black horse and buggy?"

She told me he had. I told her to go pack up while I hitched the horse to the buggy.

When I returned to the house the soldiers had surrounded it and asked me where my mother was. I ran up stairs, tried to open mother's door, when she informed me that Massa Jake had locked her in. The soldiers were hurrying me to get my mother and come on. I told them Massa had locked her in, and one of them gave me an ax and told me to break the door open. I told mother to stand back from the door. At the same time Massa Jake came in with a shot gun in his hand, but before he could raise it dozens of muskets were aimed at him. By this time I had the door open, and there stood mother with a rope around the bureau, and every loose article she could get hold of was wrapped in her straw tick [mattress case], all tied up ready for moving. She was expecting to move the whole cargo in a buggy.

I had her unpack as quickly as possible and gather up her clothes and little keepsakes, so we could be out of the yard as soon as possible. I shall never forget the courtesy shown mother by two or three soldiers, in helping her in the buggy. Being all ready, and our buggy placed in line with the other contrabands [slaves who had run away to the Union army]—for there were between one hundred and fifty and two hundred wagons, mule carts, pack horses, mules and even milk cows, we started on our journey.

Most of the southern men had gone to war, and those who were too old to go had taken the women and gone to the cities, leaving the farms and country homes virtually in charge of the colored people. I had an uncle who was left in charge of a farm three miles from town. We passed by his place on our way to Virginia, and when we came in sight of the farm we could see colored people by the hundreds, who

had gathered from other farms. The news spread like wild fire all over the country that the Yankees had come.

The "great house" was kept furnished the year round and left in the colored overseer's charge, because the family would come back and forth, sometimes staying weeks at a time. The veranda was filled with men, women and children, singing, shouting and praising God in the highest. I hastened into the yard and was soon the center of attraction. Uncle Isaac was soon by my side, picking me up and carrying me around, shouting at the top of his voice, while I was struggling to get down, and trying to drown his voice so I could tell him that he was free, and to pack up at once and go with us.

I was inviting him to liberty, yet I had not a shelter in all the world to put my head save the canopy of Heaven. But I had heard of a country where all men were free, and like Bunyan's Pilgrim [John Bunyan wrote *The Pilgrim's Progress*, an allegory of salvation] I had started to make it my home.

\* \* \*

Robinson enlisted in the Union Army as soon as they began allowing black troops to fight, and he remained with the army until the conclusion of the Civil War two-and-a-half years later. He fought in the Battles of the Wilderness, Kenesaw Mountain, Chancellorsville, Culpepper, Antietam, Blue Springs, Missionary Ridge, Nashville, and Greenville.

After the war it was very difficult for Robinson to find his family, as slaves didn't always retain the name of their last master. It took him several years to find his mother, but he never found his father. He worked as a horse-cart driver for the Nashville fire department, as a singer and banjoist for a troupe of African Americans who sang slavery songs, then for an oil company. In 1869 he went to England for a year, giving concerts and learning to read and write.

Upon his return he went to school in Nashville for three years, and in 1874 entered college, but didn't complete his degree. He worked as a teacher in Tennessee, a railroad porter, a steamboat steward, and a hotel cook in Chicago, before finding salvation in Christ in 1877. He married that year and preached in various places in Indiana until his wife's death in 1892. At that point he became an itinerant minister, evangelizing throughout the Midwest.

At some point, Robinson, who was still known as William Cowens after the name of his first and last masters, joined his mother and nine of his brothers in a reunion. His father had been a South African prince known as "Rob-o-bus-sho," meaning Robinson Crusoe. At this reunion, the entire family decided to throw off their various slave names and rename themselves after their father. As Robinson wrote in the conclusion of his autobiography, "I am prouder of my father's heathen name than of all the professed christian names that I was compelled to acknowledge while a slave."

# FURTHER READING

## I. OTHER SLAVE NARRATIVES

Practically every book-length American slave narrative can be found in its entirety at http://docsouth.unc.edu/neh/texts.html. Seven out of the ten narratives included here can be found in their entirety in *I Was Born a Slave: An Anthology of Classic Slave Narratives*, edited and annotated by Yuval Taylor, and available in two volumes—along with thirteen other narratives of note. There are many other collections of slave narratives available, as well as many individual narratives. In addition, the following books contain shorter slave autobiographies: *Slave Testimony*, edited by John W. Blassingame; *Early Negro Writing, 1760–1837*, edited by Dorothy Porter; and *Unchained Voices*, edited by Vincent Carretta. Lastly, in the 1930s the federal government funded a project in which thousands of surviving slaves were interviewed; these interviews have been collected in a number of different books.

## II. BOOKS ABOUT SLAVE NARRATIVES

William L. Andrews's *To Tell a Free Story* is by far the best literary analysis of early black autobiography. Other volumes well worth seeking are Charles T. Davis and Henry Louis Gates Jr.'s *The Slave's Narrative*, a collection of insightful essays; Frances Smith Foster's *Witnessing Slavery*, a consideration of the literary genre of the slave narrative; and

Marion Wilson Starling's *The Slave Narrative,* the 1946 study that initiated serious attention to the genre.

## III. BOOKS ABOUT SLAVERY

Julius Lester's *To Be a Slave,* Charles H. Nichols's *Many Thousands Gone,* John W. Blassingame's *The Slave Community,* and Eugene D. Genovese's *Roll, Jordan, Roll* all explore what slave narratives tell us about slavery. There are many excellent histories of slavery available, but these books are the most intimately bound up with the stories the slaves told themselves.

## IV. OTHER BOOKS OF INTEREST

The following books I not only found useful for my own research, but would also highly recommend for those interested in exploring the subject further.

Andrews, William L., ed. *African American Autobiography: A Collection of Critical Essays.*

————, ed. *North Carolina Slave Narratives.*

Andrews, William L., Frances Smith Foster, and Trudier Harris, eds. *The Oxford Companion to African American Literature.*

Berlin, Ira. *Generations of Captivity: A History of African-American Slaves.*

————. *Many Thousands Gone: The First Two Centuries of Slavery in North America.*

Foner, Philip S., ed. *Frederick Douglass: Selected Speeches and Writings.*

Foster, Frances Smith. *Written by Herself: Literary Production by African American Women, 1746–1892.*

Franklin, John Hope, and Alfred A. Moss, Jr. *From Slavery to Freedom: A History of African Americans.*

Gates, Henry Louis, Jr. *The Classic Slave Narratives.*

Higginson, Thomas Wentworth. *Black Rebellion: Five Slave Revolts.*

Jackson, Blyden. *A History of Afro-American Literature, Volume I: The Long Beginning, 1746–1895.*

Johnson, Charles, Patricia Smith, and the WGBH Series Research Team. *Africans in America: America's Journey through Slavery.*

Kolchin, Peter. *American Slavery 1619–1877.*

Olmsted, Frederick Law. *A Journey in the Seaboard Slave States in the Years 1853–1854, with Remarks on Their Economy.*

Ripley, C. Peter, et al. *The Black Abolitionist Papers.*

Williams, Kenny J. *They Also Spoke: An Essay on Negro Literature in America, 1787–1930.*

Yacovone, Donald. *Freedom's Journey: African American Voices of the Civil War.*

Yellin, Jean Fagan. *Harriet Jacobs: A Life.*